An American
ADVENTURE

An American
ADVENTURE

From Early Aviation Through
Three Wars to the White House

WILLIAM LLOYD STEARMAN

NAVAL INSTITUTE PRESS
ANNAPOLIS, MARYLAND

Naval Institute Press
291 Wood Road
Annapolis, MD 21402

Library of Congress Cataloging-in-Publication Data
Stearman, William Lloyd
  An American adventure : from early aviation through three wars to the White House /
William Lloyd Stearman.
      p. cm.
  Includes index.
  ISBN 978-1-59114-827-2 (hardcover : alk. paper) 1. Stearman, William Lloyd, date. 2.
Stearman, William Lloyd, date—Family. 3. Stearman, Lloyd, 1898–1975. 4. Aeronautics—
United States—History—20th century. 5. United States. Navy—Officers—Biography. 6.
World War, 1939–1945—Campaigns—Pacific Area. 7. Foreign correspondents—United
States—Biography. 8. Diplomats—United States—Biography. 9. United States—History,
Military—20th century. 10. National Security Council (U.S.)—Biography. I. Title.
  CT275.S668A3 2012
  629.130973—dc23
                        2011040288

20 19 18 17 16 15 14 13 12   9 8 7 6 5 4 3 2 1
First printing

Contents

Preface

"WHAT ARE ALL THESE NICE PEOPLE doing in the nasty world?" This kept running through my mind in first encountering my fellow Americans after returning, at long last, to the United States, having been away for most of the preceding eighteen years. (I left this country in 1944 at age twenty-two and returned in 1962 at age forty.) Having long lived in a postwar Europe initially semi-ruined and impoverished, and beset with the kinds of trials, tribulations, frictions, and other adversity that do not tend to make people nicer, I could only marvel at how good and ingenuous Americans seemed to be. I was a twentieth-century version of Washington Irving's famed *Rip Van Winkle*, who fell into a deep sleep before the American Revolution and awoke to a transformed post-Revolution country. I never had seen a supermarket, nor any of the increasingly ubiquitous postwar suburbs. There also had been substantial changes in family life and in society in general, not all of them exactly felicitous. Rock had replaced swing.

In short, I believed I had come to a fascinating new country, but hardly a foreign one, since my family on both sides had been here since the late seventeenth century. I was made acutely aware of the striking and significant differences between the American and European mentalities and lifestyles. Yes, there is a *European* mentality, albeit with numerous variations, into which I gained valuable insights by virtue, inter alia, of being married to a European (my first wife was from Vienna, at the crossroads of Europe). Decades later, I still marvel at how relatively well, on the whole, our country functions—with a number of notable exceptions, of course.

I grew up in the early days of aviation. My father, a World War I Navy flyer, largely developed this country's first commercial aircraft, the *Swallow*. After this, as primary designer and engineer, he partnered with Clyde Cessna and Walter Beech in the Travel Air Company, which he left in October 1926 to relocate in California, where he founded Stearman Aircraft Co. He is best known for designing the prototype of the famed World War II Stearman trainer, manufactured by the company he founded (now Boeing-Wichita), which retained his name long after he left. It is little known that he was the first president, and, in effect, founder, of the Lockheed Aircraft Corporation (now Lockheed Martin). The Lockheed Electra was initially designed by my father and then modified with the help of others. My father's last plane, the Stearman-Hammond, was probably the most foolproof airplane ever built, but was too expensive to sell. My father is quite rightly in the National Aviation Hall of the Fame, but it was largely thanks to the untiring efforts of his first test pilot that he is there. Incidentally, I always especially enjoyed hearing my father talk about his acquaintances, such as Charles Lindbergh and Howard Hughes.

I had an interesting and carefree youth, a highlight of which was experiencing life in a mid-nineteenth-century time capsule: I lived for a time with my grandparents on a farm in the remote Ozarks. I also have vivid memories of the late "Roaring Twenties" and, later, the Great Depression. American life and society have changed radically since that time.

After high school I started working as a professional cowboy and eventually ended up graduating from the University of California at Berkeley. Like most Americans at that time, I had led a fairly sheltered existence. This existence ended with Pearl Harbor. (The "Three Wars" in the title refer to World War II, the Cold War, and Vietnam.) I first left the United States as a young naval officer in the early fall of 1944 to fight the Japanese, and eventually was in the first wave of nine assault landings in the Pacific 1944–45, some major, some minor, and one that was the last amphibious assault of the war. I was scheduled to be in the first wave of the first assault on the Japanese mainland on November 1, 1945, which I most probably would not have survived. It was during the war, on the eve of a major battle, that I became what was probably the first Catholic Stearman since the English Reformation. After the war, I had the nerve-racking experience of being one of the Navy's youngest ship captains at a time when the Navy was rapidly disintegrating. Inter alia, I had to take my rickety ship through the Panama Canal without a pilot on the bridge, and had a jarring experience when I couldn't avoid smashing a pier in Jacksonville, Florida.

After the war, I went to Europe for graduate studies on the GI Bill of Rights in Geneva, Switzerland. I finally finished my studies, which later overlapped my professional work, with the equivalent of an MA and a PhD. In my subsequent nearly sixteen-year European sojourn, I experienced postwar Europe in all its devastation, hopes, successes, danger, and failures. This included an early stint as a part-time stringer correspondent covering Eastern Europe as it was being taken over by Communists. In January 1950 the Soviets tried to seize my fiancée, Eva, which resulted in our getting married six months earlier than planned. Three years later Eva gave birth to our daughter Betsy (Elisabeth Anne).

In 1950 I joined the U.S. Foreign Service in Vienna and immediately began four and a half years of negotiations with the Soviets in the Allied Commission for Austria and wound up spending a total of nine years a hundred miles behind the Iron Curtain in those great centers of espionage, tension, and intrigue—Vienna and Berlin. In November 1956, just after my Berlin tour, I had the heartbreaking experience of watching the Soviet Army crush one of the last pathetic pockets of revolutionary resistance in Hungary. Before returning to the United States, I had served in our embassy in Bonn, West Germany, during two major nail-biting crises with the Soviet Union. During the first, in the 1959 Foreign Ministers Conference in Geneva, I saw the United States almost sell out Berlin because we then believed in the "missile gap." I subsequently attended the aborted May 1960 Paris summit conference. The last crisis, following the disastrous June 1961 Kennedy–Khrushchev summit in Vienna, generated a flood of East German refugees, resulting in the Berlin Wall to stem it. This experience permanently soured me on summits.

I was alone within the U.S. government in predicting the August 13, 1961, Berlin Wall erection, committing the unpardonable sin of being right when everyone else was wrong. Such a disgraceful lapse happened again in 1981 when I alone insisted the Soviets would not invade Poland. I later more than made up for these lapses, however: in 1991 by insisting that the Soviets would never permit the reunification of Germany; in 1989 by failing to read clear signs that the Soviet empire was on the verge of breaking up; and, worst of all, in the fall of 1972, while in the White House as Henry Kissinger's expert on our enemy in Vietnam, by failing to recognize that this enemy was on the verge of defeat.

After finally returning to the United States in 1962, I had ahead of me a most gratifying tour in the State Department where I was involved in Soviet and Eastern European affairs during interesting times, including the 1962 Cuban Missile Crisis. This was followed by some twenty months in Vietnam, where I headed psychological war operations against North Vietnam and its army. I narrowly escaped ending up in a body bag, and, to this day, am plagued by tinnitus acquired by being on the receiving end of much Soviet heavy ordnance. After I returned to the State Department, official Washington was jolted by a casual question posed to me by a Soviet KGB agent—my brief moment of (albeit internal) fame. This episode, incidentally, is mentioned in three books, including Henry Kissinger's memoirs. I should add that while at State I did a stint in the "Intelligence Community," when I was assigned to State's Bureau of Intelligence and Research, which was a thoroughly disillusioning experience. My Vietnam experience ultimately led to my spending a total of seventeen years—an all-time record for an NSC professional—under four presidents on the White House National Security Council Staff (NSC). During this time in Washington, I was living in the old 1784-dated Halcyon House in Georgetown, one of the most notorious haunted houses in the East. My first top boss on the NSC staff was Henry Kissinger; under him, in January 1973, I became director of the NSC Indochina staff, covering Vietnam, Laos, and Cambodia, making me probably the most senior U.S. official who dealt exclusively with these countries. During my incumbency all of Indochina went down the tubes (for which I take only a small part of the blame). I am, to this day, both vexed and saddened by our disgraceful betrayal of our Vietnamese allies when they were finally on the verge of winning. In essence, we snatched defeat from the jaws of victory. After being involved with Vietnam continuously from November 1965 to January 1976, from the rice paddies to the White House, I have arrived at conclusions about this conflict substantially different from those of most liberals and many conservatives.

I later developed my own theories as to why the Soviet empire collapsed when I covered it in the White House under President Ford and President Bush (also later explained in detail). While I was in the Nixon White House, and unbeknownst to me, the Watergate cover-up largely evolved some fifty feet from my office. I had to read the newspapers to know what was going on. Needless to say, it was extremely disheartening for those of us in the White House when this all came out. Witnessing the rapid transition from Nixon to Ford was a surreal experience.

From 1977 to 1993 I was both a part-time and a full-time member of the faculty of Georgetown University, an experience I shall always cherish. I ended each course with a three-hour lecture on how to get the most out of life, and what's important in life, most of all: picking the right spouse and having a happy marriage; also getting the most out of college for your money; driving since 1936 without having an accident; and getting ahead in a job or other situations. Many students said it was the most useful part of their Georgetown education (available on my Web site, www.williamlstearman67.com). Of course, I would like to believe them, although I do hope they also got something from my courses themselves.

After leaving the White House in 1993, I had served in the U.S. government under ten presidents—nearly a quarter of all the presidents we had ever had. I have strong views on who were best, who were worst, and who was in between. I went on to writing and to heading an association dedicated to the unfortunately ultimately futile cause of modernizing and returning our two well-preserved reserve battleships to active service; without these battleships Marines and soldiers would have no essential, lifesaving naval fire support for a very long time. This long and hard-fought effort began in December 1994 and finally became hopeless in 2010. The major untold scandal of the Vietnam War was the documentable needless loss of thousands of American lives for want of battleship fire support.

For reasons no one can fathom, I was knighted in 1997 in an ancient papal order and became "Sir William" (a title only used within the order). Most importantly, in 1984 I made the wisest move of my life when I married my dearest and closest friend, the beautiful Joan Frances Crotty. (Eva had died a few years before.) Our marriage has been and continues to be an inordinately happy and fulfilling experience.

On my Web site www.williamlstearman67.com I have posted writings on subjects that didn't fit in this book, for example, critiques of modern art and of unguided evolution as well as a selection of inspirational writings, a description of black American progress, coping with heart attacks and melanoma, and college advice.

★ ★ ★

I would like to dedicate this book to my dear wife, Joan, without whose constant essential support it could not have been written.

I owe debt of gratitude to Dr. Stephen T. Hosmer of the RAND Corporation for having persistently encouraged me to write these memoirs and then for suggesting they be published by the Naval Institute Press.

Here I would like to thank the staff of the Naval Institute Press, especially its Director, Richard Russell, who took a chance on a book quite atypical of NIP products and who provided a great deal of helpful guidance, which clearly improved what I had originally written. Others of the NIP staff who have been very helpful include: on the production side, Emily Bakely, Susan Corrado, Marlena Montagna, and Alison Hope; in marketing, Judy Heise, George Keating, and Claire Noble.

Last but not least, I could not have written this book had my quirky computer not been kept up and running by my good brother-in-law, Sione Finau, ace IT professional with NIH.

Chapter 1

The Early Years and Family Roots

I WAS BORN IN WICHITA, KANSAS, on June 22, 1922, son of Lloyd Carlton Stearman and Virtle Ethyl (Trusty) Stearman. Only forty years before, Wichita was still a wide-open cow town like Abilene and Dodge City. My family on both sides came from a long line of Southerners dating back to the late seventeenth century when my ancestors left England, Scotland, and Wales and settled in Virginia and the Carolinas, or so my family tradition has it. My mother's family ended up, via Tennessee, in the Missouri Ozarks about forty miles north of Arkansas. My great-grandfather Stearman, a Virginian, who died when I was in high school, had studied architecture at the University of Virginia, but went north to seek his fortune, since the postwar South was an economic disaster area. He married a Yankee from New York and blended in. My father told me that my great-grandfather designed a railroad station in Chicago, and was doing quite well there when his wife was diagnosed with "consumption" (tuberculosis) that the doctor said could only be ameliorated, if at all, in a dry climate, unlike Chicago's. In any case, the doctor said, she probably did not have long to live. They then moved to western Kansas where they initially lived in a primitive sod house on the prairie. My sickly great-grandmother subsequently had ten children, nine of whom survived; she lived to well over ninety.

My grandfather Stearman, whom I adored, was the architect-builder at Frank Rockefeller's large ranch in western Kansas. (Frank was the brother of the famous John D. Rockefeller.) In my boyish eyes, my grandfather was a remarkable man indeed. He could, and often did, design a house and build the whole thing with his own hands. Several of these houses are still standing. He not only played classical music on the violin, he made violins as a hobby. Famed Austrian violinist and composer Fritz Kreisler was his (and our family's) idol, too. On the ranch, he was known for his broncobuster skills. The story goes that nary a horse could throw him. He was gentle and slightly built, but tough and wiry.

He could remember the tag end of the wide-open, rough-and-tumble cow-town days of Dodge City, Abilene, and Wichita, and I loved his tales of the Old West with its good and bad gunslingers and other assorted characters. I was intrigued that he knew a man who had been scalped by Indians and lived to tell about it. There were still Indian wars in his lifetime, and, he said, the prevailing view of Indians in those days was that "the only good Indian is a dead Indian." (This statement is attributed to Gen. Philip Henry Sheridan after his Civil War service. It's hard to imagine anyone saying this today.) To my grandfather one of the greatest villains in history was Gen. Valeriano Weyler, Spanish governor-general of Cuba, who was notorious for his ill treatment of the Cubans, much publicized in the American press, which contributed to American eagerness to go to war with Spain in 1898. My grandmother was a quiet, borderline dour lady who had studied at a music conservatory and taught piano to youngsters (including me, at times). My father was born in western Kansas in 1898.

My maternal grandfather Trusty, who died when I was about fourteen, was an ardent Southerner who, for better or for worse, made a lifelong Southerner out of me. (My father's family, which had gone north, soft-pedaled its deep Southern roots.) His father, my great-grandfather, was named Thomas Jefferson Trusty. He was born in 1828, just two years after Thomas Jefferson, very popular in the agrarian South, had died. As a child my grandfather played with slave children (like most Southerners, his family could not afford slaves, though). He was ten years old when "The War" ended in 1865—never mind that since then there had been the Spanish-American War and the Great War (later called World War I). When I told him I had learned in school that we had lost The War he said, "Billy, we didn't lose it militarily. We were starved out." He also told some fascinating eyewitness war accounts overheard from Confederate veterans' conversations. I learned early on that combat veterans of all wars generally only will discuss their war experiences with other combat veterans. I even found this to be true of myself after World War II. As a kid it never occurred to me to take notes. I wish I had. All that I can remember of his secondhand war accounts was that Wilson Creek ran red with blood for a long distance after that battle. It always intrigued me that my grandfather knew people who could remember when George Washington (who died in 1799) was still alive. This illustrates how close we actually are to our historical past.

Then, too, he and his family experienced their own share of war trials and tribulations, since nowhere else did the civilian population suffer as much as in Missouri, which, after Virginia and Tennessee, saw the most actual combat and worse, and was racked by merciless guerrilla warfare conducted by both sides. When his brother was born in 1864, after the Yankees had seized control of the area, as an in-your-face gesture toward the blue-coated occupiers, he was christened Jefferson Davis Trusty after the Confederate president. As an adult, Jeff was caught in a land fraud scheme and escaped to New Orleans, where he spent the rest of his life.

My grandfather remembered the Reconstruction period with special bitterness. Especially hard for Southerners to take was having the slaves gain the franchise while the whites lost theirs. I once believed that Abraham Lincoln and Gen. William T. Sherman were two of the greatest villains in American history. Later I came to have an extremely high regard for Lincoln and even some sympathy for Sherman, and eventually concluded that it was a good thing that the South lost the war. Most people today do not regard Missouri as Southern, though it is still a member in good standing of the Southern Governors Conference and the Southern Legislators Conference. The magazine *Southern Living*, I notice, always includes Missouri. Missouri also had statewide racial segregation, like all other Southern and border states. Historically, Missourians seemed to have been the most fanatical of all Southerners, since they began fighting the Yankees (mostly in "Bleeding Kansas") six years before the Civil War began. The twelfth star in the Confederate Flag stands for Missouri, and the thirteenth for Kentucky. Mark Twain, who was from northern Missouri, always referred to himself as a Southerner, as indeed he was. *American Heritage* (November 1991) noted that Missourian "[Harry] Truman was raised in a border state county as Southern in sympathy as any Mississippi Delta town."

It saddens me, then, to hear Missouri referred to as a "Midwestern" state, but it is located in the midst of Midwestern states and, alas, has taken on many Midwestern attributes. In all fairness, however, the Midwest has long symbolized down-to-earth American virtues and stability. The troubled South, on the other hand, always has seemed more colorful to me, with all its faults and picaresque characters, and therefore has been more interesting. This is probably why the South has produced more good literature than has the Midwest. During the civil rights strife of the 1960s, the South got a lot of bad press. Perhaps many Missourians, who also had their segregation problems, might have thought it better to be considered Midwestern—just my theory, anyway.

On the slavery issue, my grandfather did not think it could have long survived, since it was so *uneconomical*. He argued that the Northerners could pay their workers, who often were just off the boat, a pittance and work them hard. Then, when they got sick or old, they turned these workers out on the street. On the other hand, when one paid $1,000 to $1,500 for a field hand, the going price before the Civil War, you certainly should take decent care of him or her. (Relatively few people earned $1,000 a year.) Moreover, you had to provide food, clothing, shelter, and medical care, and then take care of a slave in his old age. Of course, in the upper

South where their numbers were small and were mostly under family supervision, slaves were treated better than in the Deep South with its ruthless overseers. Slaves in the upper South were "kept in line" by the threat of being "sold down river," meaning the Mississippi River, to the slave market in New Orleans. My grandfather never mentioned how slave families often were broken up by being sold. My grandfather's line of reasoning would justifiably shock, if not outrage, most people today. But he was a decent, intelligent, God-fearing solid citizen who should be judged in context of his times and region. Actually, my mother told me he long had moral reservations about slavery. He was a great admirer of presidential candidate William Jennings Bryan and could recite his famous 1896 Democratic Convention "Cross of Gold" speech in toto, which includes, "[Y]ou shall not crucify mankind upon a cross of gold," which was a pitch for free silver coinage.

I would like to pause here to note a phenomenon of which I have become increasingly aware in the nearly nine decades in which I have lived: a frequent failure to consider past events in the context of the times. This viewing the past in terms of present assumptions and expectations has been very aptly labeled "presentism" by Professor Robert J. Norrell in his excellent book, *Up From History: The Life of Booker T. Washington* (Belknap/Harvard University, Cambridge, MA, 2009). Washington was an outstanding black leader of the nineteenth century who founded the famed Tuskegee Institute in Tuskegee, Alabama, in 1881 and wrote his autobiographical *Up From Slavery* in 1901, among other achievements. Norrell defends Washington against activists in the 1960s who took to criticizing Washington as an "Uncle Tom" because they did not consider him sufficiently militant in pressing black demands, failing to realize the extremely delicate position in which the strong prevailing white prejudice of the Deep South had placed him at that time. One false step and his heroic and successful efforts to provide higher education for blacks would have been wiped out.

My maternal grandparents and their children were very well read in eighteenth- and nineteenth-century English and American literature and in translations of French, Roman, and Greek classics. They had the great advantage of my grandfather's being head of the school board, which gave him the right to take the local school's library home for the summer. My grandparents paid my mother fifty cents every time she read the Bible. The whole family knew the Bible well and could quote freely from it. People read a lot in those days, since there were few other sources of entertainment. There was no electricity or batteries, hence no radio that, in any case, had only recently reached urban areas of the country. I always have considered Abraham Lincoln to be among the very best educated of all our presidents and nearly all of his education came just from the reading he did on his own.

Since there was no high school anywhere near where my mother grew up, she had to board with her Aunt Minnie Burke to attend high school in Harper,

Kansas. When she finished high school, she started teaching eight grades in one room, which was commonplace then. She assured me that it worked very well, especially since the younger children learned so much from hearing the older ones recite. This was recently confirmed by a close friend of mine who spent eight years in a one-room school in Kentucky. (Today there are still about three hundred one-room schools in the United States, most of them in the upper Midwest, and they have excellent track records.) In those days, a general high school degree was all it took to teach. And in those days, even those finishing just the eighth grade were often better educated than many of today's *college* graduates. If one doubts this, just look at the late nineteenth-century eighth-grade final exam in the school of a small Kansas town posted on the internet. Most college graduates today would have trouble passing it. In the hardscrabble Ozarks, where my mother grew up, very few, if any, ever went to college and few even went to high school.

It was in Harper that my mother met my father, who worked as an automobile mechanic and also was a "soda jerk" at the local soda fountain. As a boy, I was intrigued with his tales of mixing large candy batches with a baseball bat.

In Harper there were already a number of early cars, which required a good bit of maintenance. As a mechanic, he was actually skilled enough to have built a complete car from scratch while still in his teens. Before long, he began studying architecture at the Kansas State Agricultural College in Manhattan, which is now Kansas State University. After we declared war on Germany in 1917, he left college to become a naval aviator and wound up at the North Island Naval Air Station, San Diego, where he flew in Curtiss N-9 and other seaplanes. Incidentally, his commanding officer there was Cdr. Ernest Spencer, the first husband of Wally Warfield Spencer Simpson, whose affair with King Edward VIII led to the major scandal of the times, the king's 1936 abdication and subsequent marriage to the twice-divorced Wally.

Had my father gone overseas to fight, he might well have found himself in combat with my future father-in-law, who was an officer in the Imperial Austro-Hungarian Navy, with which a number of U.S. naval aviators wound up fighting. Judging from letters he wrote to my mother (whom he married not long after the war), he was heartbroken when the war ended before he could get overseas. After the war, he got a job as an architect in Wichita, Kansas, but aviation was in his blood and was to be his future, and an illustrious future it turned out to be.

My mother had fortunately learned piano as a child. Her father had sold his favorite saddle horse to buy her a piano, and she often practiced while her sister Jessie and brother Tom did farmwork. After marriage, her piano playing paid off in helping augment my father's meager income by working in a music store playing sheet music for those who wanted to hear what the music sounded like before they bought it.

(NOTE: The following accounts of my father's early aviation days would have had to depend entirely on the remembered oral reminiscences of others and on my other personal memories were they not jogged, confirmed, augmented, and rendered more accurate by the following reference material: A great book entitled *Stearman* by Jim Avis and Martin Bowman [Motorbooks International, Osceola, WI, 1997] cites many of the chapter-and-verse facts about those days that I will use, most having been in one form or the other already in my memory. An article by Dan Downie, "From Rockets to Crop Dusters," in *The AOP Pilot* of May 1964, reproduced in *The Stearman Flying Wire* of May 2004, was very helpful, as was Edward H. Phillip's excellent book *Stearman* [Specialty Press, North Branch, MN, 2006], the best of the Stearman books.)

After answering a newspaper ad in 1919, my father went to work for a company building the Swallow aircraft, the first production-line civilian airplanes sold commercially in the United States. This company became Swallow Aircraft Company in 1924, after which my father designed the New Swallow, the first commercial aircraft to use the Curtiss OX-5 engine, which is the engine that had powered the Curtiss JN-4 "Jenny" World War I trainer. After the war, there were a large number of 90-horsepower OX-5 war surplus engines available at a bargain price. Not only were they superior to most other aircraft engines then in use but their relatively cheap price finally made civilian aircraft affordable and therefore marketable, since civilian engines were very expensive. (It was in 1924, at age twenty-two months, that I took my first plane ride—in a Swallow of course—sitting on my father's lap.)

In the meantime, my father had designed a new aircraft he badly wanted to build. To do so, he joined forces with Walter Beech and Clyde Cessna in early 1925 to form the Travel Air Company; both of these men later were to achieve great fame in aviation. Dad's design turned out to be a highly successful airplane. (All the planes listed above were biplanes.) Since none of these three great aviation pioneers had much interest in or talent for business, and preferred hands-on working on airplanes, the company's business was in effect run by its secretary and bookkeeper, twenty-year-old Olive Ann Mellor, who later married Walter Beech and wound up as president of his famous company when Walter died in 1950. My mother was convinced that this remarkable woman actually ran the Beech Aircraft Company even when Walter was still president, and that she was the brains of the company. Today, Olive Ann would be Travel Air's executive vice president. My father and Cessna left Travel Air in 1926 to found their own companies. Beech stayed until 1932, when he founded Beech Aircraft Company.

Fred D. Hoyt, a Travel Air salesman in California, in 1926 lured my father out to Venice, California, where Stearman Aircraft Company was born. Fred Hoyt became the Stearman chief pilot and salesman, and also became a close friend of the family. While delivering a Stearman in January 1928, Hoyt ran into severe disabling weather and bailed out over southern Idaho. He parachuted to a safe landing but froze to death seeking shelter. Tragically, he reportedly passed within fifty yards of a house without seeing it in the storm. My father was directly involved in the extensive search for him. His death was a great blow to us all. Sometime after 1960 a film was made based on this tragedy. Hoyt was succeeded as chief pilot by David P. "Deed" Levy, slight of build, dashing, handsome, and a fearless, super pilot, who greatly impressed me when I was a small boy. In his later years, he was instrumental in getting my father, by then deceased, into the National Aviation Hall of Fame.

Flying in those days was a hazardous business. I remember one morning picking up the morning paper at the front door and being shocked to read the headline, "Lloyd Stearman Lost in the Mountains!" My father had had a forced landing in the Rockies and it took awhile for him to get back to civilization. Why we weren't informed of this crash and the press was has always been a mystery to me. Even in those hazardous days of flying, my father always insisted that the most dangerous part of flying was driving to and from the airport, a view he held all his life.

The Stearman C-1 produced in Venice started out with the ubiquitous OX-5 and ended up with a war surplus (French) Salmson engine with more than two and half times as much power (in other words, 230 horsepower). A subsequent model, the C-2, was flown by Fred Hoyt in several movies, including that great silent classic *Wings*, which won the very first Oscar in 1927 and was the first movie I remember seeing. While the C-2 was a big success, the company was short of funds needed for expanding its increasingly successful business and was somewhat in debt. Interestingly, in those days there wasn't a great deal of available money in California, so my father had to take his company back to Wichita where the money was—mostly oil and wheat money—and where he had solid backing from the Wichita business community, especially from leading businessman Walter P. Innes Jr. It was Innes who played a key role in getting the needed financial backing.

I vividly remember the car trip back to Wichita in September 1927, when I was five. It was quite an adventure, especially for my little sister Marilyn Ruth (named after the much-beloved dancer Marilyn Miller and our pretty aunt, Ruth Stearman) and me. There were no paved state highways through Arizona and New Mexico, and sometimes a washed-out road necessitated a considerable detour. We encountered very few cars except in towns. The ubiquitous adobe houses were festooned with strings of red peppers. The Indians we encountered were generally standoffish, although not hostile, and never let us photograph them. I now realize that this may have been at least partly due to the last Indian war's having been fought only a few decades before. Trading posts were the only place one could buy Indian artifacts; they were a bargain, since there were then very few tourists in the area. Everything we bought there was 100 percent authentic. I still have a few things we purchased at a trading post in New Mexico. En route we stayed at "cottage camps," which had individual little cabins and were the forerunners of motels.

In Wichita we moved into a modest three-bedroom house in a middle-middle-class neighborhood. Among my fond memories of those times were ice deliveries that were made in a horse-drawn covered ice wagon. As the iceman went from door to door depositing blocks of ice in people's iceboxes, the horse and his wagon would follow. We children all followed along cadging pieces of ice to suck. It was in Wichita that I began kindergarten. In those days, all we did in kindergarten was play, socialize, and listen when the teacher read to us. We didn't learn a thing, academically speaking, not even the alphabet or how to count to ten. Anyone suggesting preschool then would have been thought insane. By contrast, my poor little niece had homework in kindergarten. I don't remember ever having much, if any, homework in grammar school. Still, I submit that we finished school far better educated than is the case today. (I recently read that Finland does not send children to any school until age seven and the results are generally superior to those in most other countries.) Also a recent study concluded that countries where the children had no homework, on the whole, did better than those countries that do, including the United States.

When my sister or I fell ill with a contagious disease, someone from the Wichita health office would come along and put a big quarantine sign on the front door with the disease noted in large letters, with different colors for different diseases. My father still went to work every day, so the quarantine had its gaps. Most people worked on Saturdays. Sunday band concerts were very popular all over the country, and one can still find little gazebo-type bandstands in small towns. Also on Sundays, in the Wichita park a large screen would be put up for free movies, which were still silent. Radio was just becoming popular. The world's first commercial radio broadcasting station went on the air in the United States in 1920. My father made our first radio, and initially we could only listen to it with earphones. The first thing I ever heard on radio was a prizefight. I believe it was Gene Tunney versus Jack Sharkey, but I'm not positive. Eventually my father rigged up a speaker so we could all listen together.

I spent a good bit of time on Sundays at the airport, which was always exciting. Sometimes it was a bit too exciting when my father would take me up and insist on doing aerial acrobatics. This may be why, although I grew up in aviation, I never had a great desire to fly. Also I saw a number of crashes, mostly at air shows. Once on a Sunday afternoon at the airport, I saw a suicidal pilot spin his plane into the ground less than a hundred yards from where I stood. I was the first on the scene. The plane was scattered all over, and there in the middle was the body of the pilot, the first dead person I had ever seen. At one Sunday air show at the airport I watched a lady parachutist jump out of a plane with a sack of flour under one arm to leave a spectacular trail in the air. Next to me stood her little boy, who was about my age. We watched, stunned, as her parachute failed to open. As she hit the ground, her poor little boy went into hysterics. These boyhood experiences did not contribute much to my becoming an aviation enthusiast. However, this did not inhibit my trying hard, after Pearl Harbor, to become a Navy flyer, just like my father had been in World War I.

Chapter 2

Living in the 1850s

MY FONDEST MEMORIES OF THOSE DAYS were of the times I spent with my maternal grandparents on their farm in the Ozarks some forty miles north of Arkansas. It was a different world, or, as one would say today, it was a (albeit spacious) time capsule. Life there had changed very little since the 1850s. I will always cherish having had the great privilege to experience life as it essentially was in the mid-nineteenth century. My grandparents were leading citizens in their little farm community of Oscar. My grandfather headed the school board and my grandmother was postmistress. However, like everyone else in that area, they had neither electricity nor running water and, by national standards, were as poor as church mice. We knew no one who had an automobile, although there were a few around. (For example, the Springfield newspaper was delivered by car.) All our locomotion was provided by horses, with either a buggy or a wagon. My grandfather would ride about on business or social calls on his saddle horse. The great thing about a horse and buggy is that after visiting neighbors in the evening, we could all fall asleep on the way home because the horse knew the way. When the buggy would stop, we would wake up and there we were, at home.

It was, however, a chore to hitch up a buggy or wagon every time one wanted to go somewhere, which contributed to the inordinate time we spent going to church on Sundays. It took us a good hour to get to Boone Creek Baptist Church, a typical Southern Baptist congregation. Then we sat through what seemed liked endless hellfire and damnation sermons by Brother Taylor, the pastor, preceded and followed by some good gospel singing, which I much enjoyed. In the summer, we kept cool in church by fanning ourselves with rounded bamboo fans carrying ads of funeral parlors. The "parking lot" was well shaded for the horses. All the fences lining the roads and dividing the fields were split rail.

I have ever since nourished a great appreciation for having hot running water. If you wanted to bathe you had to chop wood, draw water from the well, and heat it over a wood stove. When hot, we poured the water into a big zinc-lined tub in the kitchen. You can see why people rarely bathed more than once a week, if then. With no running water, we had a nice four-hole privy about fifty yards from the house. Instead of toilet paper there was a box with corncobs and a *Montgomery Ward* catalogue or two. The last pages to be used were those showing boots, knives, guns, and dresses. Beside every bed was a nightstand in which we kept a lidded chamber pot half filled with water to be used at night and emptied in the privy each morning. For washing, there were washstands with bowls and pitchers like those one now sees in antique stores. Light was provided by kerosene lamps. One of my little chores was cleaning their chimneys. It later occurred to me that my grandparents and all their neighbors lacked amenities that had been commonplace in ancient Rome.

Farm children, even when little, were expected to work. I slopped the hogs, brought in wood for the stove, looked for eggs that the free-running hens laid all over the place making every day a sort of Easter egg hunt, and did a number of other chores. The farm was not very prosperous, having no rich bottom soil, and did not produce a very good livelihood. Indeed, it was a hardscrabble existence. We raised corn, peanuts, and livestock to sell and had a garden that provided vegetables to augment the dairy and meat products we ate. Weather could wipe out a crop with disastrous results. One year no one had any Christmas present because times were so hard. My grandmother did a good deal of food "canning" (in glass containers) and made our soap. What bothered me most was a complete lack of refrigeration. The smokehouse had a fairly cool root cellar for storing perishables, but I never really got to like milk right from the cow and not refrigerated. We kept eggs in a large earthenware jar filled with water glass (silicate of sodium) that preserved them very well.

We were not far from a tiny hamlet called Oscar, which was mostly owned by the Smith family and consisted mostly of a general store and a blacksmith shop. My grandmother ran the post office, which was in the rear of the store. The store seemed to have everything: sunbonnets for the ladies (the old-fashioned kind that curled around the head), boots, knives, harnesses, hardware items, flour, cornmeal, and of course the ever-present cracker barrel located not far from the potbellied stove. Cold drinks were also there, especially the very popular Dr. Pepper, which, for distribution reasons, was not sold outside of the South until the mid-1960s. (It is still my favorite soft drink.) In front of the store was a bench where in good weather old-timers would sit and talk about everything: The War, hunting, horses, the price of grain, you name it. They would gather around the stove in bad weather. I was most fascinated by watching George Smith at his forge shoeing horses or making parts for broken farm equipment. His blacksmith shop equipment had changed little in a hundred years. I can still remember the shop's acrid smoky smell. My sister, mother, Aunt Jessie, and I went back to Oscar in 1970s and were surprised to see how little had changed. Sadly some nice old homes were falling apart and the rail fences had gone, as were the trees around Boone Creek Church, which had been cut down to make room for automobile parking.

The big event, when I last visited the farm as a child, was the Old Settlers' Reunion outside Houston, the county seat (appropriate for Texas County). We loaded up our biggest wagon with food, primitive camping gear, and tarpaulins, and made our way to the big campground outside the distant town. By the time we got there, it was full of wagons and buggies from all over the county and beyond. It was a great time for my grandparents to see old friends and family members. Of course, I just enjoyed the camping out. Two things I best remember: Confederate veterans and their sons giving the "rebel yell" at night—sometimes, it seemed, all night long—and a peepshow cranked by hand entitled "The Death of Floyd Collins." (Collins died in a widely publicized cave accident in Kentucky in 1924.) The people in the Ozarks sometimes seemed fixated on death. Another memorable adventure I shall never forget was actually happening on a moonshine still in a cave along a river—the Piney, as I recall. Moonshining provided an income for quite a lot of people in the Ozarks. I assume it was all exported, since everybody, being Southern Baptist, seemed to be a teetotaler. A great aunt, however, made elderberry wine for "medicinal purposes."

I always hated to leave the farm. The last time there, I built a log cabin out of fence rails. Bruno, the farm dog, a German Shepherd mix, was my close buddy; for a long time he would not let anyone dismantle our cabin to reclaim the rails. I had one last adventure before I left. I was out plowing with a hired hand, a chap by the name of Jack Spitznagel, who let me ride the horse back to the barn. I jumped on him with no saddle or bridle, assuming he was too tired to do anything but gently walk. The next thing I knew, he had taken off with me hanging on to his mane for dear life. He took a short cut to the barn by sailing over a rail fence. Fortunately I had learned to ride at an early age, an old Southern custom, and I managed to stay on.

I still cherish and shall never forget having had this privilege of living like our mid-nineteenth-century forefathers.

chapter 3

The Roaring Twenties, Life in Wichita, and the Stearman Company Grows

T HE STEARMAN AIRCRAFT COMPANY WAS ESTABLISHED in Wichita in 1927. By 1928 it was doing exceptionally well, starting with its C-3 series configured to carry mail or passengers, or both. The planes were used by the U.S. Mail Service, the Forest Patrol, the Peruvian Air Force, seventeen airlines in four countries, eleven petroleum companies, and sport fliers. The plane I always liked best was the Stearman Coach, which had a cabin containing both the passengers and the pilot with wraparound 360-degree view. (Only one was made.) The success of the company was reflected in a considerable improvement in our standard of living. My parents built an attractive Dutch Colonial house on Pershing Avenue in an up-and-coming residential district of Wichita. We had a young live-in maid named Opal, a Cherokee, whom my sister and I adored. (We were very upset when she married a nice firefighter and left us.) And one of Dad's customers gave us a Chow puppy we named Ching whom we dearly loved. (He was run over and killed eleven years later in California.) We also had a Chris-Craft motorboat that we kept on the Lake of the Ozarks in neighboring Missouri. A favorite toy my father picked up in New York was a small copper model of the Woolworth Building; at 792 feet, it was then the world's tallest building. (The 1931 Empire State Building reached 1,250 feet.)

These were the "Roaring Twenties" with bootleggers (the result of Prohibition) and associated gangsters and "flappers," the women swingers of the Twenties. Most women, who actually were far more conservative than the well-publicized flappers, still dressed like them, even my grandmothers. They bobbed their hair, dressed in unflattering, loose, body-disguising dresses with short skirts, and wore cloche hats. In point of fact, few women have good-looking legs and exposed knees are seldom attractive. To tell the truth, as a kid I didn't really think much about fashions. The devil-may-care attitude, cultivated at the time, was well reflected in a tune from a popular musical of the time:

> *This being a good little goody is all very well,*
> *But what can you do when you're loaded with plenty of hellll?*
> *And when you're learning what lips are for,*
> *Is it naughty to ask for more?*
> *Let a lady confess I want to be baaad.*
> *Is it naughty to vamp [entice] a man*
> *Sleep each morning until after ten*
> *Let a lady confess I want to be baaad.*

Sounds tame by today's standards, but it was daring at the time. Also symbolizing this period was a magazine called *Ballyhoo* that featured mildly off-color jokes, and corny advertising takeoffs: "Do you shave or Gillette 'em grow?" I well remember a for-then very risqué cartoon showing a nude model and a window washer looking in the open window, remarking, "I don't blame you, lady, as warm as it is." Needless to say, *Ballyhoo* did not survive the onset of the Depression (nor did the devil-may-care attitude of the Twenties).

My father had a bootlegger, but the only evidence I saw of it was a small keg of peach brandy in the cellar, which I thought tasted pretty good. One occasionally saw a person crippled by "Jake Leg," the result of drinking toxic Jamaica gin, one of the sadder results of Prohibition. (Actually, thousands died from toxic booze.) My grandmother believed that one shouldn't even eat ginger snaps because they might have contained gin.

My mother and father were both music lovers, popular and classical, so we always had the latest recordings. The musicals and operettas of the time were wonderful. Each one had at least two or three great songs that endured, which were called "Evergreens." The year 1927 alone produced *Good News* with its hit "The Best Things in Life Are Free," then *Connecticut Yankee* with "And Then My Heart Stood Still" and "Thou Swell." That year saw one of the best musicals of all time, the still-popular *Show Boat* by Jerome Kern with its "Old Man River," "Bill," and four other all-time favorites. Contrast this with the 1960 hit musical *The Fantasticks*, with only one hit tune, "Try to Remember." Incredibly, that musical ran more than seventeen thousand performances. There were also lovely American operettas by Victor Herbert, Rudolf Friml, and Sigmund Romberg. What could possibly be more romantic than Herbert's beautiful songs, "Kiss Me Again," "Thine Alone," and "My Dream Girl"?

And then there were rousing and sentimental songs left over from the recent Great War (which came to be known as World War I): "Over There," "Smiles,"

"Long, Long Trail," "Tipperary," and the poignant "Roses of Picardy." Songs were singable and music was musical. Since the Gay Nineties were less than thirty years in the past, many songs of that period were also still popular: "Daisy Bell" ("Bicycle Built for Two"), "The Band Played On," "When You Were Sweet Sixteen," "Kentucky Babe," "After the Ball," "Hot Time in the Old Town" (a big favorite during the Spanish-American War), and, on the serious side, the still popular "America the Beautiful." "The Star Spangled Banner" did not become our national anthem until 1931, which was the year I turned nine. In the meantime, in school we mostly sang "America" (My Country 'Tis of Thee) or "Columbia, the Gem of the Ocean," which I have always thought should have become our national anthem. For one thing, it is much easier to sing than "The Star Spangled Banner."

The movies were still silent, with Al Jolson's *Jazz Singer* breaking new ground as the first "talkie" in 1927. The first movie (they didn't call them films then) I remember was that marvelous silent World War I classic *Wings* with Gary Cooper, Clara Bow, Richard Arlen, and Buddy Rogers, which, as noted earlier, won the very first Oscar for a film. When I saw it again more than fifty years later I was amazed at how much of it I had accurately remembered. It was about two brothers who were pilots in the same American pursuit squadron in France. One brother was shot down behind German lines, but managed to get to a German air base where he stole a Fokker and headed toward his base. On his way back, his brother unknowingly shot him down. His Fokker crashed into a farmhouse in which he died in the presence of his brother and Clara Bow, as I recall. In World War II something similar almost happened when Captain Bruce Carr's P-51 was shot down behind German lines. Carr managed to steal a German Focke-Wulf and successfully made it back to his base after having been repeatedly fired on by American troops.

The good times for the Stearman family were about to end. The prospering Stearman Aircraft Company was, alas, a prime target for a takeover. (Yes, they had them even then.) The pursuer was United Aircraft and Transport that controlled several airlines consolidated under United Airlines, and that owned Pratt & Whitney engines, Hamilton-Standard propellers, and the following aircraft companies: Boeing, Hamilton, Sikorsky, and Vought. United bought all the Stearman stock and took it over in August 1929. My father remained president and work began on a new plant. Then came the big stock market crash on Tuesday October 29, 1929. By the end of this slide the market reportedly had lost 40 percent of its value. Times became hard, but Stearman continued to survive by taking in maintenance and component work from other companies and producing planes on order. Naturally my father lost money in the crash. He even managed somehow to lose money *before* the crash. Too bad my much-more-savvy mother didn't handle the finances, but wives rarely did this in those days. (That is why I let my financially astute wife handle our finances.) However, somehow we did manage to have a fairly decent standard of living throughout the Great Depression.

One of the most disheartening things I remembered about the Great Depression was seeing men wearing ties and three-piece suits going from door to door begging for food. Times were really very hard for many people, especially for workers and farmers. At the height of the Depression, more than a quarter of our workforce was out of work. (In some places unemployment was up to 80 percent, I have heard.) Also very sad were all the cases when people lost their life's saving when a bank collapsed. Thank heavens for the subsequent Federal Deposit Insurance Corporation, which now helps safeguard bank accounts against such disasters. Incredibly, this lifesaver was initially opposed by President Franklin Roosevelt. Also, many lost their farms when they couldn't pay mortgage and other debts. Farm prices were very depressed. I remember someone having the bright idea of dumping milk to keep the price for milk up—this at a time when people were going hungry. I had the impression that during the Depression there was a much greater spirit of charity and camaraderie than either before or after the Depression. In a way, camaraderie took a different, but still strong, tack after the attack on Pearl Harbor.

In December 1930 my father was eased out as president. His faithful secretary Lillian P. warned him, but my father did not believe that there were those plotting against him (my very perceptive mother believed it, though). Notable among the plotters was Vice President Earl Schaefer. Schaefer was a West Pointer who had a great deal more political and administrative savvy than did my father, who was mostly interested in designing. My father departed Stearman in June 1931, but left behind a number of designs yet to be built, including his Model 6 that, with later limited modifications (see below), became the famous World War II Stearman trainer, built by Stearman-Boeing (PT-17 in the Army Air Corps and N2S2 in the Navy). Most of our service flyers, as well as Royal Navy and other nations' aviators, learned to fly in that trainer.

Stearman engineers Harold Zipp and Jack Clark had been assigned to convert the Model 6 to the Model 70 that was to be developed as a military trainer. Ever-faithful and very knowledgeable Stearman test pilot (originally hired by my father) David "Deed" Levy, concerned that my father was not getting all the credit he deserved for the origins of the Model 70, several years ago sent photos of the Model 6 blueprints showing the penciled-in changes Zipp and Clark had made, for publication in the Stearman Restorers Association newsletter. This successfully proved that, in general, the changes were not major. Unfortunately, the most major change was a narrow cantilever landing gear that caused ground-looping that rarely plagued earlier Stearmans. (Ground-looping occurs when a moving plane's wing tip touched the ground, flipping the plane around.)

There are hundreds of Stearman trainers still flying, and these great airplanes have a wide following. I have heard that in 1930 my father had worked with Jack Northrop on his revolutionary all-metal Alpha low-wing monoplane that sounded the eventual death knell of the fabric and wood biplanes. I believe my father's prime interest was in its cantilever wings. He was to design his next plane along these lines. In 1931, the year my father left Stearman, the Northrop Aircraft Corporation was united with Stearman, and Jack left the company, because he didn't want to leave California for Kansas, for which one could hardly blame him in those days.

Then it was back to California for us, where my parents spent the rest of their lives.

chapter 4

Back to California and the Birth
of Lockheed Aircraft Corporation

IN 1931 AIRLINE OWNER WALTER T. VARNEY and my father formed the Stearman-Varney Corporation for the purpose of designing a new airliner. We moved to Piedmont, California, an attractive suburb above Oakland, and my father went to work on his old drawing board with his drafting tools and his trusty slide rule, designing what eventually became the famous Lockheed Model 10 Electra. I saw the first design lines put on paper; after its initial flight in February 1934, I actually flew the (already airborne) plane myself. My father began with a single-engine single-rudder design that, with some later input from other engineers including Chief Engineer Hall Hibbert, became the familiar twin-engine twin-rudder first Electra, then the only American all-metal low-wing transport plane. This was the plane in which Amelia Earhart mysteriously disappeared over the Pacific in 1937 and in which British Prime Minister Neville Chamberlain flew to Munich in 1938 to meet with Adolf Hitler, with whom he concluded the infamous Munich Agreement, soon to become synonymous with diplomatic appeasement and sell-out.

As the initial design neared completion, the question arose: Where should it be built? There were two main choices: the bankrupt Lockheed Aircraft Company in Burbank, California, or the bankrupt Viking Flying Boat Company in Connecticut. The new company's chairman of the board and treasurer, Robert Gross, and his brother, Vice President Courtland Gross, were both from Connecticut and naturally argued for the latter choice, which, incidentally, was owned by Bob Gross. My "steel magnolia" mother, on the other hand, said there was no way she would ever move to Connecticut, and insisted it would be Lockheed or forget it. My father felt the same way and was bolstered by my mother's determination. This was not a family conflict, since both had enjoyed Southern California where Stearman was founded. He prevailed by virtue of being the designated president, and being strongly supported by his good friend Thomas Fortune Ryan III, who had provided a good bit of the financing and was a principal backer. Moreover, the company was being formed for the primary purpose of building the nation's first all-metal, cantilever-winged airliner which my father was then designing. In any case, the Lockheed name survived and the plane was built in Burbank. My father was only thirty-four when he became the first president, and, in effect, founder of the new Lockheed Aircraft Corporation, which is now the huge and diverse Lockheed Martin Corporation, the world's largest defense contractor.

Designing was my father's first love and forte; despite the responsibilities of being president, he remained directly involved with many design changes, including those mentioned above. For example, he was present at the plane's wind tunnel tests at the University of Michigan in Ypsilanti that were partly conducted by a student, Clarence L. "Kelly" Johnson. Based on these tests, inter alia, Johnson recommended that substituting two smaller twin rudders for one large rudder would increase stability. My father was very impressed by young Johnson, so I always assumed he was responsible for Johnson's eventually coming to Lockheed during his watch. "Kelly" Johnson would later become famous as the legendary head of Lockheed's famed "Skunk Works" that successfully produced highly classified military and other super-secret aircraft, including the famous U-2 spy plane.

My father was an enlightened employer who paid his workers above-union wages; the employees called him by his first name. I've always believed that they respected him because they believed, correctly in most cases, he could probably have performed any of their tasks at least as well as they could. In his early days, he actually built airplanes with his own hands, as did his onetime partners Clyde Cessna and Walter Beech. As CEO (president) of Lockheed, my father earned only $4,800 a year (about $73,400 in today's dollars). Granted that Lockheed was not a very large corporation then, but it did have an excellent worldwide reputation; moreover, he was not only CEO but also was directly involved in design, engineering, and production.

Compared with the sometimes-inflated compensation for many American CEOs today, even in small companies, my father's compensation seems pretty pathetic. It was probably no more than six times that of the average worker in his plant. (In 1980, executives of large companies made about forty times the average worker's wage. In 2008 this ratio had ballooned to 320 times [*Washington Post*, February 8, 2009].) My father did acquire a very sizeable amount of Lockheed stock, that, alas, he sold for a dollar a share when he left Lockheed in the 1930s, because he thought it would go under, which it probably would have were it not for the upcoming outbreak of war in Europe in 1939. This resulted in eventual British purchase, beginning in 1938 and well into the war, of some three thousand Hudson bombers; the Hudson was an offshoot of the Electra. Had he just held on to this stock, Stearmans would not have had to work for generations. Moreover, at the time he sold it, we really didn't need the money. My much-more-financially astute mother thought this sale was a mistake, but my father, unfortunately, never listened to her in such matters, which is another reason why I let my financial savvy wife handle all our finances. (My wife's father was an accountant, among other professions.)

My parents rented a nice three-bedroom California Spanish-style house in the Toluca Lake section of North Hollywood, where some of the movie stars lived. The house had a large backyard with a big walnut tree, great for a ten-year-old boy who loved to climb trees. Also, the northeast end of Toluca Lake was not developed, and one of my friends and I built a raft there and pretended to be Huckleberry Finn. In those days, the San Fernando Valley was scarcely developed and was filled with walnut groves, orange orchards, and ranches. Although it's hard to imagine today, at that time Southern California was really a great place to live, with few cars, no smog, and actually not a whole lot of people. The Los Angeles River, which wound its way through the Valley, had not yet been channelized to prevent floods, and had some great little swimming holes, as well as plenty of watercress and edible crawfish. Nearby, Camel's Back Mountain was wonderful for climbing and exploring. It was great fun, too, sneaking under fences into movie lots, especially at nearby Universal, to play among the sets.

As the production of the Electra got under way, the company finished and sold some of the uncompleted or leftover original Lockheed planes that had round fuselages of plywood formed in halves in large concrete molds and then fitted together. They were actually pretty good airplanes. It was in one of these that beloved humorist Will Rogers and pilot Wiley Post died in a crash in Alaska in 1935. I always liked Wiley, who wore a black patch over his missing eye. He loved to Indian wrestle: two men would lie on their backs in opposite directions with arms and raised legs interlocked. The winner forced the loser's leg down to the floor. I never saw Wiley lose.

In any case, it was difficult getting any new enterprise under way during the Great Depression, which had been exacerbated by the Federal Reserve's ill-advised tight money policy and then globalized in 1930 when President Hoover signed the disastrous Smoot-Hawley Tariff Bill, which was followed by tariff retaliation abroad. This played a significant role in Hoover losing the 1932 election. However, contrary to popular belief, the election of Franklin D. Roosevelt made some things even worse. Soon after his 1933 inauguration, his administration began promoting ill-conceived legislation and programs hostile to business that severely worsened the business climate in the United States. And healthy businesses were the only way unemployment could be reduced. Economist Amity Shlaes, chronicler of the Great Depression, noted, "New Dealers attacked . . . the entire business community—

'princes of property' as Roosevelt called them. Washington's policy evolved into a lethal combo of spending and retribution" (*Washington Post*, February 1, 2009). Thanks to Roosevelt's New Deal policies, our double-digit unemployment rate, at about one-quarter of our workers for some time, remained a serious problem until we engaged in the large-scale war production resulting from the outbreak of World War II. There is now widespread agreement among economists and historians that Roosevelt's economic policies actually prolonged the Depression. As one of his closest associates reportedly noted, Roosevelt had scant knowledge of economics, and that manifested itself repeatedly during his administration. One of Roosevelt's most harmful programs, the National Recovery Act (NRA), was actually declared unconstitutional in 1935 by the U.S. Supreme Court. I experienced these New Deal economic depredations at firsthand by listening to my poor frustrated father fulminate against the latest nonsense out of Washington. The only person in the White House with whom he would do business was White House Press Secretary Steve Early, whom my father trusted and respected. How dealing with my father fitted in with Early's job description has always been a mystery to me. My father wanted nothing to do with any of the rest of them, including the president himself.

All of my father's beefs against Roosevelt were dwarfed by his outraged reaction to FDR's order in early 1934 to have the Army Air Corps take over delivery of airmail from the private contractors who had been doing a reasonably good job, considering the technical limitations of the time. Some in Congress thought their profits were too high. My father saw this move as not only still another New Deal swipe at private enterprise, but also correctly predicted it would be a disaster. He was then an officer in the Army Air Corps Reserve, and, in addition, was otherwise well acquainted with Army aircraft airmail limitations, since at Stearman he had designed and built a number of strictly airmail planes. The Army Air Corps pilots and its aircraft were totally ill suited to this mission that, to top it all off, had begun at a bad weather time of the year. Army pilots crashed right and left. Three were killed in one day, raising a hue and cry against the whole operation. By summer, private contractors had again taken over airmail delivery. There was a bright outcome of this whole botched operation, however: members of Congress and others realized that our Army Air Corps was in bad shape because its appropriations had been drastically cut. With this realization came a steady strengthening of the Army Air Corps. For example, its appropriations doubled in the next two years. Moreover, one general later remarked that this experience provided "the best possible" training for our pilots who flew in World War II.

To his credit, however, Roosevelt to a great extent restored hope to the disheartened American people through his charismatic personality and his words of encouragement, such as "The only thing we have to fear is fear itself." His "Fireside Chats," thirty speeches that were broadcast on the radio, were often great morale boosters. He got many unemployed men off the street through his Works Progress Administration projects, which included everything from interviewing former slaves to building roads (and even to paying instructors in the art of fencing). And the Civilian Conservation Corps, run along Army lines by Army officers, was a boon to many young men and did a lot of good in the field of conservation, among others. It also provided good training for the officers and other participants that was soon to come in handy.

Roosevelt presciently built up our fleet and took other measures to strengthen our national defenses. He was very proud of our fleet. It always struck me as preposterous that he was rumored to have known about Japanese plans to attack the fleet at Pearl Harbor and did nothing to prevent it, because he wanted to get us into war. He did rightly want to get us into war, indeed, but against Nazi Germany, not against Japan. Hitler did Roosevelt and the world an enormous favor by foolishly declaring war against the United States, on December 11, 1941, four days after Pearl Harbor, apparently believing Japan, in turn, then would attack the Soviet Union, which it never did, in effect double-crossing its Axis partner Hitler. Being at war with Japan would have made it otherwise difficult for us to go to war with Germany. Even as it was, probably most Americans believed that the war against Japan should take priority over the war in Europe. Those of us who fought in the Pacific certainly thought so. Roosevelt, fortunately, had other ideas and was right.

When Hitler gained full power in Germany in 1934, my father became very alarmed, insisting that Hitler would ignite another major war in Europe. The vast majority of Americans would have disagreed with him. However, unlike most Americans, he was well aware of what was going on in Europe through his business contacts there. His knowledgeable contacts also included his Dutch acquaintance Tony Fokker, whose famous World War I planes were the mainstay of the Imperial German air force and who had moved to the United States in 1922. Of course, he personally knew the former German World War I aces and other flyers who took over Hitler's Luftwaffe. On occasion, we had Europeans to dinner at a time when that continent was ten travel days away. The dinner conversation was always enlightening, but not always encouraging. My father was especially fond of the two Royal Dutch Airlines (KLM) representatives "Curley" Venendahl and Kuhn Parmentier, who did business with him. He had heard that when the Germans overran the Netherlands in 1940, they had escaped to England and had joined the Royal Air Force.

My father was the only gentile anti-Nazi I knew of at that time. Since anti-Semitism was widespread in the United States, the average American seemed not to be overly concerned about Hitler's anti-Semitic campaign, and therefore was not too disturbed by his patently outrageous persecution of Jews in Germany. One of my father's very best friends, Sam Metzger, was Jewish. Sam was also active in aviation. I always thought this friendship was largely responsible for my father's outspoken distaste for Nazi ideology and that it reinforced his conviction that Hitler was a dangerous madman. My father was devastated when his old friend Ernst Udet (pronounced OO-det), a World War I ace and one of the greatest stunt pilots of all time, became a senior Luftwaffe general. He later exculpated himself in my father's eyes by committing suicide in disgust. Sometime after the war, Udet's story was made into a play and then a film, *The Devil's General* (Der Teufelsgeneral) by German playwright Karl Zuckmayer. It now seems incredible that, for a long time—indeed until the end of World War II when the horrors of the Holocaust became known—throughout the United States there were a large number of hotels that would not accommodate Jews. Also, most clubs and fraternities excluded Jews. In fact, up to the early 1960s there existed, even in our nation's capital, residential areas that had covenants directed against selling real estate to Jews and to some non-Caucasians. (Although, by the 1960s, the courts had ruled they were not legally binding, buyers, even Jews, still signed them to facilitate a home purchase.)

I suspect that the post–World War II revelations about the Holocaust aroused a sense of guilt in many Jewish Americans for not having done more to help rescue Jews. At one time, in fact almost up to the outbreak of war in 1939, Hitler might well have let most, if not all, Jews under his control leave. There were many sad stories of Jews leaving Germany, but with no country accepting them (the United States accepted only a limited number), returning to Germany where most ultimately ended in death camps. In defense of American Jews, I would say this: First, no one in his wildest nightmares could possibly have imagined that, in a supposedly civilized country like Germany, an unspeakable atrocity such as the Holocaust could be perpetrated. Second, it was probably feared that admitting sizeable numbers of European Jews would only exacerbate anti-Semitism in the United States.

I would like to interject here concern about how the Soviets have succeeded in labeling Nazism as "fascism." Since Soviet propaganda labeled those on the right or even middle of the political spectrum "fascists," as Nazism's heinous crimes became well known the fascist epithet became an increasingly effective way to discredit those who opposed Communism, including all those on the right. While fascism and Nazism shared some characteristics, such as being antidemocratic, antiliberal, militaristic, nationalistic, and tyrannical, there also were fundamental and significant differences. Nazi is short for National Socialist German Workers Party, hardly the name a fascist party would adopt, and one indicating a decidedly left orientation. Indeed, Hitler, though militantly anti-Bolshevik, reportedly was influenced by Karl Marx and his party was very much worker oriented. While Nazism was murderously anti-Semitic, fascists, who were on the extreme right wing, were somewhat anti-Semitic but, except for those under German control, would not have murdered Jews. Thus equating Nazi Germany with fascist regimes severely dilutes the horror with which everyone should view the former.

Fascists also were not militantly anti-Christian, especially not anti-Catholic, as were the Nazis. Several European countries and Japan had fascist-type regimes in the 1930s and 1940s, but the salient and longest-lasting European fascist regimes were in Italy under Benito Mussolini and in Spain under Francisco Franco. Initially opposed to Hitler, Mussolini later became a Hitler ally and eventually fell under his total control after being deposed in Italy in 1943. Franco believed he needed German and Italian support to win the Spanish Civil War; although technically neutral in World War II, he sent "volunteer" troops to aid the Germans on the Eastern Front. This cooperation with Nazi Germany ended in 1943. Nevertheless, after the war, Franco's Spain became a pariah state. Eventually Franco succeeded in gradually transforming Spain from his strict authoritarian rule to a democracy, something that never would have occurred to Hitler.

I grew up in an atmosphere that encouraged interest in foreign affairs, especially in Europe. I remember being shocked by the abortive July 1934 Nazi putsch attempt in Austria that resulted in the murder of Austria's chancellor, Engelbert Dollfuss, in his office. Another shocker, later that year, was the assassination by a Macedonian terrorist of Yugoslavian King Aleksandr I and French Foreign Minister Louis Barthou in Marseilles. I recall that none of my young friends had the least interest in these notorious events. This disinterest probably applied to most grown-ups as well. Contributing to my interest in foreign affairs was my mother's love for foreign films to which she usually took me along. As I remember, they were much more realistic and engaging than Hollywood's products. At that time, however, I never dreamed I would someday be engaged abroad as a professional diplomat. I am sure that my early exposure to and interest in Europe had much to do with my later going to Europe and subsequently joining the U.S. Foreign Service.

I used to think that my father knew everybody worth knowing—not because he was ever a name dropper, but because I often heard him describe his encounters with the rich and famous to my mother or to friends. For example, Dad loved to relate his latest encounter with Howard Hughes, the notoriously eccentric entrepreneur, film producer, aviator, and builder of one of the world's largest airplanes, the Spruce Goose (which only flew a short distance), and ultimately a billionaire. Hughes preferred to do business from phone booths and would show up for board meetings, that my father attended, in tennis shoes, no tie, and dirty white duck trousers—this in a day when men all routinely wore ties and three-piece suits. He also never wanted to be touched and became increasingly eccentric with age.

Dad loved telling about his lunches with Charles Lindbergh. (Lindbergh, in 1927, was the first person to fly solo over the Atlantic and was widely idolized here and abroad.) My father and he always lunched at some out-of-the-way greasy spoon café to escape adulating fans who sometimes would even pull off his buttons for keepsakes. My father never described any conversation they had, probably because "Lindy" was singularly taciturn. I'm sure they only talked about getting his Lockheed ready to fly. Lindbergh became much more reclusive after his baby boy was kidnapped and murdered in 1932. He and his wife Anne Morrow subsequently moved to England to escape publicity and didn't return until 1940. On his return, he became a prime object of controversy as the result of his involvement with the pacifist America First campaign and his evident sympathy for Germany, where he had received a medal from the Nazi regime. His wife Anne Morrow Lindbergh wrote a book, *The Wave of the Future*, which envisaged the ultimate triumph of totalitarianism and created a figure of speech. Given Lindbergh's seeming retiring nature, I was astonished to learn not long ago that after the war he had fathered children with three different women in Germany.

The Lindbergh kidnapping trial of the accused Bruno Hauptmann was a national sensation. I think there will always be uncertainty about Hauptmann's guilt, since he got anything but a fair trial. In January 2006 I learned from a History Channel documentary that Hauptmann's famous defense attorney (hired by notorious newspaper mogul William Randolph Hearst) was convinced his client was guilty and wanted to see him end in the electric chair—just the kind of guy you want representing you when facing a possible death sentence. (Also, Hauptmann was German, which did not garner him much public sympathy.) My Grandmother Trusty was very worried that my sister and I might be kidnapped, since my father was then fairly well known. We all pooh-poohed this, but I also learned from the same History Channel documentary that at that time there had been a rash of children kidnapped for ransom.

My parents got to know a number of movie stars. This led to my having a "thrill that comes once in a lifetime" experience. At one Saturday afternoon matinee, a number of others in my age group and I saw a movie starring Ken Maynard, my all-time favorite cowboy star, whom I considered far superior to Tom Mix, Hoot Gibson, and all other also-ran cowboy stars. In this movie, Ken had somehow managed to force a tree full of outlaws over a cliff. I thought that had to be the greatest feat any cowboy had ever accomplished, and so did all my friends. The next day, lo and behold, who showed up at our house for lunch—Ken Maynard himself! When I asked him how he had managed to topple all those outlaws over the cliff, he shrugged it off with an "aw shucks, it was nothin'" instead of disillusioning a ten-year-old by describing how such stunts are choreographed in Hollywood. Maynard was quite an accomplished stuntman and rode a horse he named Tarzan.

Among the most improbable of my father's friends—or close acquaintances, in this case—was the budding author Irving Stone. My father was especially taken by one of his recent successes, *Sailor on Horseback*, a biographical novel about that colorful adventurer and writer Jack London. His other meticulously researched and very well-written later biographical novels include *Lust for Life* about the famed artist Vincent van Gogh, *Love Is Eternal* about the tragic Mary Todd Lincoln, and his masterful biography (later a film) of Michelangelo, *The Agony and the Ecstasy*. They are truly great books and, as I noted, exceptionally well researched. Stone was quite liberal and enamored of the New Deal. My father, on the other hand, was conservative and hated the New Deal and Roosevelt in general. After each visit by Stone, my father would swear he would never have "that damned Communist" over again. Some weeks later, Stone would show up again for dinner. He eventually bought our Graham-Page roadster with a rumble seat. (Rumble seats were folded down where trunks usually are and would be folded upright when in use. They were, in effect, outside rear seats.)

Growing up in a musical family, I took piano lessons after school once or twice a week. I was first taught by my grandmother Stearman, who had graduated from a music conservatory and was quite demanding. Later, my mother took up my musical education. My whole family seemed quite musical. My father, like his father, not only played the violin fairly well—he also could, and did, make violins. My mother was a fairly good pianist and later in life taught other children how to play. Surprisingly, my mother found that the advent of TV encouraged children to learn the piano. My sister Marilyn developed a very good singing voice. On occasion, the whole family would gather around the piano for a songfest, usually singing favorites from the 1890s and early 1900s such as "My Darling Clementine," "She's Only a Bird in a Gilded Cage," "She's More to Be Pitied Than Censured," "The Daring Young Man on the Flying Trapeze," "Rose of Washington Square," World War I songs, and all of Stephen Foster's lovely songs, which have, unfortunately, fallen into disrepute for being considered politically incorrect. It was always great fun. People used to sing a lot. It's a pity this great pastime has largely died out. Maybe it's because popular music has become increasingly unsingable. The highlight of my musical education came when my mother took Marilyn and me to a Hollywood Bowl concert that featured a Sergei Rachmaninoff composition with Rachmaninoff himself at the piano. Rachmaninoff's face reminded me of a tired Saint Bernard dog, especially his eyes, and he had unusually large hands. We were sitting in the front, and I overheard him tell one of the musicians how tired he was. He died ten years later.

We used to listen to radio quite a bit. We children had our favorite shows. Over time, these included *Little Orphan Annie* sponsored by Ovaltine and whose theme song was, "Who's that little chatterbox? The one with pretty auburn locks? Whom do you see? It's Little Orphan Annie." Then there was *Jack Armstrong, the All-American Boy*, an all-around high school athlete, sponsored by Wheaties and whose theme song was, "Wave the flag for Hudson High, boys. Show them how we stand. Ever shall our team be champions, Known throughout the land!" Then there was the Lone Ranger and his trusty sidekick Tonto who was announced (to the tune of the overture from the opera *William Tell*) with "A fiery horse with a speed of light, a cloud of dust, and a hearty 'Hi-Yo, Silver!' . . . The Lone Ranger." Tonto always called the Lone Ranger "Kemo Sabe," which supposedly meant trusty scout.

Then there were the family radio shows. Favorites were shows with great comedians like Jack Benny, Fred Allen, and Amos and Andy; soap operas like *Myrt and Marge*, the adventures of two single working women, and *One Man's Family* about an upper-middle-class family who lived on the San Francisco peninsula. I remember being especially intrigued by Paul, the reserved and somewhat mysterious oldest son who had seen combat in World War I. Then there was the wonderful *Sherlock Holmes* series with those great actors Basil Rathbone (Holmes) and Nigel Bruce (Watson), sponsored by George Washington coffee. I can still visualize scenes from the "Hound of the Baskervilles" episode. Radio stimulated the imagination, just as TV tends to deaden it. We were fond of the *Firestone Hour* that featured sentimental favorite songs like "My Rosary," and "Manhattan Merry Go Round," which should have been called the Parisian Merry Go Round, given that it favored popular French music. All in all, in those days radio was an incredibly wholesome and enjoyable form of entertainment.

My generally happy boyhood in Southern California drew to a close with the advent of my becoming a teenager and our moving to Northern California.

Chapter 5

Observations on the America of My Youth, the Late 1920s to the Early 1940s

WHEN I SEE HOW OVERPROGRAMMED most American children are today, I marvel at how carefree children used to be. Very little of our free time in any way included adults or organized activities. The only exception, in my case, apart from later becoming a Boy Scout, were weekly free fencing lessons by a florid-faced, roly-poly, but light-footed French instructor, Monsieur Couderc, who was paid by the Works Progress Administration and who always smelled of garlic. Actually, fencing eventually became the only sport at which I really excelled. (Saber became my specialty.) Monsieur Couderc was a real pro to whom I have always been grateful, demanding as he was.

Most of our daylight activities were spent outdoors, unless the weather was really bad. Parents often had to order us indoors. We made our own fun and games. These activities usually took place in backyards and in vacant lots that were plentiful in residential areas during the Depression. A favorite pastime was pickup baseball games. As with all our activities, we did not want adults within one light year of our ball games. When I returned to the United States in 1962, I was saddened to discover that adults, mostly fathers, had taken over kids' baseball by organizing it into Little League facsimiles of professional baseball, organized and dominated by adults. Or maybe there were a lot of fathers who wanted to play ball vicariously through their children. Maybe because of more prosperous times or population pressures, vacant lots had disappeared. I found it sad to see these little kids in uniforms playing scheduled games, with adults on the sidelines giving advice and encouragement or reprimands. I found it incredible that some of these kids were even traded among teams.

We were all experts at amusing ourselves with simple games like marbles, tossing pennies or milk bottle tops to a line, mumblety-peg (flipping a knife so it would stick in the ground), and a host of other little games. We also were keen on what today would be outrageously politically incorrect games involving toy guns in cops and robbers, cowboys and Indians, or just plain warfare. We usually used cap guns, but often also engaged in fights with rubber guns. Rubber guns fired large rubber bands cut from discarded inner tubes that used to be in all tires. The guns themselves were long pieces of wood—the barrels—nailed to a small block—the grips—that had a spring clothespin attached in back. The rubber band was attached to the "muzzle" and then pulled back and stuck in the clothespin. To fire it one had only to depress the clothespin. They stung a bit, but were otherwise harmless. In our war games, complete with trenches, our favorite weapon was missiles obtained by pulling up wild grass in vacant lots and compacting the attached sod into firm little balls stabilized by a grass tail when thrown.

Of course, we all had BB guns with which we mostly shot at tin cans, but never at each other. Strangely, all this early gunplay did not turn us into criminals or psychopaths. At the age of seven I had use of my first real gun, a .22 rifle. Coming from a long line of shooters and hunters, I was thoroughly indoctrinated in gun safety, like most of my generation who had guns. Two basic gun safety rules were drummed into us: (1) Always assume a gun is loaded. (2) Never ever point a gun at anything you do not want to kill. We had few gun accidents, and we certainly didn't shoot at anybody—until we had to in the upcoming war.

It is illustrative that at a time when street crime against ordinary citizens was virtually unknown, gun control was in large measure absent. Anybody could buy any kind of gun through the mail, including fully automatic Thompson submachine guns. The first federal gun control law, the Firearms Act of 1934, required the registration of these submachine guns, as well as sawed-off shotguns and other guns that were used exclusively by outlaws and, far too belatedly, by law enforcement officers.

In my time, things had advanced beyond the "children are to be seen, but not heard" stage, but we were still far from being the center of attention, as children are today. For example, I do not remember ever having more than half a dozen or so toys, including my beloved Lincoln Logs. I do not recall ever getting more than two presents of any kind for Christmas, and not because my parents were poor. That seemed to be the norm at all levels of society. My parents gave us love, attention, and discipline instead of things. Also, they were our parents, not our friends or buddies. The idea of playing with our father, such as tossing the old football around, would have appalled most of us. I did go hunting and fishing with my father, but that was different. We always assumed that our parents knew more than we did and were far better equipped to make the family decisions. Fathers were respected as the head of the family, even when mothers actually quietly called the shots, in stark contrast with today when the father is all too often regarded as the oldest child in the family, or at least as a bumbling, somewhat comical incompetent. Families had meals together whenever possible. As a result of this kind of stable family life, I believe we felt far more secure than children do today.

Absent then was the intense competition that plagues kids today. As I have noted elsewhere, we didn't have homework, and the subject of school was rarely raised by my parents, probably because my sister and I got reasonably good grades. Of course, children who were doing poorly were heavily leaned on by their parents. If children ever got into trouble in school, they got into double trouble at home, unlike today when parents so often give teachers a hard time when they try to discipline their little darlings. Parents backed teachers to the hilt. I should add that we were spanked when we deserved it. This was usually for deceiving, disobeying, or disrespecting our parents (or grandparents) or for just plain being naughty. My mother preferred using switches and my father a razor strop (which he also used to sharpen straight-edge razors). I never held a spanking against my parents, since I felt I had been bad and deserved the punishment. In my case, however, spanking was quite infrequent. Now people are appalled at the very idea of spanking, which is called "hitting," a highly loaded word that encompasses everything from harmless spanking by hand of a child's well-padded behind to potentially lethal slugging of a child with a baseball bat, a prime example of the social tyranny that is creeping into our language. There were very few discipline problems in school. In fact I never knew anyone who had been sent to the principal for misbehaving. In those days principals did not hesitate to administer corporal punishment that was usually followed by another spanking at home.

I never knew of any mother who worked outside the home; they certainly existed, but mostly at a level of society I did not know. (As late as the 1950s, I have heard, only 7 percent of mothers worked outside the home.) Also, I never knew of any children whose parents were divorced, and this was in Southern California. Divorce was something that movie stars did when they wanted to change partners at a time when living together out of wedlock was not acceptable but divorce generally was tolerated. Of course, this sometimes resulted in women remaining in abusive relationships "for the sake of the children" when they should have bailed out. However, not having acquired any outside work force or professional skills, they often felt compelled to remain for the financial security needed by them and their children.

On the whole, women with a husband who was an adequate breadwinner and with children who opted to work outside the home were stigmatized for letting someone else care for their children, whereas today feminism has succeeded in stigmatizing stay-at-home moms who devote all their time to raising their children.

I should add here, however, that most professions at least prior to World War II and a number thereafter excluded women, whereas now virtually all professions fortunately include women. Until well after World War II, for instance, women were generally excluded from medical schools in this country, whereas even in Vienna, long a bastion of male chauvinism, women had long been going to medical school. Now American women are the majority of students in med schools.

Another important factor explaining stay-at-home moms in the pre-1960 decades was the absence of today's commercialism and consumerism that encourages a need for material things one could easily do without: household gadgets, entertainment equipment, the latest car when the present car will easily do, and on and on. Most appliances, moreover, seemed to have lasted much longer than they do today. We did without—although of course many if not most of these things did not yet exist. On the other hand, except for homes (fewer than half of American families owned their own home then) and cars, people generally did not buy anything they could not afford to pay cash for. Some things were bought on installment plans, but people wouldn't have dreamed of going into debt for things they really did not absolutely need. I still feel this way, and, fortunately, so does my wife. Also, people usually only shopped when they actually needed something. Today, shopping is encouraged by malls and a great deal of advertising, and has become a prime form of entertainment. When I left Europe in 1962 Europeans still had the same attitude toward consumerism as we used to have in America.

Washington Post columnist Richard Cohen (March 3, 2009) had it right when he wrote, "The [American] people of the 1920s and '30s were tough, hard. They did not expect all that much from life, and they had learned to expect next to nothing from the government. In contrast, we [today] are soft and coddled." I would add to this that the vast majority of American men went to work right after high school (as did I) and married when they could afford to support a wife. This was usually in their early twenties. (My father married my mother at age twenty-three; he previously had some college and wartime service.) Americans thus matured much earlier than is the case today. For example, except on farms where every hand counted, I never heard of a grown man returning to live with his parents, as is often the case today.

I still remember what a great improvement it was to replace iceboxes with refrigerators, which we called Frigidaires, the brand name of the most popular first ones, or fridges. Fridges had a big ventilated cylinder on top. I also remember the improvement when we replaced carpet sweepers with vacuum cleaners, and washboards and tubs with washing machines. Dryers came much later, so we still had to hang out our wash on a line. Incidentally, this outdoor-dried wash always smells fresher than clothes coming out of a dryer; also, line-dried clothes last longer than those dried in dryers.

I do not recall ever being bored as a child, as so many children seem today, nor did I ever hear this from my friends. In fact, I do not recall ever being bored in my entire life, and I am sure this holds for most of my generation.

As to crime, it was mostly confined to notorious bank robbers like John Dillinger, "Pretty Boy" Floyd, and Bonny and Clyde and to mainly Chicago-based gangsters who thrived on selling bootleg liquor during Prohibition with rival gangs fighting over the business and killing each other in the process. Al Capone was the most notorious of the lot. Less well publicized were the lower profile but highly pernicious crimes committed by the mostly East Coast–based Mafia that had existed since before World War I. Actually, all this crime made for titillating newspaper reading, but little affected the average citizen who was rarely the victim of these outlaws and then almost never by design. Compared to the sad fate of many cities today, our big cities were remarkably safe. You could walk around late at night anywhere in any big city in the United States without worry. I remember as a midshipman in 1943, walking in Central Park in New York at one in the morning without a care in the world.

From all I have written so far, one might conclude that, in respect to lifestyle in my youth, all was relatively idyllic in our country, apart from the Great Depression, of course, but there was a dark side that we tried to ignore or of which we were not very conscious. For example, public mob lynchings, of which there have been none since shortly after World War II, were so commonplace as to be back page news, if covered at all. Most were in the South and most victims were black; many whites were also lynched and many lynchings occurred in the Midwest and elsewhere in the United States. For example, six months before Lincoln's 1909 hundredth birthday in his hometown of Springfield, Illinois, five thousand witnessed the lynching of two black men accused, but not tried or convicted, of raping a white woman. I remember hearing of a particularly revolting lynching in San Jose, California, in the early 1930s. My mother told me how, before World War I, a black man was burned alive before the statue of justice in Springfield, Missouri. While only a tiny percentage of the American population ever participated in a public lynching, the fact that lynchings were tolerated at all represented an unspeakable tolerance of barbarism in its worst form. Lynching had been fairly widespread in the Old West, but as a rough form of frontier justice in the absence of courts of law; most commonly, the victims were lynched for stealing horses, rustling cattle, or killing someone not in self-defense. Racism usually didn't enter into the equation.

Racist-based lynching got significant encouragement after the Civil War when the increasingly lawless and eventually disbanded first Ku Klux Klan sought to keep the newly liberated blacks "in their place." Lynching was defended in D. W. Griffith's famous 1915 film *The Birth of a Nation*, a film that President Woodrow Wilson reportedly praised. That the revived version of the Klan, founded in 1915, has been allowed to flourish so long in this country is a national disgrace. For example, on August 8, 1925, forty thousand Klan members in their robes and hoods paraded down Pennsylvania Avenue from the Capitol to the White House. In a number of places the Klan has had considerable political clout. The Klan has always been anti-black, anti-Semitic, anti-Catholic, and generally anti-foreign. We have come a long way in that groups holding such views today are confined to the lunatic fringe with very little influence or power, although Klan members, up to not long ago, have been involved in private lynchings and other crimes against blacks and white civil rights activists.

Whenever anyone asks me if I would like to return to those "good old days," though, I always say no, and for one good reason: antibiotics. This word symbolizes to me the enormous medical advances we have made in the past seventy years. People used to routinely die of illnesses that now are considered not terribly serious. For example, many died of influenza, pneumonia, and other common illnesses that usually are successfully treated with antibiotics. And then we did dumb things that would horrify any physician today. For example, beginning in the late 1920s, shoe stores had fluoroscopes into which you would place your feet to see how well selected new shoes fit. They fascinated us children because we could look down and see the bones in our feet. Then someone in 1946 discovered that every time someone placed his feet in one of these machines he absorbed the radiation equivalent of twenty lung x-rays. Shoestore fluoroscopes had ended by 1960. Actually these were just gimmicks that contributed next to nothing in terms of selecting shoes that fit.

There was widespread cigarette smoking, which gained great popularity among our troops in World War I and carried over into peacetime, mostly among men. Women usually didn't smoke. Even then, however, people were aware that this was a very unhealthy habit. In fact, cigarettes were commonly referred to as "coffin nails", as in, "Every cigarette you smoke is a nail in your coffin." I became a heavy cigarette smoker during World War II. I still don't know how anybody can be in a war and not smoke. Combat tends to make one nervous and anxious, to say the least, and a cigarette can help alleviate these feelings.

While on the subject of health, I would note that, unlike today, one saw relatively few overweight people, and rarely, if ever, obese or morbidly obese people. Also there were virtually no rail-thin women with anorexic figures. People ate more sensibly. They ate regular meals and healthier snacks. There was little fast food available and this was mostly limited to little hamburger or root beer joints, and most people got more exercise than they do today. On the other hand, in 1940 life expectancy at birth was 61.4 years for men and 65.7 years for women. In 2008, however, the figures were 75.4 and 80, respectively.

While on the subject of what was wrong those days, one must say that when it came to protecting the environment, Americans were both clueless and indifferent. For example, in 1934–35, dust storms devastated plains states such as Kansas and Oklahoma, where extensive grain production and the elimination of native wild grasses had disturbed the topsoil. As a result, when the region was hit by drought conditions and high winds, the area turned into the notorious "Dust Bowl" from which thousands of ruined farmers escaped to California with their belongings piled on old cars and trucks. Many eventually flourished in California. These Dust Bowl refugees were featured in John Steinbeck's classic *Grapes of Wrath*. Our lumber industry was destroying vast forests through "clear-cutting" every tree in sight without any replanting. While there weren't many cars to pollute the air, most home central heating burned coal, which is very polluting. Also large game animals, such as deer and bear, became quite scarce except in some parts of the West. By contrast, today there are deer in every state except Hawai`i, and in many places they even have become a pest. And bears have made a dramatic comeback and have even been spotted in suburbs outside of Washington, DC. A number of animals, for example buffalo, once on the verge of extinction, now thrive. Our relatively recent discovery of the vital importance of protecting the environment is certainly one of the major advances of our time.

I had the great misfortune of being in the Los Angeles County school system when it was suffering under the baleful influence of that misguided, famous "educator" John Dewey whose aversion to "elitism" and "authoritarianism" gave birth to "progressive education" that was then plaguing the L.A. County school system, as it was later, beginning in the 1960s, to plague school systems throughout the United States to this day. The main tenet of progressive education was and continues to be an emphasis on "learning how to think" as opposed to memorizing facts and figures—such memorization always being prefaced by the pejorative adjective "rote" indicating a mindless process. As I once wrote in the *Washington Post*, "Learning to think without having memorized the requisite facts is like trying to run a computer without the requisite software." I still like that analogy. This is why, to this day, I cannot spell, since my grammar school teachers didn't have us memorize correctly spelled words at a time when all kids should be learning this most basic skill. At least I had learned the multiplication tables, so, unlike so many younger people today, I don't need a calculator to multiply 6 times 6 or even 2 times 2. At age twelve, I spent a year at a small military school, and that year advanced me a year ahead of my peers in public school. One thing I must say is that we were all raised to be very patriotic, which most of us remained despite all the warts and blemishes revealed about our country by subsequent research and publication often produced by disenchanted academics.

Chapter 6

We Move North

I AM NOT ENTIRELY SURE WHY MY FATHER LEFT LOCKHEED in the mid-1930s. My guess is that, while he always insisted on heading any company he joined or helped form, he wasn't really cut out for or interested in the kind of administrative work being a CEO inevitably entailed. I also had the feeling that Chairman Robert Gross was keen on being president. My father's first love was designing and then supervising the building of aircraft. Also, he didn't think Lockheed was going to survive, and it probably wouldn't have, had it not been for the outbreak of war in Europe in September 1939. A military derivative of the Electra, the Hudson Bomber was sold to the Royal Air Force, and that no doubt saved Lockheed. My father simply wanted to get back into designing and then building a new airplane. On behalf of the U.S. Department of Commerce, he went out to review an easy-to-fly aircraft built by Dean Hammond who then lived in Ann Arbor, Michigan, and who had built a revolutionary twin-engine two-tail beam aircraft. The whole project intrigued my father, who joined with Hammond and completely redesigned his plane, giving it a very stable tricycle landing gear—unusual and pioneering then, but standard on most aircraft today (probably encouraged by this innovation)—and substituting one pusher engine for the original two. They agreed to build it in the San Francisco area and wound up with a factory south of San Francisco near the airport.

This tricycle landing gear, twin tail booms, pusher-engine Stearman-Hammond was a smashing technical success, but ultimately a financial failure. It was so simple to fly that anyone could fly it with little instruction, and thousands did. You simply steered out to the runway with an auto-like steering wheel, lined up with the runway, and then pulled both the throttle and the steering wheel all the way back, and up it went. Once in the air, one simply steered it right or left with the steering wheel only, no rudder pedals or joystick to bother with. To go up, pull back on the steering wheel, to go down, push it down. About the only way to crash it was to run into something flying horizontally. It couldn't stall. It could safely land at seventy-five miles per hour at a 45-degree angle. The three dangling landing gears could take the shock. As an experiment, with a pilot on board only to give instruction, an eleven-year-old boy who had never been in an airplane before got in, took off, flew it around Los Angeles, and landed without the pilot once touching any controls. It was unquestionably the world's safest airplane. The trouble was twofold: it could seat only two, and it cost about $35,000 (about $438,000 in today's dollars)—and this was during the Depression. The Navy bought some and equipped them to be flown pilotless by remote control for experimental purposes. This was one of the earliest UAVs (unmanned aerial vehicles) that are now a mainstay of our armed forces, in fact. Alas, however, there weren't enough private purchasers to keep the factory afloat. The company only sold about twenty airplanes.

The upside of this chapter in our life was that we lived in Burlingame on the San Francisco peninsula, a delightful community that had one of the very best public high schools in the nation. Indeed, some rich families who lived in adjoining affluent Hillsborough sent their offspring there, even though they could have afforded any private prep school in the country. For example, families with students in my school were members of the canned fruit family, the Doles, and of the family that made nearly all jukeboxes in the United States as well as organs, the Wurlitzers. Their extended family back in Milwaukee also made Schlitz and Pabst beer. My good friend was Raimund Pabst Wurlitzer. At a time when nationwide only about 15 percent of high school graduates ever even started college, our class in Burlingame had more than 90 percent *finishing* college. I very much liked high school, especially math, science, and foreign languages. I studied Latin and French and taught myself German. I long have been convinced that the most important phase of one's education is high school. Here is where one gets most of the basic knowledge one needs. College only builds on this. I hold this view with even greater conviction after having taught at the university level for sixteen years.

Since there were no school buses, we either walked or bicycled to school, which was about a thirty-minute walk away. Actually, I had a daytime-only driver's license at age fourteen, having learned to drive at age twelve. Not even the many affluent parents I knew bought cars for their offspring, even when they were in college. A few students had scraped together enough to buy and restore an old Model T Ford or a more modern Model A. The Model T, the world's first mass-produced auto, was, by today's standards, curious and primitive indeed. It had three pedals: one for two speeds forward, one for reverse, and a third for braking. All three pedals activated bands that, when applied, gripped the crankshaft at selected spots.

Reverse was more powerful than the two forward speeds, which sometimes led to people backing up hills.

In the 1920s and into the 1930s there was a wide selection of automobile makes. My father always preferred Packards, which looked like Rolls Royces. All cars, even the most modern and expensive, were unsafe by today's standards. They often had high centers of gravity that led to tipping over. Their brakes left something to be desired, and tires often blew out or went flat, but cars then could go almost as fast as today's cars. For example, we had a Packard that could do well over 100 miles per hour. Seatbelts did not come into general use until well after World War II. My father installed airplane seatbelts in his cars in the 1950s, years before auto seatbelts finally became easily available. Our generation was, in general, quite conservative in behavior, and those at Burlingame were especially so. Anyone who smoked cigarettes was considered a deadbeat. Marijuana was something only lower-class Mexicans and big band musicians smoked. Famous drummer Gene Krupa, for example, was rumored to be a marijuana smoker. All other drugs were beyond the pale. Sex was something we only talked about but didn't practice.

We had formal black-tie proms and considered jitterbugging infra dig. (I still do.) We all knew how to dance, having been sent to dancing school at age fourteen. We had the privilege of later dancing to big-name bands that came to San Francisco hotels to play, including Tommy Dorsey, Harry James, Benny Goodman, and Glen Miller. Later I also danced to them at the famed Palladium Ballroom in Hollywood. I made some very good friends in high school, many of whom did quite well after their service in World War II. For example, one good friend, Rollin Myer, introduced condominiums to the United States. He initially went broke in the complicated pioneering process, but eventually recovered to do quite well. As a generation, we were very individualistic and would have shunned like the very plague large crowds of young people, unlike later generations who flock lemming-like to such places as Fort Lauderdale on Easter breaks. The crowded masses of young people at Woodstock or later at mosh pits would have been viewed as scenes from Hell resulting from very bad dreams. Kids also didn't then emote hysterically at popular music performances, as they often do now—although I do remember that when a skinny little guy sang a solo with Dorsey's band, most of the gals would stop dancing and push toward the stage with audible sighs of delight. The vocalist was Frank Sinatra.

We didn't drink hard liquor, but did drink wine and beer, which was considered part of eating among the Europeans who set the tone in San Francisco, where we often went to dine. I have fond memories of Ripley's French semi-basement restaurant with candles and checkered tablecloths where for seventy-five cents one got a tureen of soup, a large bowl of salad, half a roasted chicken, vegetables, cheese, fruit, dessert, and a large carafe of red wine. (Seventy-five cents would be about $10 in today's money.) I always had a stein of beer with my meals at that great old German restaurant Schroeder's on Front Street. (It's still there.) High school and college students were never "carded" when drinking at restaurants. I dearly loved San Francisco, simply called the "The City" by natives to this day. In San Francisco the sizeable European population, especially the French and Italians, had great influence and set the tone. The City of Paris was our leading department store. The City had some of the best French restaurants in the world outside France, and there were many good Italian restaurants. The large and thriving Chinatown always fascinated me. We used to go up there to buy noodles and other great Chinese specialties.

The San Francisco Opera House hosted some of the best opera in the country. I saw my first opera there, *Der Rosenkavalier* (still my favorite opera), with famed Lotte Lehmann singing the role of the *Feldmarschallin* and Eric Leinsdorf, a newcomer from Vienna, conducting. It was magical and unforgettable, even though I stood the whole time at the back of the top balcony, which was all I could afford. A favorite radio show was Josef Hornig's delightful *Viennese Echoes*, which played music that made me long to visit Vienna. (When I finally did visit that city, I wound up living there and marrying a Viennese.) From both of my parents I had acquired a great love of music, classic and popular, and Vienna was the music capital of the world.

Then there was the German House, a four- or five-story building that housed the some forty-three German-speaking German, Austrian, and Swiss clubs and organizations in the City. Once a week, Raimund Wurlitzer and I used to go up there to sing with the German *Maennerchor* (men's choir), which sang old German songs, and to drink beer. This was a scene right out of pre–World War I Germany. It was a great way to practice German, which I was teaching myself at the time. All in all, San Francisco, without doubt, was this country's most cosmopolitan city. The City looked both to Europe and to Asia. With some justification, San Franciscans considered the New Yorkers provincial for believing that the world revolved around their city. I might add that San Francisco was probably our most tolerant city where discrimination of all kinds was at a minimum. This led to a more visible homosexual community than found elsewhere in the country.

There were, however, dark spots in the City. For example, more than thirty years after the famous 1906 earthquake and subsequent fire, there were still vacant lots in downtown San Francisco where one could still see the remains of destroyed buildings in foundations with steps leading to nowhere. San Franciscans always have referred to just the fire, not the earthquake. I recently learned on the History Channel that the then-mayor of the City decided that, for public relations reasons, the fire sounded less menacing because it could be countered, whereas an earthquake was an act of God over which people had no control. Thereafter, and to this day, it became the fire.

The Depression seemed, in a way, more entrenched in San Francisco, since the strongly unionized workforce was driving new businesses to set up in non-union Southern California. Exacerbating the problem were serious 1930s waterfront clashes between the striking longshoremen, led by Harry Bridges, a known Communist from Australia, and the police, especially during the general strike of 1934, which Bridges was instrumental in fomenting.

The American people seemed little concerned about the troubling storm clouds forming on distant horizons in Europe and Asia. Somewhat of an exception was the Spanish Civil War, which began in 1936 when Gen. Francisco Franco moved against the shaky government in Madrid with troops he had commanded in North Africa. This began what many later came to see as a rehearsal for World War II. The Spanish government, the so-called Loyalists, before long became dominated by Spanish Communists loyal to Moscow and to Stalin. For example, this government sent Spain's entire gold reserves to Moscow for "safekeeping"; this later went to pay for military equipment sent to Spain from the Soviet Union. As Norman Friedman explained in his excellent book *The Fifty-Year War: Conflict and Strategy in the Cold War* (1999), Spain was "the first attempt by the Soviet Union . . . to gain control of another country." The Soviet Union provided aircraft and pilots and other forms of military assistance. Far more publicized was the larger and much more visible military support provided by Germany and Italy to Franco's forces. World opinion was shocked by the 1936 bombing of the northern Spanish Basque city of Guernica by German bombers, labeled an atrocity and immortalized by Picasso in his famous mural. Widely touted as a "terror" bombing, it actually had a solely tactical military objective.

To some degree, American public opinion was polarized by this tragic and bloody civil war. Conservatives, and most especially Catholics, supported Franco who had the support of the Church in Spain simply because the far-left Loyalists had declared war against the Church, executing thousands of priests and nuns, even a bishop or two, and burning or desecrating churches where they held sway. Liberals, on the other hand, tended to support the Loyalists and hailed as heroes members of the Abraham Lincoln Battalion (not brigade), which consisted mostly of American Communists from urban areas. The Battalion was part of the International Brigade headed by dedicated Stalinists who were wont to execute Brigade members who proved to be "left-wing deviationists" such as anarchists, Trotskyites, and Socialists, reflecting Stalin's purges that were then racking the Soviet Union. Certainly, Franco was no choir boy and executed his share among those supporting the Loyalist cause. In the long run, however, Franco's victory in 1939 was by far the lesser of two evils. A Communist victory would have been a major prolonged disaster for

Spain and most certainly would have invited a German and Italian invasion and occupation. Spain already had lost nearly seven hundred and fifty thousand people in its war. Franco skillfully managed to keep Spain out of World War II and, after years of a strict dictatorship, eventually led Spain incrementally toward its present first successful democracy, for which he now gets little credit.

I had always been interested in events abroad, especially in Europe. This was not only unusual among my peers but also among the population at large. In today's shrunken world, it's hard to imagine how distant all these dramatic events abroad seemed to most Americans. Remember that in California we were at least ten travel days away from Europe and even farther from Asia. We were certain that our isolated geography would always protect us from any attack from abroad: we were right as far as the continental United States was concerned. We didn't then regard Hawai`i as part of the United States, but even there no one ever expected an attack. As a people we were largely unconcerned when Japan began overrunning China. The infamous 1937 Japanese "Rape of Nanking" did not arouse much resentment.

One of my high school friends had attended the 1936 Olympics in Berlin and came back full of enthusiasm for what he had seen in Germany. He especially noted there was full employment, in contrast to our widespread unemployment, and that a "fresh wind" was blowing through the country. Nazism was very youth oriented, and that too impressed him. Nobody could then foresee where this all would lead, although my father was convinced from the beginning that the Nazi regime would lead to no good, and probably to war.

Americans, on the whole, also were not overly upset by the March 1938 German Anschluss occupation of Austria and the subsequent occupation of the Czechoslovak territory following the notorious 1938 Munich meeting with Hitler, to which British Prime Minister Neville Chamberlain flew in a Lockheed Electra. A real shocker and surprise was the August 1939 German–Soviet Nonaggression Pact, which gave the USSR the eastern part of Poland and control of the Baltic States and Finland, setting the stage for World War II. This initially really nonplussed Communists all over the world. In the United States Communists began agitating against our fighting their newfound ally, Germany, with their "The Yanks are NOT coming" slogan. I will never forget picking up the *San Francisco Chronicle* from my doorstep the morning of September 2, 1939, and reading that Germany had invaded Poland. Two days later, France and Great Britain declared war on Germany, and World War II was on.

During the month of August 1939 two high school friends and I set out for Canada in an aging coupe pulling a small trailer with our food and sleeping bags. Vancouver, British Columbia, our first stop in Canada, was clearly foreign, more like an English city than any American city. The British Union Jack flag was flying everywhere. Workers, wearing typical English pulled-down working-class caps, were going to work on bicycles. The main department store, the Hudson Bay Company, had only British and Canadian goods for sale. As far as we could tell, there was nothing there from the United States. Canadians smoked Sweet Caporal cigarettes, not Camels or Lucky Strikes. The nearby Lion Gate Bridge was proudly touted as the "longest suspension bridge in the British Empire." Unlike today, Canada then was clearly a country distinct and different from the United States. When it lost its British qualities, it lost its distinct character. From Vancouver, we went east to Alberta Province via the Trans Canadian Highway, which was a two-lane gravel road. One could drive a whole day seeing only a few people, usually Native Americans. One afternoon, we all went to sleep at the same time as we drove and wound up in a ditch. It was our good fortune that a rare truck happened by an hour later and pulled us out. We camped out the whole trip and had a generally marvelous time. This was my first visit to a "foreign" country.

When graduation time came the following June, unlike all my friends I didn't go to college, but went to work on a cattle ranch instead.

chapter 7

Life on the Ranch and College Days

Ican't remember exactly why I, unlike most of my friends, did not go to college after high school. It was probably because I didn't have enough money for college and had to work. As noted earlier, at a time when only about 15 percent of American high school graduates nationwide even started college, most graduates of Burlingame High finished college. I liked high school and got very good grades. I most probably would have been accepted into virtually any college of my choice in the United States, since competition for college acceptance was far less than it is today. However, a great uncle who had a cattle ranch, the Lazy S (the S was on its side), a relatively small spread east of the San Francisco Bay Area near Livermore, offered me a job punching cattle at a dollar a day and "found" (bunk and meals) for a ten-hour day, a wage that had not changed since the Civil War. Since I had always liked to ride, the idea of making a living on a horse greatly appealed to me. My parents with their rural background were of the opinion that when a boy turned eighteen he was a man and on his own. They subsequently never offered me any advice or counsel; moreover, I was expected to earn my own way. In any case, there wasn't much money on hand because Stearman-Hammond was failing.

I would like to digress here to note that one of my favorite cousins, Bob Crow, took another route when he graduated from high school. He went to Canada to enlist in Canada's famed Princess Pat [Patricia] Regiment, since Canada, as part of the British empire, went to war when Great Britain did, in September 1939. In recent times, American men fled to Canada to escape the Vietnam era draft, and now American military deserters are doing the same thing to escape service in Iraq. Then, however, a number of Americans went to Canada to *fight*—to fight

Nazi Germany. I thought they were nuts, since I was dead set against our getting involved in the European War. I was part of a generation that widely believed we had been snookered by British anti-German propaganda into getting involved in World War I.

We antiwar types agreed with the wag who said, "All we got out of that war was out." We had read Erich Maria Remarque's *All Quiet on the Western Front* (1929) and had seen the 1930 film, which humanized the German soldiers, which had been dehumanized by anti-German propaganda in World War I. We also had read H. C. Engelbrecht and F. C. Hanighen's *Merchants of Death* (1934), which described how arms manufacturers and dealers had profited by selling to both sides. Many of us, in short, were disillusioned with that war and saw the second war simply as a continuation of the first. I believed I had gotten the best birthday present ever when, in 1941, on my nineteenth birthday, Nazi Germany attacked Communist Soviet Union. I thought, aha, the Commies and the Nazis will kill each other off, and I won't have to go to war. (The Communist Party line immediately shifted from "The Yanks are NOT coming" to "Open a second front now!") Unlike antiwar activists during the Vietnam War (and to some extent the Iraq War), we were not antimilitary. Indeed, we greatly admired World War I heroes, the flying aces, men such as Alvin York, "the Lost Battalion." In any case, subsequent events dramatically proved that we had been profoundly wrong in our opposition to a war with Nazi Germany.

Bob's mother, who was my mother's sister, went to Vancouver and, with the help of an American consul, got Bob out of the Princess Pats and brought him back to the United States. After Pearl Harbor, Bob enlisted as a medic in the U.S. Army; this was the most hazardous duty of all since medics have to collect the wounded on battlefields when all other soldiers were hunkered down in foxholes. He eventually got the Bronze Star for bravery. He was fortunate indeed that he had left the Princess Pats, since it was sent to Hong Kong where it was captured by the Japanese in 1942. One of my State Department bosses on the Soviet desk, John Guthrie, joined the Princess Pats in 1941 and spent the war working in a Japanese coal mine. He once told me that he was amazed that he had never tired of eating rice.

The Lazy S was not only shorthanded in cowpunchers, but also "shortpawed" in mousers, so I took the family cat to the ranch with me. I soon discovered that the life of a cowboy is singularly unglamorous. I started the day at the crack of dawn milking a cow, which I did not find easy. My cat would always show up for a milk handout and in time brought kittens with her. I did get to ride a lot, but I generally spent my time on such mundane tasks as riding fence lines to see that they remained intact, rescuing calves from bogs or other hazards, and doing other uninteresting chores around the ranch. I did learn a good bit of carpentry when we built a new horse barn, though. My horse was a calm, untiring quarter horse. Once when I had finished spraying for barn insects, I jumped up on my horse holding the sprayer just when the spray piston slid out between the unsaddled horse and me. I drove its handle into the poor unsuspecting horse, which violently bucked me off in an arc that landed me on my face in the dirt. Not badly hurt, I did what one must always do when thrown from a horse: I got back on and rode off with only a hackamore (bridle without bit).

There was once a bit of excitement when it was reported that there were cattle rustlers in the area. I felt the need to be armed, and the only gun I could afford was an old Model 1873 Winchester .44–40 rifle. As it turned out, I never encountered any rustlers, which was just as well, since I would have been hopelessly outgunned. In any case, I also bought the old Winchester in case I spotted a deer while riding around. In fact, I was later told by old cowhands that, even in the heyday of cattle ranching, cowboys usually did not carry a gun, unlike in the movies. (When we ever had time, we cowboys would go into town to watch a Western.) The highlight of my cowboy days was a big old-fashioned roundup at a nearby large ranch where a number of us from other ranches joined in the task. At a roundup we prepared a sizeable number of calves to join the herd. We would heel- and head-rope them and stretch them on the ground to immobilize them. I did head-roping, but could never master the fine art of roping a running calf's hind two legs. Once a calf was immobilized, we branded it, clipped off the tip of one ear, and made a perpendicular cut into the same ear. This was called earmarking. We then bobbed off its horns and covered the stumps with a kind of tar to prevent infection. Next we castrated them if they were males. We later broiled the removed testicles on the branding fire and called them "Rocky Mountain Oysters." They tasted great. In later years, all this was done in chutes, because roping and roughing up the calves made them lose weight.

The Lazy S was located in hilly country that was nicely scenic, but not ideally suited for cattle. (I would guess that this whole area has been subdivided by now.) We had a relatively small herd so it didn't matter much. One cowboy lived in a house on the ranch and others came in from nearby ranches when needed. I lived in the ranch house, since, being a small ranch, we had no bunkhouse. Our resident cowboy was from the old school, although he was only in his thirties. I was delighted that he actually knew most of the authentic old cowboy songs like "Bury Me Not on the Lone Prairie," "Red River Valley," and "The Old Chisholm Trail" (with ribald, if not raunchy, verses I had never heard before); he was full of other authentic cowboy lore, too. In all, it was a fairly happy time, but I could see that there was really no future in punching cattle. Moreover, it wasn't very interesting or rewarding work, and the pay was miserable. So I decided to go to college. I still think it's a good idea to work at something before going to college; my opinion on this is even stronger after having been a college professor.

I borrowed enough money from my great uncle, at the going interest rate, to enter the Colorado School of Mines (that we called just "Mines") for the spring semester. Mines turned out to be an exceedingly grueling and demanding school. We had to carry an inordinately heavy course load of math, science, and engineering unrelieved by any liberal arts studies, even English. The reason Mines was so demanding was that a mining engineer often was expected to work in isolated locales and had to be self-sufficient in all kinds of engineering. By the time a student graduated, he (it was then an all-male school) was qualified in mining, electrical, mechanical, civil, and chemical engineering. This made it by far the most demanding engineering school in the country. In the summer, we first took a summer field course, and for the rest of the summer were expected to gain employment in a mining-related job. After completing the summer surveying course, which I loved, I went up to the Climax molybdenum mine high in the Rockies looking for work. It was early July and there was still snow on the ground. The mine didn't have the greatest safety record, so I decided against it. Moreover, by then I had decided I didn't want to work underground as a mining engineer and preferred to become a geophysics engineer who always worked aboveground, searching for minerals beneath the surface. (Geophysics was being pioneered in Germany at that time, and all our instruments and most of our reading material had come from that country.)

I then headed out to the Kettleman Hills oil fields on the eastern edge of California's San Joaquin Valley; an aunt and uncle of mine lived in nearby Avenal, and I could stay with them and save money. Since I have always suffered from acrophobia (except when flying), I didn't want to work high up on drilling rigs, so I got a job as a roustabout working on the ground. This was far more dangerous than being up on high because things kept falling off the derricks and other structures, and we didn't have hardhats at the oil fields in those days. I never knew anybody who worked in the oil fields for any length of time who hadn't lost at least a finger or toe or two and sometimes a hand, foot, or arm. At times we were working in the sun when it was well over 105 degrees in the shade. We had to take salt tablets every hour. Anyway, I survived intact and made fairly good money for my continued education.

In addition to the very heavy course load, as first semester freshmen at Mines we were subjected to considerable hazing. For example, we all took the same chemistry class, and every Friday afternoon the sophomores were waiting for us as we left this class and formed a long gauntlet that we had to run while being beaten with heavy Army belts, then part of the Army ROTC uniform. (ROTC was obligatory for freshman and sophomores.) At the end of the semester, we had to run the "All School Gauntlet," which was a quarter of a mile long around a field house track. During that run we first-semester freshman were beaten with belts by every other student in the school. There also had been plenty of extemporaneous hazing during that miserable first semester. I speculated that the powers that be at this school saw hazing as a way to toughen us up for a tough profession.

In addition, my best friend from high school days, Bill Granfield, and I pledged the Sigma Alpha Epsilon fraternity in which we pledges were regularly beaten with barrel staves and sometimes even with wire coat hangers. Needless to say, we all suffered from very sore bottoms. There was precious little time for social life and hardly any women we could date in our small town of Golden, located at the eastern foothills of the Rockies. When we did have a bit of free time, we would get sloshed on beer from a local old, small, brick brewery that brewed the now-famous Coors beer. I think we students drank a sizeable percentage of Coors's total output. We either bought it by the keg from the brewery or guzzled it by the glass in the badly misnamed Chocolate Shop.

On the afternoon of December 7, 1941, a group of us was sitting in the SAE (Sigma Alpha Epsilon fraternity) living room listening to records or reading when we heard that Pearl Harbor had been attacked. Our immediate reaction was, "Those Japs must be out of their minds to attack us. Their flimsy aircraft will fall apart in midair and their tinny ships will be sunk wholesale." One must remember that in those days everything made in Japan—toys, for most people—was synonymous with junk. (As the war progressed, of course, we had a rude awakening.) We had no idea of how devastating the attack had been. So we all believed that the war could not possibly last more than six months, and that if we didn't want to miss it, and that included all of us, we had to enlist immediately. Many men at Mines had the same feeling. Of course the war also gave us a chance to escape the academic thralldom of Mines. Frantic faculty members pleaded with us to stay in school, and I assume a number did, at least those seniors who were going to graduate as second lieutenants in the Army engineers the upcoming June. As soon as the fall semester ended, however, Bill Granfield and I headed for California and recruiting stations.

When the Japanese had been rampaging all over China, we did not take any serious action, but when, in 1940–41, they moved into French Indochina, the United States and our Allies imposed a blockade on the shipment of scrap iron, rubber, and oil to Japan to counter rampant Japanese aggression in Asia. The Japanese considered this a virtual act of war, since this move seriously threatened to destroy its economy, a fact not wholly appreciated in Washington. The Japanese, however, clearly had moved into what is now Vietnam to use it as a base for operations against the resource-rich Dutch East Indies to the south. Having defeated the mighty but feckless Russia in a 1904–5 war and acquired Korea (then called Chosun) and a good bit of Manchuria, Japan began to pride itself on being a world power. In 1937 Japan invaded North China, which did not sit well with the United States. Japan became greatly concerned about being largely dependent on indispensable oil from a not-very-friendly or dependable America and wanted the oil independence that the oil fields in the Dutch East Indies could provide.

Given our newfound hostility in the form of the blockade, they feared that we would oppose this move by interposing our fleet in the area. To prevent this, they sought to destroy our fleet at Pearl Harbor, but had the bad fortune to have missed our carriers that just happened to be at sea; much of our fleet remained intact. Japanese leaders, out of touch with reality, considered the Japanese to be intrinsically superior to soft Americans whose will to fight, they believed, eventually would be exhausted by intense prolonged and bloody battles in the far-distant Western Pacific area. But they also believed that war with the United States was inevitable and that it was best to strike it sooner rather than later before American armed forces became stronger. War thus came about in large measure as the result of profound miscalculations and a misreading of intentions in both Washington and Tokyo.

I have long been fond of telling students and other audiences that we got into World War II because of Vietnam. They would first regard me as somewhat balmy until I explained myself. Persistent rumors that President Roosevelt knew about the pending Japanese attack and did nothing to prevent it are patently absurd. Roosevelt—quite correctly, as it turned out—wanted to get us into a war with Germany. As noted above, through a profound miscalculation, he clearly failed to recognize how serious a blow he had landed on Japan with his 1941 embargo. I believe he actually would have done anything to stave off a Japanese attack, since a war with Japan was the last thing in the world he wanted. Moreover, he loved the Navy and was especially protective of its new ships that he had ordered built. In the final analysis, he was neither base enough nor stupid enough to have been guilty of such perfidy. I am sure that Roosevelt must have been as astonished as we all were when Hitler declared war on us four days after Pearl Harbor. Finally, FDR got the war he really wanted.

There has been much justified consternation about our wartime relocation of Japanese, including U.S. citizens with Japanese heritage, on our West Coast to relocation centers in the interior of the country. Obviously this was a clear injustice perpetrated on innocent people. As always with past events, however, one must consider the context in which this occurred. After Pearl Harbor, most Americans were furious at Japan and the Japanese. Moreover, we thought the Japanese in California did little to assimilate, considered them to be standoffish, and did not especially like them. I never felt this attitude was racist, since we liked the Chinese Americans among us. There was genuine concern that some Japanese might engage in espionage and sabotage of defense plants and installations in California. In point of fact, relatively few Japanese in the United States were in any way disloyal to this country. In fact, some of the most courageous and effective troops we had in

World War II were those highly decorated Army infantry units composed entirely of Japanese Americans. These units suffered heavy casualties fighting for this country in Europe. The most outstanding of these Japanese American units was the famed heroic 442nd Regimental Combat Team, which became the most decorated unit of its size in American history.

My parents had moved to Los Angeles where my father was running a defense plant, and I moved in with them again, something I had never expected to do, but which was a practical wartime temporary arrangement. Soon after Pearl Harbor my main ambition was to enlist as an aviation cadet in the Navy and become a Navy flyer, as my father had been in World War I. The Navy thought this was a great idea and was preparing to make my swearing-in a recruiting public relations event, since most naval aviators were then getting their primary training in Stearman N2S2s and, moreover, I was carrying on a family tradition. This was in early 1942. I passed the flight physical with flying colors, except for clogged eustachian tubes that were essential to equalizing the air pressure inside and outside of the ear with rapid changes in altitude. Try as they could, Navy doctors could not blast my tubes open. Ultimately I could not pass the required flight physical. Today I bless my eustachian tubes every time they give me trouble when I'm flying: everyone I knew who joined that first post–Pearl Harbor class of aviation cadets was dead within a year because the normal two-year training time (it's still two years) was reduced to a fraction of this time due to the urgent need for Navy aviators. In retrospect, I am not at all sure that I would have survived the shortened training and I may well not have survived early combat. Fortunately, as it turned out, I had one great alternative: the Navy V-12 program, which enabled college students to remain in school to largely complete their education before being commissioned as ensigns. The Navy, unlike the other services, placed great weight on having college-trained officers. This enabled me to return to college and hopefully graduate before being called to active service to eventually become commissioned an ensign.

I am sure that my eagerness to enlist greatly pleased my interventionist father who must have been more than upset by my antiwar convictions, although we didn't discuss it very often. As I have noted, my father thought we should have been supporting the British from the very beginning of the war. I knew he was very unhappy with Charles Lindbergh for cozying up to Nazi Luftwaffe generals and especially for his leading role in the America First isolationist, antiwar movement that I, alas, also supported. In fact, he no longer wanted to have anything to do with Lindbergh. (Lindbergh, however, later redeemed himself in my father's eyes by flying some fifty combat missions in the Pacific theater as a civilian testing Lockheed P-38 fighter planes.) My father seriously thought of volunteering for the Army Air Corps, especially after two of his best friends joined up: Tom Ryan (mentioned in Chapter 4) who became a colonel in the Army, and Fred Hewitt who became a commander in the Navy. My mother successfully discouraged my father from following suit.

After the humiliating surrender of all our forces in the Philippines, on April 9, 1942, and other military setbacks, American morale hit an all-time low. It was greatly boosted, however, when, on April 18, sixteen B-25 bombers, under the command of Maj. (later Gen.) Jimmy Doolittle, bombed Tokyo and other Japanese cities. Where these planes came from was a secret. Asked about this, President Roosevelt said, "They came from Shangri La," a fictional utopia in the Himalayas featured in James Hilton's popular 1933 novel (later a film), *Lost Horizon.* (Roosevelt subsequently named the Maryland presidential retreat Shangri La; it since has been renamed Camp David.) My father was a close friend of Doolittle's and knew about the raid ahead of time. He told me that it was launched from a carrier (USS *Hornet*) and that the pilots had practiced carrier takeoffs on a runway with the dimensions of a carrier deck painted on it. Doolittle, my father, and a number of other World War I flyers had formed an association called the "Quiet Birdmen," a misnomer if ever there was one. Among the most notorious of the lot was Doolittle, whose wild, boozy parties got him banned from a number of hotels in the prewar years, according to my mother. Doolittle had been an exceptionally good test pilot and famous air derby participant, winning many races.

The V-12 program required that I be in college, so I entered the University of California at Los Angeles (UCLA). While there, I worked as a part-time service station attendant. I wore a white shirt, pants, and overseas cap and had to perform full service, since this was before self-service was introduced. At one point I worked in my father's defense plant as a spot welder making ammunition boxes on a production line. It was good experience learning how production line workers fared. I could see how they would get fed up with it. I later got another summer job with the California State Forest Service as a blister rust control worker in the Sierra foothills east of the state capital, Sacramento. Blister rust had devastated the forests; it was spread through wild gooseberry plants. Our task was to completely eradicate these troublesome plants, roots and all, and create a gooseberry-free belt across the Sierras. It was very hard work, but the food was good and the pay wasn't bad.

We also doubled as firefighters when there were local forest fires. This could be very dangerous if we were caught in a crown fire, which leapfrogged over the firefighters and trapped them. We were constantly short of workers, so every Saturday evening we would take a truck to Sacramento and gather up drunks on skid row and dump them in our truck. (Imagine the outcry if anyone tried that today.) When these hijacked men sobered up, they were stuck way up in the middle of nowhere. They had to work if they wanted to eat and be paid, and they actually were paid a fair wage. In point of fact, it did them a world of good to be "off the sauce" for a week and be well fed and cared for. On the next Saturday skid-row run we offered to return any of them to Sacramento who wanted to go. Some opted to stay with us, since they felt better than they had in a long time.

I didn't care much for UCLA or for the local SAE chapter, so I transferred to the University of California at Berkeley that most people simply call "Berkeley" or "Cal." My friend Bill Granfield also enlisted in the V-12 program and went to Stanford, Cal's arch rival. I liked Berkeley very much and was especially taken by the great bunch of brothers at the local SAE chapter. I was a math major and a history minor. When I began actually taking liberal arts courses, I thought I'd died and gone to heaven. After grueling Mines, these courses were not only a piece of cake, but also very interesting. Berkeley had a fabulous history department. For American history I had the famed Professor John D. Hicks, who wrote one of leading American history college textbooks, *The American Nation: History of the United States, 1865 to Present* (1937). Hicks's lectures were absolutely fascinating. In fact, many who were not even taking his course would stand in back of the large lecture hall and simply listen. For German history I had the famed Raymond Sontag.

I had a great roommate, David Clark, who years later headed the *Sunset Magazine* book section. Another favorite brother, Phil Knox, became a top officer of Sears. Both Dave and Phil long remained cherished friends of mine. Social life at the SAE house was great. We had a lot of fun gathering around the piano and singing college and other songs and generally whooping it up. We were fined for using bad language at meals, but this was dropped at lunch on "Dirty Friday" when we all loved to sing bawdy limericks. The texts we sang, however, never had any four-letter words. In fact we simply didn't use such words, nor did most people in those days. Our parties were outstanding and very boozy. I remember at one party knocking off a fifth of Scotch and winding up passed out on the second floor of the Theta sorority house behind us. How I got there, no one knew. One thing was certain, I had had nothing to do with any of the sisters there. In fact, shortly thereafter I even began dating a Theta. I should add here that I am sure that most of my SAE brothers finished college without ever having had sex, as incredible as this may sound today. I suppose Berkeley, even then, was somewhat liberal, but, if so, I wasn't aware of it. There certainly was no apparent antiwar agitation, except for a small group of Communists who, prior to the June 1941 German attack on the Soviet Union, were promoting the "The Yanks are NOT coming" line, urging the United States to stay out of a war against Stalin's Nazi allies. After we got into the war, their line quickly changed to "Open a second front now!" obviously to help the beleaguered Soviet Union. Then there was the Communists' Twentieth Century Bookstore right on the edge of the campus (a fact I later pointed out to my Soviet colleagues in Vienna to show how free we were).

I must say that the professors at Berkeley were very understanding when it came to the performance of their war-destined male students. I never heard that draft boards were granting student deferments, as they did during the Vietnam War. Those of us in the V-12 program, the ROTC, or the Army Student Training Program (ASTP) were exempt from the draft because we were already in the service, however. The Navy, which, unlike the Army, placed great store in having college-educated officers, was true to its promise that its V-12 and ROTC students were intended to become officers. The Army, to a large degree, reneged on its similar promise when it needed more personnel. For example, after our losses during the grim December 1944 Battle of the Bulge, the Army simply pulled ASTP students out of school and put them into the ranks as privates. In the spring of 1943, all the V-12 students were placed on active duty as apprentice seamen (the lowest rating). We donned bell-bottom sailor uniforms and moved into the large International House at the upper end of Bancroft Avenue on which the SAE house was located. I never knew, nor really cared, what happened to the House's previous occupants. We kept going to our same classes, but now we were in uniform.

In the fall, my class of V-12 students was pulled out of school and sent to a pre-midshipman school boot camp in Portsmouth, Virginia. At the time, I was one semester shy of credits needed for my BA, but good old Berkeley eventually gave me the one semester's credits for midshipman school, so I could later go to grad school. I was going to be in uniform for the next three years.

Chapter 8

I Go to War

WE TRAVELED BY VERY CROWDED TROOP TRAIN from California to Portsmouth, Virginia. Our boot camp at Portsmouth was new and not all that bad. We learned to drill, to shoot a 1903 Springfield rifle, and a few other things that raw recruits are required to learn. We were supervised by lower-rated sailors who enjoyed the momentary opportunity to lord it over future officers. In late November 1943 a number of us and I were transferred to the U.S. Naval Reserve Midshipman School at Columbia University in New York City. The school had taken over a number of student resident halls, and I was assigned to Johnson Hall. For the first month we were on a kind of probation. Those considered qualified were then appointed midshipmen, while the rest went to the fleet as sailors. The discipline was very tight and the course load extremely demanding. One instructor told us that in four months at the school we were to receive as much seamanship, gunnery, and communications instruction as the Annapolis middies got in four years; I believe he had attended the Naval Academy at Annapolis, Maryland. In addition, we had other courses such as leadership and ship and aircraft identification, which later turned out to be critically important. Not surprisingly, having grown up with airplanes, I was one of the best in aircraft recognition, something that was later to save lives.

I found New York strange, vibrant, and fascinating. One could walk for blocks in some parts without hearing a word of English. The city also was awash in people in uniform. Since we midshipmen had officers' uniforms, we often were saluted by enlisted sailors and soldiers, which we enjoyed, even though we were not yet entitled to this courtesy. We much enjoyed being invited to spend part of a weekend with affluent families in upscale Westchester County north of New York.

These good people wanted to do something for those in uniform and probably believed that it was "safest" to invite future naval officers into their homes. My old friend Bill Granfield, whom I called "Granny," had already been commissioned a Navy Supply Corps officer and was stationed at the Supply Corps facility at 90 Church Street in lower Manhattan. He hated it and longed to get into combat.

I was commissioned an ensign on April 13, 1944, in St. John the Divine Cathedral on New York's upper west side. Prior to that, we all had taken a competitive exam in math and mechanics to qualify for a plum assignment to the Tactical Radar School in Hollywood Beach, Florida. To my utter surprise I was one of the few chosen. When I got to the school in Florida, I discovered that we were being trained to run a ship's combat information center, usually located somewhere in a ship's bowels and loaded with radar and communications equipment. This was to be the ship's eyes, ears, and brain. To me this meant seeing the war on a radar plan position indicator (PPI) scope. That did not appeal to me in the least. Moreover, I had heard that we were planning a major amphibious invasion of France. I just had to get in on that historic event, so I applied for a transfer to the Atlantic Amphibious Command (PhibLant).

I quickly got my wish. I was to report within a week to the amphibious training base at Little Creek, Virginia, in the Norfolk area not far from Portsmouth where I had been as a sailor, to train for landing ship medium (LSM) duty. LSMs were some 208 feet long with a beam (width) of thirty-four feet and a maximum displacement (weight) of nearly a thousand tons. The bridge and other superstructure were located on the starboard side, as with carriers. They had a large open well deck for tanks and other vehicles. The bridge, pilot house, and gun tubs were lightly armored. When I saw a photo of this ungainly ship and learned they were going to be deployed only to the Pacific, I decided I had to get out of this assignment. I took a train to Washington and stayed at an Allied officers' club that had been set up by private donors in an old brownstone mansion on Dupont Circle. I decided to call my father's old friend Adm. Charles Emery Rosendahl, the Navy's chief lighter-than-air (i.e., dirigibles) officer and advocate, to get me out of the assignment and have me assigned to the Atlantic destroyer fleet. Unfortunately, the only phone I could use at the club was located at the end of the bar. I got right through to the good admiral: he was cordial but uncooperative. When I told him that I planned to stay in the Navy (true at that time) and needed destroyer duty, the admiral told me that on no other ship would I get as much valuable seagoing experience as on an LSM (and he proved to be absolutely right). He closed with "Give your dad my best regards"—all this within earshot of half a dozen sniggering officers at the bar. Talk about humiliation! I gave up and reported for duty at Little Creek. At some point I learned that Granny had gotten his wish for a combat assignment, and in spades. He had somehow finagled a transfer to the submarine service. Nothing would do but that I join my best friend. Fortunately for me the amphibious force had priority over everything else. A quarter of all the officers in the submarines service were killed in action, the highest rate of any branch of any service. Granny eventually experienced exactly the same kind of terror so graphically portrayed in that greatest of all war films, the German *Das Boot* (1981) (pronounced "boat").

At Little Creek everything and everybody were in Quonset huts, which did prepare us psychologically for overseas duty. We trained on a small fleet of LSMs, mostly in the nearby Chesapeake Bay. Future LSM crews were formed at Little Creek, and I was assigned to a crew headed by Lt. Kenneth D. Higgins from Athens, Tennessee, who had already completed a Pacific theater combat tour on a carrier. He was going to be our skipper until after the war. We learned nearly all we needed to know about LSMs. I was slated to be the ship's gunnery officer, which I liked. I was especially interested in gunnery training at nearby Dam Neck where aerial targets were towed by a slow aircraft just offshore past the firing range. There we were introduced to the latest in fire control for 20-mm and 40-mm rapid fire antiaircraft guns, using the Mark IV gyroscopic sight. It worked great on the range, but was to prove to be all but useless in combat. At the end of our training, we all were lined up in a morning formation by crews, when a messenger gave me a telegram that I read to all assembled. It notified me that I had been classified 1A and was to report to my draft board for immediate induction. Big laugh all around! By that time I had been in the Navy for well over two years. I noticed a big difference being an officer in the Norfolk area from my treatment when I was there as an enlisted man at nearby Portsmouth in boot camp. Rumor had it that the local citizens had signs in their yards reading, "Dogs and sailors keep off the grass."

We all headed by train to Houston, Texas, where our ship, the future USS *LSM 67*, was undergoing final work at the Brown Shipyard preparatory to its commissioning. We were lucky to catch the ship before all the work was completed so we could cajole workers into making small but useful changes. In due course, the ship was formally commissioned and began its shakedown cruise in the Gulf of Mexico. We had only five officers and fifty-five men, so by that time I had been given the additional duties of communications officer and supply officer. Before long, because I had been a math major in college, I also became navigator, normally the function of the executive officer, the second in command. I am afraid I was a bit delinquent in my duties as supply officer, since we headed out to sea on the shakedown with an inadequate supply of toilet paper, of all things. We somehow made out without having to use our charts as a substitute, but I had begun my tour of duty somewhat under a cloud. During our shakedown there was a submarine alert in the Gulf. I had assumed that we had pretty well eliminated the U-boat threat off our coasts. If there really was a German sub in the Gulf, it must have had a remarkably gutsy or a totally clueless skipper.

As noted, our ship had five officers and later included our group's doctor. (There were six ships in a group, which roughly corresponded to a squadron of destroyers.) The captain, Lieutenant Higgins, had been an attorney before the war. Second in command was Lt. (jg) Sid Horman, the executive officer, who had been in business. Both, I believe, were commissioned at an officers' candidate school. The rest of us had gone to midshipman's school. Next in rank was the engineering officer Ens. Art Ostrowski. As I noted above, I was the gunnery officer, with collateral duties as supply and communications officer and, before long, navigator. All were married except me, a fact that would eventually prove to be both a boon and a bane to me. Later we took on board our group doctor, "Doc" Kieffer, an obstetrician in civilian life.

Well before President Truman integrated the services in 1949, small ships like ours were already integrated. At first, the ship was home to one black, Courtney, who was a steward's mate—in effect, an officers' servant. Later, a second black sailor joined. Both men served in gun crews when we went to battle stations. They lived and ate with the rest of crew. In fact, Courtney's best friend happened to be a blond, blue-eyed white signalman from the same hometown: Longview, Texas. They were inseparable buddies. Our crew came from a rich mixture of ethnic backgrounds: Greek, Polish, Italian, Hispanic, Armenian, German, Irish, African, and Anglo-Saxon. All, however, were first and foremost good Americans. The best educated was Allan Talmud of New York, who was the ship's yeoman or secretary. Our head cook had owned a restaurant and our most senior storekeeper had owned his own business. In all, we were blessed with an outstanding group of enlisted men. Fortunately we had some regular Navy petty officers who held things together when the others were demobilized. I got to know a good bit about our sailors' private lives by censoring their letters, a chore that I did not relish, but that was necessary for security reasons. (Officers censored their own letters.) The saddest events in their lives were when they received "Dear John" letters from their girlfriends or fiancées. ("Dear John, I met the nicest fellow and we are now engaged. I'm sure you will understand. . . .") Naturally, I never discussed what I read with anyone, unless a medical or mental problem was revealed. We officers slept and ate in our small wardroom where our bunks were behind a thick curtain separating them from our dinner table. The captain had a cabin so small that he couldn't sit at his desk when his bunk was down. The ship was completely self-contained. We made our own freshwater from seawater, and we had a small store, fully equipped hospital facilities, and more-than-ample food supplies.

Finally we had orders to sail for the war zone in the Pacific and we headed south to the Panama Canal. At the officers' club at the Coco Solo submarine base on the Atlantic side of the canal, I bought a quart of Canadian Club whiskey for $1.80 (about $26 today). We made it through the Canal and headed into the Pacific.

Under way we took advantage of our spacious now-empty tank deck to play volley ball and other games. Underway water poured in between the bow doors, forming a small swimming pool. The crew also greatly enjoyed watching two officers pummel each other with boxing gloves. The two fighters were always the same: the youngest officer and I. I foolishly took up boxing at Berkeley in line with the martial arts instruction we were receiving as V-12ers. I was a lousy boxer (light heavyweight class). Actually, the only sport I ever excelled in was saber fencing, which I did at Mines. Had I not been sick at the finals, I might well have won the Rocky Mountain Intercollegiate championship in saber, since I had twice bested the aviation cadet from nearby Lowrey Field, who won.

Another brief diversion was an old nautical custom of initiating those who had not crossed the equator when we did so. The minority "shellbacks" who had already crossed the equator, including Ken Higgins, initiated the rest of us who hadn't. Since we all were going to have considerable spare time on our hands before we entered the war zone on the other side of the Pacific, I took advantage of this time to finally read Leo Tolstoy's great classic *War and Peace*. It so happened that, right before I saw my first combat, I had read the description of principal character Pierre's impression of his first encounter with actual war, at the 1812 battle of Borodino, where the Russians were defending against Napoleon's offensive. The stark authenticity of that scene is a prime example of Tolstoy's genius and of why this book is widely regarded as the greatest work of fiction ever written. I was not surprised to learn, years later, that Tolstoy himself had experienced combat as a Russian officer in the Crimean War (1853–56).

After what seemed like an interminable time, we finally put in for refueling and replenishment at the small Polynesian island of Bora Bora northwest of Tahiti in the Society Islands. Bora Bora was a true island paradise like people read about but doubt really exists. It is surrounded by lagoons; in its center is a high vertical walled volcano plug that always seemed to have a cloud around its summit, even on clear days. Life there was effortless and laid back. Food abounded in the forested parts that produced bananas, breadfruit, and other edibles that we thought were for the taking, including semiwild pigs and chickens. (It turned out that the inhabitants considered all this food theirs.) The lagoons provided plenty of fish. The climate was perfect and there had apparently been no appreciable illness or disease before the arrival of the Europeans. (It was a French colony.) The Polynesian women were attractive, as was instantly discovered by the small band of sailors who manned the facility. When there was no ship to service they were shacked up with these women. Some of those stationed there actually turned down chances to return to the United States on leave or transfer, and I can understand why. It was a tug of war between those of us who wanted to prolong our stay in this fabulous place and those stationed there who wanted us out as soon as possible so they could get back to their women and their totally relaxed, unmilitary way of life. It's a great pity that this island paradise could not remain in this near original pristine state, but it unfortunately has since been destroyed by tourist-related commercialization.

One day, some of our crew went into the jungle area in search of bananas and came out with a huge stalk of bananas that they were carrying alongside a lagoon when an outrigger canoe with several islanders came by, spotted our people, and started to chant in English, "You steal our bananas. You steal our bananas." Our sailors slunk away, but hung on to the bananas. Since the bananas were seemingly growing wild, we thought they were there for the taking. We should have realized that almost everything the people ate on the island, even the chickens and pigs, was "wild," so they had a right to complain about our lifting their bananas.

Before very long, to the great relief of the island's Navy contingent, we had to face up to the fact that we were supposed to be going to war. We set sail for the war zone, by then mostly in the Western Pacific area. (Due to this above-mentioned commercialization, now only the massive volcanic plug that looms over the island and the lagoons seem unchanged. Hardly anything else is recognizable. Sometimes one can't stop retrogression.) We steamed through a South Pacific area that had seen a great deal of combat in the previous two years, but first stopped for another refueling at our large base on Espiritu Santo Island, southeast of battle-torn Guadalcanal.

From there we headed west across the South Pacific. On the way, I experienced one of the most hair-raising moments in my life. It happened while I was on the bridge as officer of the deck on a midnight to 4 AM watch. In this part of the ocean, anything moving on or close to the surface leaves a bright fluorescent track at night. As I looked around me, I was suddenly terrified by a fluorescent streak on our starboard beam heading right for us amidships and at a normal torpedo speed. There was no time to do anything but call out to those on watch and then brace myself for a blast I knew could tear the ship apart and kill many of us. Nothing happened. I then looked to the port side, expecting to see the track continue because the torpedo had been set too deep, given our unloaded shallow draft. There was no track. I looked again on the starboard side in time to see another track headed at an angle away from the bow. It was a dolphin. Dolphins love to frolic in ships' bow wakes.

We finally put in at Hollandia, New Guinea, in the part claimed by the Dutch. Our troops stationed there insisted that New Guinea was the only place in the world where you could be up to your knees in mud and choking on dust at the same time. Indeed, it was the worst place I had ever been. I can't even remember why we were there. Maybe we had to refuel again. By the time we arrived, Australian troops were ably cleaning up remnants of Japanese fighters there. I believe it was at that time that we went to Manus Island off the coast of New Guinea where we had a repair base and dry dock. It must have been there that I visited HMAS *Australia,* the flagship of the Royal Australian Navy that was being repaired after having taken a kamikaze (suicide aircraft) hit on its bridge in Leyte Gulf that had killed the captain, the fleet's commanding admiral, and almost everyone else who had been on the bridge. Some of its officers invited me on board for a drink. As in the British Royal Navy, they could drink on board ship, something that had long been banned on U.S. ships. They insisted on treating me to their famous beer, which I later learned could be up to 15 percent alcohol. I quaffed this great-tasting beer as I would have a far weaker American beer, and it took two officers to get me safely down the gangplank. I don't remember how I got back to my ship. Maybe my new Australian "cobbers" (buddies) got me home. I must say that since then I have always had a preference for real (usually not exported) Australian beer.

For some reason we next put in at the small island of Morotai, then part of the Dutch East Indies, which later became Indonesia. It was there we encountered our first action. Those stationed there invited us to see a movie on their outdoor screen. We were seated on the trunks of coconut trees enjoying a movie comedy when a stick of bombs detonated around us. We flattened out and then took off for our ship. I never found out if anyone was killed or wounded. We had apparently been hit by one of the solitary Japanese aircraft that often harassed our installations at night, known as "Bed Check Charlies." We then took off for our final destination, Leyte Island in the Philippines, the first island that we had invaded and that was still in the final stages of being liberated from the Japanese. It was a good thing that we hadn't arrived sooner because the LSM flotilla that we were to join was engaged in some fierce action in Ormoc Bay west of Leyte.

The Japanese were desperately trying to reinforce their troops who had been pushed back to the western part of Leyte. We were trying to outflank them by landing troops south of where the Japanese were coming in. Just before dawn, two LSMs carrying some of these troops plus tanks hit the beach. Due to a navigational error or some other cockup, they landed on a beach held by the Japanese. When they were fired upon, they realized their mistake, pulled off the beach, and then ran into each other. They did eventually manage to escape, however. Later that morning, two LSMs were taken out by kamikazes. There, but for having loitered a bit here and a bit there, would we have gone. I have to say that our skipper, Ken Higgins, was not the type to deliberately delay getting into the fray.

Before I take us into the war, I would like to make a point. Combat in war is so far removed from any other human experience that it hardly can be described. It has to be experienced to know it. Even then, it is so surreal and grotesque that it is hard to grasp, even while it is being experienced. This was especially true in our war at sea where we experienced attacks that were so sudden and usually unexpected that it was not always possible to know exactly what was happening. In any case, witnesses to combat action often have a *Rashomon* moment when they try to describe it. (*Rashomon* is a classic Japanese film made in 1950 in which several people witness a crime, but each describes it differently because of the way they have filtered it through their own experiences.) I say all this because, while I will do my best to describe actions in which we were involved, I cannot guarantee that someone else might not have a different version of these same events. My personal descriptions will usually be subjective and derived from impressions I had at the time. I should add here that while we did encounter some fierce and horrific combat, this was sporadic and not too frequent. What we went through, in any case, could hardly be compared to that endured by the good infantrymen and tank crews whom we landed on hostile shores. They had to stay in the fight while we could sail away.

Leyte Gulf was a busy place, to say the least, and was the staging area for subsequent landings in the Philippine Islands. About nine weeks prior to our arrival, we came very close to losing the toehold we had gained at Leyte and that began our campaign to liberate these islands as Gen. Douglas MacArthur had earlier promised when he had declared, "We shall return." What was very probably the most heroic and courageous action in U.S. Navy history saved the day when, off the island of Samar, immediately north of Leyte, three destroyers and four smaller destroyer escorts, with only 5-inch guns, which had been screening small "jeep" carriers, stood off an infinitely larger and stronger Japanese fleet of four battleships, six cruisers, and ten destroyers. That Japanese fleet included the *Yamato*, the largest battleship in the world, with 18-inch guns. The spirited and persistent attacks by our small ships and aircraft from the small carriers, at the cost of one carrier, two destroyers, and one destroyer escort sunk, effectively blocked the Japanese fleet just forty miles from its objective, Leyte Gulf.

After the war, the Japanese fleet commander, Vice Adm. Takeo Kurita, reportedly explained that he had been warned of an impending large air strike, no doubt referring to the large carrier strike force commanded by Sen. John McCain's grandfather, Adm. John S. McCain, which, closing in from the east, had gotten within striking distance. So instead of just steaming ahead and wiping out our sitting duck transport and other ships and vulnerable shore installations, which he most certainly could have done, he opted to protect his fleet from anticipated concentrated air attacks. Similar attacks had recently cost him one super battleship and other ships damaged, so Kurita retreated up the San Bernardino Strait north of Samar from whence he had come the night before. (Some months later, I conned our small ship through this strait and found it somewhat tricky even in broad daylight and with radar. I could only marvel at how the Japanese had managed to bring those huge ships through the strait at night, presumably without radar.)

Tacloban, the capital of Leyte, was run down and poor, with mostly unsubstantial houses and buildings, except for its incongruous "opera house." It had become General MacArthur's headquarters, and I actually once saw him standing on the porch of his quarters, looking more like a statue than a real human being. At some point, I happened to have business in Tacloban that kept me there overnight. I ate an early supper at some mess and then went to a Quonset hut at the air base reserved for officers, picked a bed, and went to sleep; I was awakened an hour or so later by bombs exploding on an immediately adjacent airstrip. I grabbed a helmet and quickly jumped into a slit trench just outside the hut's entrance. I was soon followed by an older officer who told me in no uncertain terms that I had his helmet. He said, "Taking a man's helmet out here is like stealing a man's horse where I come from in Texas." I apologized profusely and handed the helmet back to the irate colonel. By then, bombs had stopped exploding. Later, I learned that just after dusk, a Japanese aircraft had tagged on to an Army fighter squadron returning to its base at Tacloban. When the squadron had landed, the enemy plane bombed it. Everybody complained that this was inexcusably sneaky. I thought to myself that it actually had been pretty damn clever.

On Christmas Eve 1944 another officer and I, contrary to all regulations, had dipped into the ship's medicinal alcohol, mixing it with pineapple juice. We were feeling no pain when the ship's honking alarm sounded general quarters, calling all hands to their battle stations. The fleet around us was under air attack. As gunnery officer my battle station was on the bridge. Up I went and wound up witnessing a spectacular nighttime display with countless tracer rounds and airbursts from all kinds of antiaircraft guns. I had never seen a fireworks display anything like it and, in my slightly inebriated state, was really enjoying the whole thing, which later made me feel a little guilty. This is definitely not the sort of thing one should enjoy. I should note here why I hadn't broken out my $1.80 bottle of Canadian Club on this occasion: By this time it was worth $80 (about $950 today) so I couldn't afford to drink it. Later, a sergeant from the 503rd Parachute Infantry Regiment offered me a captured Japanese officer's samurai sword for the bottle. These swords were then going for about $300 (about $3,500 today). He had it back at his base camp with his belongings. We never closed the deal because he was killed in combat before he could get back to his base.

By this time we were preparing for the largest amphibious landing of the Pacific War: the invasion of Luzon, the principal island where the capital, Manila, is located. This was the real prize of the whole Philippine campaign. As communications officer I usually was the one designated to pick up operations plans. As soon as I had this one in my hands, the first thing I did was check to see where we were going to land. The whole operation was centered on Lingayen Gulf where the Japanese had landed in 1942 in their quest to take Luzon. We were going to land on White II on the left flank of the landing operation. This was not good, since this landing beach was in view of a small mountain range that angled off from the beach area. I correctly guessed that that beach is where the enemy could position a lot of artillery to give us a very hard time. I had a bad feeling about the whole thing. The enemy seemed to be and indeed was strongest where we were going. Later it was speculated that this left flank is where the Japanese had the most success when they invaded, so they weren't going to let this happen to them.

Before we took off on this operation, an air attack somewhere else in Leyte Gulf had gotten us to general quarters in a somewhat isolated part of the Gulf when two fighter planes came flying low over the water almost directly toward us. Skipper Ken Higgins ordered me to fire on them, which I refused to do because I believed they were friendlies. Higgins then shouted, "This is a direct order. Fire or you're in hack [arrested and confined to quarters]." By then, however, anybody could clearly recognize the unique gull wings of the two F4U Corsairs. Higgins said nothing more, nor should he have. My aircraft recognition training had paid off. Given the slow speed, low altitude, and course of these aircraft, we had a good chance of shooting them down or at least of severely damaging them. Attacking fellow Americans is one of the great tragedies of any war. Months later, we came very close to downing one of our own planes, as I describe below in this chapter.

At some point, I met a Royal Navy (RN) aviator stationed on board a nearby RN carrier who had learned to fly in a Stearman. When I told him it was designed by my father, he invited me on board for dinner as the captain's guest of honor. All of the aviators on board had learned to fly in Stearmans. I was intrigued that the wardroom had a fireplace with gas logs, of all things. Of course, we all drank toasts with real liquor.

We finally began heading north to our invasion destination in a ship formation that reportedly was eighty miles long. Most of the trip was uneventful. An unusually bold, if not suicidal, Japanese destroyer skipper took his ship out of Manila Bay, as we passed the Bay's entrance, to attack this huge formation. I watched the whole thing on our pilothouse radarscope and saw the destroyer's blip disappear as the hapless ship was sunk.

We did have a major scare later on when an enemy plane attacked our column of ships coming up from behind us, dropping bombs and strafing as he went along, coming in low right at us. I could swear it got so close I could see the pilot. Fortunately it was shot down just in the nick of time. (We couldn't shoot for fear of hitting ships behind us.) Ken Higgins who was always on the bridge at general quarters saw this threat, as did I. When the plane was splashed, he turned to me and exclaimed; "Stearman, these people are trying to *kill* us!"

Later we had a bizarre experience when a Japanese plane at some distance approached our formation transmitting a correct daily U.S. IFF (identification friend or foe) code that we could read on our radar scope. We never learned what happened to him, and could only speculate on how he broke our IFF code.

The Catholic Church holds that non-Catholics who lead good lives can be saved if their ignorance of Catholicism is "invincible." I had been moving toward becoming a Catholic for some years and had finally concluded that this was indeed the True Church founded by Jesus Christ. In other words, my ignorance was no longer invincible. Since I thought there was a good chance I might not survive this operation—and, in fact, I came very close to not surviving it—I became a Catholic, probably the first Catholic Stearman since the English Reformation in the sixteenth century.

I'm not too certain of the exact sequence of events, but I believe it was as we first entered Lingayen Gulf that we spotted the good old *Australia* back in action to provide fire support. I explained to others on the bridge that I knew and much liked some of that ship's officers. Then, right at that moment, a kamikaze hit its bridge with the same tragic results as had befallen this ill-fated ship earlier in Leyte Gulf: this attack killed the admiral fleet commander, the ship's captain, and nearly everyone else on the bridge, probably including officers I knew. It was sickening. The December 23, 1945, final postwar report of Rear Adm. Daniel E. Barbey, the commanding officer of the Seventh Amphibious Force (which included us), explained why ships like the *Australia* were especially singled out for attack during the Lingayen Gulf operation: "Fire support and minesweepers suffered substantial losses during the preliminary and preassault bombardment. If the enemy had concentrated air attacks on transports [that included us] with the same effectiveness achieved against supporting ships, *the Lingayen operation might not have succeeded*" (emphasis added).

After entering the Gulf, we assembled in accordance to where and when we would hit the beach. LSMs were especially designed to carry tanks and troops in with the first assault waves. Although they had less than a fourth of the displacement and were only two-thirds the length of the LSTs (landing ship tanks), LSMs had twice the propulsion power. LSTs, the workhorses of the amphibious forces, were often referred to as "large slow targets." The LSMs were faster and more maneuverable and ideally suited to their mission. As I recall, we had on our ship at least six Sherman tanks as well as various other vehicles such as jeeps. Then, too, we accommodated the tank crews and, as called for, infantrymen to protect the tanks. The landing was scheduled for 9:30 AM January 9, 1945. There were 43,599 troops and their supplies that were to be landed that day. As usual, the operation opened with a substantial naval and air bombardment. Going in to the beach there was nothing in front of us but the enemy.

By the time we hit the beach, the enemy was probably still in a state of shock from the preliminary bombardment and kept well hunkered down. At first, we didn't encounter a lot of resistance. We quickly unloaded our tanks, vehicles, and troops on dry land and took off. Before hitting the beach, we had dropped our stern anchor and winched it in to pull us off the beach. What followed was really the hair-raising part of the operation. We then took on our post assault role as supply lighters. Because we were relatively fast and maneuverable we got the extra hazardous loads to take ashore. From ammunition ships and tankers we took on some 350 tons of gasoline and artillery and mortar ammunition, piled up in our open tank deck, and headed for the beach. Things had radically changed for the worse. Good old White II beach was under fire. We came in with shells landing all around us sending up thin geysers of water.

Scared out of my wits but trying not to show it, I suggested to Ken Higgins that we really ought to find a safer beach to land all this stuff. In no uncertain terms, he said we had orders to take this stuff onto this beach and that's what we were going to do, come hell or high water. We landed and shortly thereafter we were strafed by an enemy fighter plane. I didn't see it, but crew members who did guessed that its tracers were passing over the ship at about mast level. Had any of those hit our load we would have been splattered all over the landscape. The same held true for the artillery and mortar rounds that were falling all around us. I just happened to look over to the LSM on our port side at the very moment a round hit its signal bridge, disintegrating a young signalman in a cloud of greasy smoke. This was all pretty unnerving. We finally got our cargo unloaded and headed out to sea with artillery rounds following us for about two hundred yards and getting progressively closer until we finally pulled out of range. In his report cited above, the 7th Amphibious Force commander noted, "Fortunately, opposition was light *except on White II*" (emphasis added).

When my mother died, I discovered that she had saved all the letters I had sent home from the war. The following are excerpts from one dated January 15, 1945, which described the above action on the first day of the landing.

Dear Mom, Dad and Marilyn,

As you might have guessed, "Little Willy" made the big Luzon Show. It was a marvelously well planned and carried out operation. Our Air Force did a wonderful job of knocking out the Jap air force. . . . We arrived fairly early, watched the "big boys" shell the beach then went in. Amazingly little opposition was encountered on the beach though a few spots were pretty hot! I was scared as hell going in. . . . By the Grace of God, we escaped without a scratch. Several times we escaped being blown to "smithereens" only by minutes. . . . We're extremely lucky to have come out so well, as a lot of others didn't. You people back home just can't realize what war is like. I didn't 'till I got bombed, strafed & shelled & saw some people get killed and wounded, & compared to the Infantry I'm still grossly unqualified to say that "war is hell"—War is sure a lot different in actuality than in the movies. It's nasty business, gnawing fear and uncertainty, things happen so fast & suddenly you don't know what happened. You never see the enemy. I've just had a touch of it & it's enough for me.—I wish to hell I were home. Maybe I don't have enough guts for this kind of thing, I hate getting shelled worse of all—you don't know where they're coming from or where they're going to hit & there's absolutely nothing you can do about it. However an air attack is different. I actually got a big thrill out of having my guns open up on a Jap plane. He was too high & out of range, but it gives us all a wonderful feeling to be shooting back for a change. . . . These LSMs are great for the job; so we're the "work horses" of the Amphib. On the 1st trip in we beached, got our outfit out on dry land & pulled out in 7 minutes flat. . . .

Love to all,
Bill

There seems to be an unwritten rule among those in combat never to admit one is afraid. And there is a good reason for this, most especially among officers: fear is contagious and demoralizing. It's contagious fear that results in disorderly pell-mell retreats in battle, for instance. Since officers censored their own letters, I could at least tell my family how scared I was, even if I couldn't tell anyone else. I kept feeling that I had to be one of the great cowards of World War II. It wasn't until the war was over and I talked to other combat veterans that I realized that *everybody* is scared in combat.

We operated almost exclusively with infantry units that we landed on hostile shores along with supporting tanks and other vehicles. I always felt guilty that I was not among those poor guys who had to go ashore and stay in the fight. To this day, I still feel somewhat guilty for not having had it as bad as the footsloggers in the infantry. Everyone I know thinks I'm nuts for feeling this way, but there you are. The soldiers, on the other hand, couldn't wait to get off the ship and pitied us that we had to stay on her. Their reason was, "You can't dig a foxhole in a steel deck." Still, for years after the war, I would dream about the war. In one dream I would be a coward. In the next, I would do something madly heroic. Dream analysts would have fun with my case. Even scarier than combat was coping with heavy stormy seas, with some bringing solid water onto the bridge that was more than thirty feet above the waterline. The ship's bow must always be held into the sea to avoid broaching and possibly capsizing. That can be especially tricky and difficult with smaller ships like ours. Fortunately, LSMs had a substantial metacentric height, a measure of a ship's ability to recover from rolls to the side, which made them quite stable in rough seas, unlike top-heavy destroyers that more easily capsized, sometimes doing so in bad storms.

For some time we continued bringing supplies, mostly ammunition, onto White II. Beginning the second night, the Japanese started shelling the beach nightly with what we guessed was a 10-inch howitzer. One evening, we were unloading ammunition when the truck that was working with us broke down; there was no other to replace it with at the time. Ken Higgins wisely decided to pull off the beach and anchor offshore. Early the next morning we came back to exactly where we had been, close to the port side of an LST. When we got alongside her again, we noticed a great gaping hole in her side at the waterline with little packages of breakfast food floating out of a storage hold. The night-firing howitzer had nailed the LST. More importantly, when we lined up the hole with where we had been that night, it became clear that this round would have landed square on the ammunition on our tank deck blowing us all sky high. Our Guardian Angel was working overtime that night. We could never spot this gun from the air, so the Army sent a regimental combat team into the mountains where it discovered and destroyed a large howitzer mounted on a track that enabled it to be hidden in a cave or shelter by day.

Of the subsequent landings we made on Luzon, the one I most remember was taking Olongapo at the head of Subic Bay north of Manila, on January 30. Olongapo is located at the base of the Bataan Peninsula; our operation was intended to cut off this peninsula. Bataan had a very special significance for all of us, since it was the site of the infamous April 1942 "Bataan Death March" resulting from the Japanese force-marching some seventy thousand American and Filipino prisoners of war (POWs) sixty-three miles to a prison camp. En route, as many as sixteen thousand died from starvation, dehydration, beatings, torture, and other mistreatment. After the war, the Japanese general responsible for this atrocity was executed by Allied order. In the force steaming up the Subic Bay toward our objective, we were in the right column with nothing between us and Bataan but a single U.S. destroyer that kept pace with us as we steamed along. Every time I glanced over at the fateful peninsula, I saw the destroyer's stars and stripes with Bataan in the background. We were moving inexorably to avenge the tragic victims of the Death March. To this day, I can hardly picture this scene without tearing up with emotion.

We discovered another Japanese atrocity when we landed on Palawan, the westernmost island of the Philippines. Before we landed, the Japanese had driven some 140 American POWs held there into an underground air raid shelter, filled it with gasoline, and then set it on fire, machine-gunning any who tried to escape.

When we discovered this, we vowed not to take any prisoners alive. Of course, when the war ended we did, but our treatment—in fact our total neglect—of prisoners was conditioned by our outrage at what happened on Palawan.

Most of our other landings in the Philippines were in the central Visayan group of islands. They were, for the most part, relatively uneventful, although one never knew for sure what to expect. In one operation, on February 21, 1945, in the Mindanao Sea close to Cebu Island, a destroyer, the USS *Renshaw*, about seventy or eighty yards off our starboard beam, was torpedoed by a midget submarine that broached as a result of the underwater explosion resulting from blowing up one set of the destroyer's fireroom boilers; this explosion produced a geyser of smoke and steam shooting high up over the ship. I was sure everyone in that compartment was killed. (I later learned that seventeen sailors were killed and twenty others wounded.) When the sub broached, we all shot at it, and it promptly disappeared. I never knew whether it was sunk or managed to slip away.

On October 27, 1945, President Truman reviewed the first postwar Navy Day sail-by from the deck of the completely repaired *Renshaw*. Not long after Manila had been captured, we put in to Manila Harbor at night. The harbor was filled with sunken ships, which made navigating through them a nightmare. Without radar it would have been impossible. Manila was largely in ruins, thanks to stubborn resistance and widescale destruction by Japanese troops. We saw newly liberated Americans and other civilians who had been interned in Manila's Santo Tomas University. They seemed to be in fairly bad shape, clearly suffering from malnutrition.

After Lingayen Gulf, most of the action we saw was in the form of air attacks. I mentioned earlier that I trained with the Mark IV gyroscopic sight, which did fine on the Dam Neck range when shooting at slowly towed targets. This sight had an illuminated reticle that, when held on the target, would solve your fire control problem by correcting for the target's speed. The trouble was that when one slewed the gun to meet the target the reticle disappeared. The contractor tried to correct this problem by enabling one to lock the reticle until one was on target. By the time this was done, however, the target was long gone. In other words, this very expensive sight was a piece of junk on which the Navy spent countless millions mounting it on all the 20-mm and 40-mm guns in the fleet. Maybe some got it to work, but I doubt it. We simply went back to using good old tracers, which also had their problems. When it looked like they were on target, they were actually curving behind targeted crossing aircraft. Speaking of guns, as gunnery officer and consummate gun nut, I managed to get our entire complement individually armed with rifles and pistols in addition to light machine guns and antitank bazookas so that if we were ever hung up on a hostile beach we could defend the ship as a well-armed infantry company. These guns did come in handy when the Japanese started to attack our anchored or moored ships with swimmers pushing harmless looking objects that were really bombs. We shot up a lot of floating boxes, especially the ones moving against the current. I acquired all these weapons from Army quartermaster sergeants by trading ice cream powder for guns. (Actually, the powder made great ice cream.)

We worked with some outstanding infantry units such as the 503rd Parachute Infantry Regiment and the 24th Infantry Division. But my favorite outfit, from a personal point of view, was the Australian 9th Division, which was one of the units most instrumental in stopping Field Marshal Erwin Rommel and throwing him back at El Alamein in North Africa in the fall of 1942, thus winning one of the most crucial battles of World War II. The Aussies were a great bunch of characters, especially the officers, whom we somehow managed to accommodate in our small officers' wardroom. They were all witty raconteurs with great tales to spin. I later regretted that we never got them to talking about El Alamein. They had a number of amusing stories about the famed Australian, Gen. Sir Thomas Blamey, though. My favorite of those stories was the one about the time the general was asked to intervene with Australian wharfies (longshoremen) who were handling supplies for Australian troops overseas and who insisted on getting danger pay (pronounced dyen-ger pie) for handling ammunition. General Blamey walked up to the wharfies who were supposed to load the ammunition, raised a box of ammunition over his head and, as wharfies scattered in all directions, dashed it on the concrete wharf exclaiming, "Here's for your bloody danger pay. Get back to work." And they all did.

This reminded me of a labor problem we had earlier encountered. We had been on an operation that kept us at general quarters around the clock for quite some time and we were all tired and cranky when we got to Leyte Gulf where we were to refuel. We were told to use a certain tanker, which we sought out and hailed. We were then told that, because it was Sunday, their crew, far better paid than our crew, wasn't working. We would have to take on the fuel without their help, since we had to take off soon and couldn't wait until Monday. One gun captain asked for permission to open fire on the tanker (of course, not granted). At some risk, our sailors had to jump on board the tanker with lines to tie us up and then had to get the fuel on board us. I have always had the greatest admiration for those heroic merchant seamen on the extremely perilous North Atlantic run. For those in the Pacific, however, their life was generally a piece of cake, and we had little respect for them.

We had a unit of the 9th Division that manned the division's relatively small-bored organic twenty-five–pounder artillery. The division was headed for Borneo, pretty small potatoes compared with fighting the German Wehrmacht led by its best general, Erwin Rommel. This was certainly their attitude when we hit the landing beach. Our Aussies went ashore and promptly set up a tea station as the

Japanese were melting back into the jungle. Meanwhile, all their guns and equipment remained on the ship, leaving us a sitting duck should the Japanese manage to set up some artillery. To get their attention, I went up to the bridge, pointed to where the enemy was disappearing, and on the bull horn let out the recently learned cry of the Australian kangaroo hunters: "Ho, Ho, Ho, There the bloody bastards go!" This greatly amused them, and they came on board and took off their things, so we could get the hell out of there. One thing that intrigued me about this operation was that, as I had been told, aircraft had spread DDT on the prospective battlefield because the area was so disease-ridden.

After the Aussies were established, I visited the area they had captured to see how they were making out. Two things struck me. One was the discovery that they had liberated a camp where a number of British Commonwealth POWs were held. When I was there, liberated POWs were stoning to death the Japanese prison camp leader who was tied to a tree. No one moved to stop them because the POWs had persuaded the Aussies that he richly deserved this grim fate. The other thing was that tea stations had been set up all around their defense perimeter.

I was later told that the Aussies' casual attitude toward fighting this enemy got them in trouble when a midnight Japanese "banzai charge" broke through their loosely manned perimeter, reached the port in Brunei Bay and caught the U.S. Navy officer port director in his tent where he was reportedly nearly cut in two by an officer's samurai sword. The charge was apparently broken up by a U.S. Army engineer unit using the .50-caliber machine guns mounted on their trucks. Our initial landing in Brunei Bay had begun with our sneaking in before dawn hoping to surprise the Japanese defending what until very recently had been an important naval base of theirs. As we crept toward them in the semidarkness, I was shocked to just make out a giant mine bristling with detonation horns slipping alongside not much more than two feet or so away. It was being pushed gently away by our bow wake. Since we were preserving radio and signal silence, I could not notify the ship directly astern of this danger. Fortunately, the mine didn't detonate against any ship. I later learned that we Allies, as well as the Japanese, had planted a number of mines in this bay. In other words, we had come close to being hoisted with our own petards. I should add one anecdote here: On the eve of our first landing with the Aussies, I told the officers on board, "Tomorrow when you hit the beach, we will all be rooting for you." This was followed by peals of laughter. Finally one of them explained that rooting was Australian slang for fornicating.

It was during this operation that we came very close to downing one of our own aircraft. Just at dusk, we were taken under attack by Japanese *Betty* light bombers that some believed might have been based at Saigon some seven hundred miles away. (The Japanese had made quite good use of what is now Vietnam with a large naval base at Cam Ranh Bay and an air base at Saigon. Twenty years later, both were important U.S. bases. After the Communist victory in 1975, Cam Ranh Bay became a Soviet naval base.) We were firing away, one after another, at the Japanese aircraft when another plane flew over that we assumed was also an enemy plane. One of my gun crew captains excitedly reported, "Our tracers are going right between the [two] tail booms." At that point I yelled, "Cease firing." The Japanese had no aircraft with twin tail booms, whereas we had two, the Lockheed P-38 fighter and the Northrop P-61 Black Widow night fighter, which is what we came within a hair of shooting down and that was clearly in pursuit of the attacking enemy planes.

My father was one of an ad hoc team of experts who examined captured or downed enemy aircraft. One he examined was a Betty that he found very well made, almost as good as comparable U.S. light bombers. He was struck that parts that did not need to be finished weren't. Also Army Signal Corps people told me that Japanese field telephone and radio equipment were substantially better than ours. As I noted earlier, Americans had long regarded everything made in Japan as junk. We were learning better.

As communications officer, among other roles, I was responsible for our codes and ciphers, which were strictly tactical strip ciphers and hand-operated code machines that were secure for relatively short periods of time, unlike the far-more-sophisticated electric coding machines found on larger ships. Every once in a while, I had to get upgraded versions of what we held, usually from larger ships. Once I had picked up our updated codes and ciphers and hitched a ride back to our ship's location in a Navy TBM torpedo bomber. I was sitting in the back in the gunner's seat. Before long, we were flying above solid cloud cover. Sometime later, the pilot noted that he was almost out of fuel, probably due to a fuel leak. He said to prepare to bail out, since we would soon go down. The radioman and I slid back the canopy and were getting ready "to hit the silk." I was very concerned that we might be over enemy-held territory and that I would not be able to destroy all this classified material in the musette bag slung around my neck quickly enough once I was on the ground. I was packing my trusty M1911 .45 Colt automatic pistol with which I could hold off only a very limited number of Japanese, if any. As luck would have it, suddenly there was a break in the cloud cover and we went down through it to discover we were in sight of an airstrip with U.S. aircraft nearby. We landed almost dead-stick. It turned out that most but not all of the terrain we had just flown over was in friendly hands.

I had long believed that our ship, which we affectionately called the *Fighting 67*, had been in the first wave of *seven* assault landings in World War II. After recently reading Admiral Barbey's final report (mentioned above), I discovered there had been *nine*. Only one person in our entire flotilla of some twenty ships received any kind of decoration for bravery: our skipper Ken Higgins, who received a Bronze Star. I had always assumed it was because he took in those explosive loads under fire during the first day of the Lingayen Gulf operation. In 2007 I managed to acquire the citation for his award and was surprised that it simply mentioned outstanding performance in all the principal operations we had been in. Now one doesn't even have to be in combat to get a Bronze Star. I suppose our only real claim to fame, as a ship, is that we were in the first wave of what I believe was the very last assault landing of World II, at Sarangani Bay on the southern tip of Mindanao, the second-largest island in the Philippines.

This landing was a small operation. I doubt if more than two battalions of infantry were involved. We had only one destroyer providing fire support, but had fantastic close air support from Marine Air Group (MAG) 24 flying those superb F4U Corsairs. The pilots were mostly a bunch of kids, many still in their late teens. I had previously much enjoyed their rollicking company in their hooch "officers' club." They had some great songs which they love to belt out. I, at twenty-two, thought they were awfully young. They may have been young, but they were gutsy and they were very good. I remember when one of them was about to attack a target behind Japanese lines he was told a machine-gun nest behind our lines needed to be taken out. This pilot almost in mid-dive switched targets and knocked out the machine-gun nest without harming any friendly forces, which were all around the target. In all the war, I had never seen combat flying like this. One advantage Marine aviators have is that the officer on the ground directing their strikes is also an aviator and all Marine aviators had gone to infantry school, as I recall. Alas, the Army Air Corps/Force was never very good at close air support, at least in the Pacific war. Naval aviators, especially the Marines, were far better. I could never understand the rationale behind this last amphibious operation, since these Japanese were cut off and in no position to do any harm. Our casualties were light, but some always get killed or wounded in any operation like this.

On June 18, 1945, it was decided to invade Japan's home islands of Kyushu and Honshu. In early July 1945 we were told that we would participate in the first landing on the Japanese mainland. As usual, I was the officer who picked up the operations plan for this landing. I first ascertained that Operation Olympic, as it was called, would take place on November 1, 1945, and that we were again to be in the first assault wave, this time on Kyushu Island, the southernmost of the Japanese mainland islands. After ascertaining exactly where we would land, I flipped to the intelligence annex. Very soon I felt sick to my stomach because I didn't see how we could possibly survive what awaited us when we hit the beach. For openers, the report listed five thousand kamikaze-capable aircraft and an enormous amount of artillery and other weapons plus a large number of defenders. In other words, I had just turned twenty-three and most probably had less than four months to live.

The enlisted men in our LSM group (squadron equivalent) began to realize that a very hairy operation must be in the works when officers were getting drunk whenever they weren't on duty. This was facilitated by all our ships being beached, so officers could walk ashore to makeshift officers' bars on the beach for beer and cheap bourbon. On occasion we would break out beer for the enlisted men to drink ashore, but they were also drinking *tuba*—fermented coconut juice popular among Filipinos. Before long, the troops we were going to transport had been identified.

Being, in effect, on a kind of "death row" from the early part of July to mid-August 1945 was certainly the most traumatic period of my life which compels me both to explain why Operation Olympic posed such a deadly threat to so many, both American and Japanese, but also to help clear up the many misunderstandings about the efficacy and morality of dropping atomic bombs on Hiroshima and Nagasaki in August 1945. Fortunately, I am now able to draw on the recent, most definitive work to date, on U.S. plans and expectations for the 1945–46 invasion of the Japanese main islands. I am referring to the extensively documented and thoroughly researched book, *Hell to Pay: Operation DOWNFALL and the Invasion of Japan, 1945–47* by D. M. Giangreco (2009); research of this book uses both Japanese and U.S. sources. I almost entirely use this document in the following description of what we would have faced on November 1, 1945.

The overall invasion of Japan was labeled Operation Downfall; the operation was divided into the initial landing on Kyushu, Operation Olympic, and the subsequent March 1946 Operation Coronet landing on the main island of Honshu near Tokyo. After the war we discovered to our chagrin that the Japanese high command knew exactly where and nearly when we were going to attack and were more than ready for us. As noted above, I was shocked to discover in our operations plan intelligence annex that the Japanese had more than five thousand kamikaze-capable aircraft. In fact, it turned out that they had some 12,700 and, instead of the pilot shortage we anticipated, they had more than eighteen thousand ready to fly. (They had also hoarded large quantities of aviation fuel for the final defense of the homeland.) Counterintuitive as it might seem, the deadliest of the kamikaze planes were some 2,000 old biplane trainers. Being mostly of wood, they were largely immune to detection by radar or proximity fuzes and could sneak in undetected at night to attack our ships. Also, having so much wing surface, they could usually only be shot down by killing the pilot or knocking out the engine. The Japanese also had some eight thousand hard-to-spot fast suicide boats to attack our shipping. When the war ended, there were already 917,000 enemy troops on Kyushu, whereas we counted on having 452,198 troops there by X-Day *plus two weeks*. In war, however, it has long been axiomatic that the attacking force should have numerical superiority over the defending one. On Okinawa (an island twenty miles wide and sixty miles long), for example, the defending Japanese troops were outnumbered by us five to one, and it still took us eighty-three days from April 1 to June 22, 1945, to defeat them after they had finally lost most of their troops, some 130,000 killed in action (KIA). Our Okinawa campaign KIA totaled some 12,613 including 7,613 Army plus more than 4,900 Navy kamikaze victims. (By comparison, as of June 20, 2010, our total KIA in Iraq since 2003 had been 3,488. Our total KIA in Afghanistan since 2001 had been 817. [In single months in Vietnam we had this many KIAs.]) This suicidal tenacity on Okinawa was a clear indicator of what we would face in invading Japan.

Even more daunting than the opposition described above, was the terrain we faced. The 7th Amphibious Force, which included our USS *LSM 67* of which I was the gunnery officer, was to land on the east coast near the city of Miyazaki. When asked for his assessment of this landing beach, Maj. Gen. Hugh J. Casey pointed to a contour map and noted that this beach abutted sheer cliffs and stated, "anyone sending landing craft ashore there was a murderer." At this point it was also noted that second-echelon loadings exactly duplicated those of the first echelon on the assumption that the first echelon would be "wiped out." We were, as always, to be in the first echelon, probably due to land our usual load of six Sherman tanks and several vehicles plus some infantry. The beach was covered by extensive well-concealed and well-protected artillery, including large guns taken from battleships. Those troops who managed to escape being trapped on the beach faced a well-fortified enemy on the high terrain above the beach. Everywhere we landed and everywhere we would continue to fight, the enemy occupied the high ground, always an advantage in battle. Bear in mind that our landing ships (and troops and supplies on other ships in the fleet) would be constantly subjected to kamikaze attacks before they even reached the beach. Because of the kamikaze threat, most of our aircraft present would be devoted to protecting the carriers and the fleet in general, leaving too few to provide essential close air support. Also our most modern battleships were reserved to protect carriers instead of providing gunfire support, this task being left to pre–World War II battleships.

Even before we knew what we actually faced in Operation Downfall, we still expected to suffer heavy casualties. For example, the July 1945 Shockley-Wright War Department study projected 5 to 10 million Japanese dead, and 1.7 and 4 million U.S. casualties, including four hundred thousand to eight hundred thousand KIA. Former President Herbert Hoover, working with Army Intelligence, predicted half a million to 1 million KIA, figures that were not contested by President Truman or his top advisers. Even before they knew about the atomic bomb, the most senior Japanese officials predicted that up to 20 million Japanese could die in defending their homeland. Bear in mind that the total number killed by the atomic bomb attacks on Hiroshima and Nagasaki was about 118,000. In 1945 firebombing had killed 178,000 Japanese and rendered some 8 million homeless. In the closing months of the war, Asians, military and civilian, from Indonesia through Manchuria, were dying at the rate of some four hundred thousand a month.

Should we have opted, as the Navy at one time suggested, to blockade Japan and to destroy its transportation system, millions of Japanese would have starved to death. Given all this, how could one possibly argue that ending the war with the two atomic bombs—and it took two to make the emperor's case for ending the war—was not intrinsically more desirable from a moral point of view than any feasible alternative? In addition to everything else, this no doubt saved my life, for which I have been eternally grateful to President Truman. In any case, the war was over, thank God.

I cannot close this chapter without a tribute to GI Jill who did so much to bolster our morale. She came across like a wholesome girl-next-door who began each radio show with "Hi-ya, fellas! This is GI Jill with the GI jive." She would then play hit tunes interspersed with cheery comment. We all loved her. The enemy's Tokyo Rose was often good for laughs, but sometimes it was amazing how very well informed she was about our operations.

Chapter 9

After the War Was Over

WORLD WAR II OFFICIALLY ENDED ON SEPTEMBER 2, 1945, with the surrender ceremonies on the USS *Missouri* anchored in Tokyo Bay. Our next mission began: picking up Japanese POWs scattered all over the islands where we had been operating. On the eve of each operation, we prayed that the troops we were picking up had received the word from the emperor to surrender, since the few U.S. troops we had with us could not have protected us from the far more numerous hostile Japanese we could have encountered. The key decision not to depose the Japanese emperor was a masterful one, but it was not easily taken since, to the American public, Emperor Hirohito was widely reviled, even on a par with Hitler. It was to our enormous advantage that the highly revered—indeed worshiped—emperor personally broadcast the order to surrender, on August 15. Among the reasons he cited for Japan's surrender was, "the enemy had begun to employ a most cruel bomb." Although there was within the Japanese military considerable resistance to surrendering, the emperor managed to prevail, but it was a close-run thing, as the Brits would say. The significance of this is well illustrated by continued resistance as late as the 1970s of isolated Japanese soldiers who did not get the word from the emperor to surrender.

We packed the Japanese troops in like sardines on our tank deck and did nothing to alleviate their thirst, hunger, or ailments, such was our bitterness toward their treatment of American POWs. At least we did them no physical harm, as we had once vowed to do. In the course of these operations, I had a fascinating conversation with a Japanese general we had taken on board, who said he had commanded most of the troops against whom we had been fighting. I later concluded that he could have been Gen. Sosaku Suzaki, commander of the Japanese

35th Army, responsible for the central and southern Philippines. The general spoke good German, which he had learned at the German Staff College in Potsdam in the 1930s. I spoke passable German and had studied military German at Berkeley, so we communicated fairly well. I must say that I, a lowly lieutenant junior grade in the Navy, got quite a charge out of interrogating the former enemy commander.

We went over a number of engagements we had both been in with my asking him why certain moves had been made. I was especially interested in why the Japanese kept reinforcing their troops on Leyte through the Ormoc Bay after it was obvious that this was a hopeless cause. In fact, I had walked along this beach and noted that one could practically have stepped from one Japanese landing craft to another for miles. This was obviously a sore point with the general. He was clearly very bitter that he had had orders directly from Tokyo to retake Leyte at any cost, and there was nothing he could do but obey, much to his disgust. When it was time for him to leave, I shook his hand and saluted him, a kind of knee-jerk military courtesy, I suppose. For this I was given a hard time by my fellow officers, but I just shrugged it off.

Soon we were back in Manila, which was beginning to return to life. Among the first enterprises to crop up were clubs catering to American troops. One evening our crew descended on the newly opened Piggy Wiggy Club and was having a great old time when one crew member loudly complained that he was being cheated by the club, whereupon our more-than-somewhat inebriated crew set about wrecking the place. It soon occurred to them that the MPs (military police) might soon show up and get them all thrown into the pokey. They then made a beeline for their ship, which was nested outboard a merchant freighter. They had no trouble going up the freighter's gangplank, crossing the ship, and dropping down into our ship—all but our most portly crew member who had passed out on the dock. Someone persuaded a crane operator on the freighter to hoist a cargo net and drop it on the dock, whereupon our passed-out sailor was rolled into the net and hoisted up. As luck would have it, he came to in midair and began screaming bloody murder until he was lowered onto our tank deck. Later I learned that my father's old friend (now colonel) Tom Ryan, who had put up much of the money to start Lockheed, was provost marshal for Manila. If our crew had been arrested, the case would surely have gotten to Tom, who would soon have discovered that I belonged to the same ship as my delinquent crew members, since I would probably have been the one to try to bail them out.

Before long, the Navy found a mission for us: moving Filipino constabulary forces to outlying islands to help quell a growing insurrection. This was probably the newly budding Communist-led Hukbalahap (or Huk) rebellion, which went on for years, until it was brought under control in 1954 by Ramon Magsaysay, who had become minister of defense when the Philippines obtained independence from the United States on July 4, 1946. Magsaysay was ably assisted in this campaign by the legendary Col. Ed Landsdale, who later put his Huk experience to use in Vietnam. The Philippine population was enormously grateful to us for having liberated them from the Japanese, who had generally treated them harshly, if not cruelly. Everywhere we went we were greeted with "*Mabuhay*, Joe!" which I took to mean victory, but recently learned meant "welcome." I believed that we had prematurely thrust independence on the Filipinos who would have been happy to have remained under our benevolent protection. We had promised them independence for 1944, but the war postponed this. It later occurred to me that Roosevelt probably wanted to push independence as part of his campaign to end French and British colonialism.

After we had dropped off all of our constabulary passengers where they wanted to go, we wound up on a lovely little island with no orders to do anything else but stay put. It was party time for the good old *Fighting 67* and its merry crew. The local village, with its fairly good little band, loved to put on dances for us, attracting a number of comely local lassies who liked to dance and were very good at it. We had a lot of dances. The bandleader was especially intrigued with the then-popular "In the Mood" that "ends" about three times, then starts up again. He liked this novelty so much he played the piece with about six false endings. Then some of us began to "go native."

I must add here that Ken Higgins had acquired enough points to leave and had returned to civilian life. Had he still been captain, I am sure we soon would have left the island and reported for duty at the closest Navy installation. Demobilization points were based on length of service, especially in combat, and on married status. Maybe Sid Horman also left, but I'm not sure. That would have left Art Ostrowski in command and me second in command. Anyway the command structure had become totally relaxed. I spent the day fishing with the local fishermen, dressed in shorts, tennis shoes, and my issue tropical helmet. These fishermen had an unusual technique. They fished a number of channels formed from coral deposits. We would position ourselves at one end of channel with our nets and another fisherman would work his way down the channel with a small dead octopus on a long stick with which he would chase the fish down the channel and into our nets. It was great fun and we caught quite a number of fish.

We had another pastime that I am ashamed to describe, that led to our undoing. Every evening there passed over the ship large flights of large fruit bats, or flying foxes, as some called them, with wingspans up to three feet. We took to shooting them down, first with rifles. Then we tried machine guns with tracers. The bats were dropping all around, and we were having a great old time, however terrible this sounds in retrospect. Then one evening at sunset, a destroyer appeared on the horizon, saw all this shooting and signaled us, "Are you under attack?" We explained this was a bit of sport shooting and then thought little of the incident. Clearly the skipper of the destroyer hadn't forgotten; he had our call sign, LSM 67. In a couple of days, we got orders to proceed to the nearest naval installation for further orders. The party was over, but it was great while it lasted. In any case, it was about time for us to go home and be of use in U.S. waters. I believe it was in late November when we headed for San Francisco via Pearl Harbor.

We reached Pearl Harbor sometime in December. As soon as I went ashore, I headed for the nearest uniform shop to buy my campaign ribbons and battle stars. To my amazement, the first shop I came to was owned and run by a Japanese man. I had assumed that all the Japanese had been sent off to camps in the United States as were all the West Coast Japanese. That was not the case in Hawai`i, however: there were simply too many of them. As noted earlier, with the benefit of hind- sight, the evacuation of the Californian and other Japanese seems terribly unfair and unjust. Once back on American territory, my bottle of Canadian Club whiskey was again worth $1.80 so I could afford to drink it. Another officer and I killed the bottle on New Year's Eve. Back to my campaign ribbons: I was eligible for only three ribbons, with battle stars plus the Victory Medal. My wife's grandfather, who was in the trenches in World War I and was badly gassed, was mustered out with only a postwar Victory Medal ribbon.(The Purple Heart was not awarded in that war.) Now one sees people in uniform who have never left the States wearing three rows of ribbons.

We steamed under the Golden Gate Bridge and into San Francisco Bay on January 11, 1946. My parents' close friends, the Hewitts, had a townhouse over- looking the Bay near the Golden Gate, and as we steamed by I could see my parents waving pillow cases at us from the Hewitt balcony. I had the conn (that is, I was "driving" the ship) coming in with a pilot on board and soon had a fight with him because he wanted to anchor us far from shore. Because we did not have a small boat large enough to make it safely to shore, we had to hitch rides from larger ships' boats. So it was essential to be inboard of those ships and closer to shore, and I succeeded in getting us anchored in a better location. I soon hitched a ride to shore and went to the nearest telephone booth to report our presence to the Navy port director.

Who should answer the phone but a German POW who spoke no English. For one minute, I thought, good grief have we defeated the Japanese and lost to the Germans? I am sure that the POW on the other end of the phone was equally surprised when I answered him in German. I was immediately connected with the port director's office, which unfortunately already had steaming orders for us. Art Ostrowski had already transferred command of the *67* to me and quickly left the ship to return home to Pennsylvania. Thus, at age twenty-three, by default I became one of the youngest ship captains in the U.S. Navy, and this at a time when the Navy was rapidly falling apart through our rapid, if not helter-skelter, demobilization. After the exchange with the port director's office, I took a taxi to the Hewitt's for a joyful, if subdued, reunion with my parents, who were then living in the upper San Joaquin Valley in the small town of Dos Palos where my father had established a crop-dusting business.

We had experienced a great deal of action, probably more than any other LSM, and suffered from a good bit of ship wear and tear. We badly needed a shipyard availability to overhaul our main engines, check our hull, and effect various other repairs. I soon found out that our ship was destined to be scrapped eventually, so we were not eligible for shipyard repairs, or for much of anything except fuel and supplies. I also soon found out that we were to take on a load of steel pilings at Port Hueneme, about thirty miles northwest of Los Angeles, to take to Green Cove Springs, Florida, on the St. John River upstream from and due south of Jacksonville, where they would be used to build docking for decommissioned Navy ships. My father visited the ship and was appalled at its dismal condition. I then took off for a visit to Dos Palos, taking along a large tub of New Zealand butter, since butter was still scarce in the United States. There I ran into several combat veterans with whom I could relate, and we told each other how scared we had been, which took a therapeutic load off our minds.

Back in San Francisco, I had a singularly embarrassing experience. I took an old high school girlfriend to the famed Top of the Mark cocktail lounge where there was also dancing. At the door I was carded. I must say I was not only embarrassed but fit to be tied. Obviously with the rank of lieutenant junior grade and campaign ribbons with battle stars I had to be over twenty-one. I always suspected that I was carded by a former enlisted man who was getting back at an officer. It was absurd that the captain of the *Fighting 67* should be subjected to this indignity.

Still early in 1946 it was clear we could tarry no longer in San Francisco Bay, and we were ordered to leave immediately for Port Hueneme. I filed a protest with the port director, truthfully declaring that the ship was in no shape to put out to sea, a fact that would soon become evident. My protest was ignored, and I had no choice but to get under way. If I'd known then what I know now, however, I would have refused to budge until all our work order requests had been filled, even at the risk of a general court marital.

When we were off Port Hueneme I realized that getting into the port would be tricky. The somewhat narrow channel leading into the port that extended out to sea was lined on both sides by rock jetties. Since we had an offshore cross current, I had to very carefully calculate where the current would take us at the point we entered this rock-lined channel. (A larger ship would not have had this problem.) A miscalculation would have resulted in our bottom being torn out on the rocks, and we would have been finished. We lucked out. I started out upstream on the current, lined up the channel right at the last minute and went in with full power to barely make it safely into the port. Fortunately our main engines were still performing fairly well even though both were actually on the verge of conking out. In any case, the thing was a white-knuckle experience if ever there was one. Once in port, we took on some three hundred tons of steel piling, which I feared could have capsized us had it shifted. The load was well lashed down with chains, but still I was worried. Steaming out of the channel was easy and soon we were out to sea. We had by then lost most of our experienced petty officers and all our officers with any seagoing experience. What were left were officers right out of midshipman's school who had never been to sea. This meant that only I, the captain, was qualified to stand an officer of the deck watch under way. For the time being, I was going to have to live on the bridge.

Off the coast of Mexico, where we encountered some fairly rough seas, things started to go wrong. First our radio went out, then our radar—and I no longer had any technicians on board who could repair them. As I recall, our sextant must have been broken, also, since I was navigating by dead reckoning—that is, I determined our position by keeping track of speed and course changes. Then one afternoon, I was dozing off on the bridge when an enlisted man on watch woke me up with a shout that we were listing to port. Sure enough we were listing to port. My first thought was, What if our load shifts and breaks loose? My most senior machinists mate and I donned dungarees and started checking the bottom compartments, beginning at the bow. We discovered nothing until we got to the stern where the ship's largest compartment, the after-steering flat, looked like a swimming pool. A seam by the port screw's drive shaft had cracked, making an opening about five inches wide and more than two feet long. The water was pouring in at a good rate. We quickly brought in our two electric pumps that got things under control before long and eliminated our port list. Then our port main engine conked out on us. Since the electric pumps got their power from generators connected to and dependent on the main engines, I prayed the starboard engine would hold. At this point, by the way, I had enough points to become a civilian again, but I was stuck with this ill-fated ship as long as it was steaming, since there was no one to relieve me.

By now, I was letting a couple of officers take the con at night while I slept on a bunk in the radio shack two decks below the bridge. Every evening I would write in the Night Order Book detailed instructions for the officers on watch on what the ship should be doing throughout the night. If there were the smallest deviations from my orders, say a small change in engine revolutions per minute or few minutes' change in the time of course shifts, I would wake up in an instant and call up to the bridge to ask what was wrong. It was eerie, to say the least. We finally made it to Panama City, where we no sooner had entered the harbor when our starboard engine gave up the ghost and quit. To make matters worse, everywhere there were signs, "Underwater Cables, Do Not Anchor." We still had way on, but without power there was not a lot of control over the ship. We had hoisted a breakdown distress signal and were headed for a Liberty Ship in the harbor when a tug came to our rescue and took us to a dock where we had power for our pumps and where we were to spend some time getting the ship back into shape, more or less. Had our last engine gone out on us while still at sea, we could well have sunk. With the buoyancy we would have lost with a fully flooded steering flat, our heavy load, which we could not jettison, would surely have pulled us down.

We tied up and I left the ship to see if we could get any help from the Navy. We were unaware that there is a very high tide on the Pacific side at Panama as opposed to a relatively low tide on the Atlantic side at Colón, so when I returned, the ship was hanging on its lines to the dock because the tide had gone way out. The officer on duty was obvious asleep at the switch. I was not too surprised, but still royally ticked off that the Navy would give us no help whatsoever. We were on our own. Our resourceful crew members somehow rigged diving masks out of gas masks we had been issued and had somehow got caulking material to plug up the big split in the after-steering flat. Our remaining (regular Navy) machinist mates tore down both engines and we had engine parts all over the ship. I marveled that they were actually able to get both engines to running again—not perfectly, but running. I took some time off each day to enjoy myself, mostly at the exclusive Club Union with a nice veranda on the harbor. The Club welcomed U.S. Navy officers and the drinks and food were quite affordable. I also enjoyed exploring the ruins of Old Panama, which had been laid waste by the English pirate Morgan in the seventeenth century. Before long we were ready to get under way. I took on board a Canal pilot, as was required, and we headed for the Canal.

On the Pacific side, the Canal zigzags a bit through the mountains, which necessitates several course changes involving lining up ranges up on hills on each course and shifting just in time from one set of range markers to the next. The ship responded so sluggishly when we made the first course change that the pilot announced that he had been a Canal pilot for twenty years and had never run a ship aground, and he wasn't going to spoil his record on a "rust bucket" like our ship. With that he left the bridge and went below to the wardroom. I had studied our charts on the Canal and had pretty well memorized the course changes. Also, I knew how to compensate for the ship's erratic performance. When we got to the huge Gatun Lake, the pilot came back to the bridge. At this point there was no longer a need for a pilot, since there was nothing simpler than steaming across the lake and then throwing a line to one of the waiting "mules" (hauling vehicles) that would pull us through the locks on the Atlantic side. To this day, I am wont to boast that I may have been the only ship captain in history to take a ship though the Panama Canal without a pilot on the bridge, and that is true, in essence. When the pilot finally came back to the bridge he was no longer needed.

Our next destination was Jacksonville, Florida. Before we entered the harbor there, I took on board a local pilot and headed for a dock designated to us right next to downtown Jacksonville. I was making a pretty good approach against the current, but still had a bit too much way on, so I ordered all engines to stop. We were still going too fast as we approached the dock, so I ordered, "All engines back." Nothing happened. By this time desperate, I ordered "ALL BACK FULL." Nothing happened. We hit the dock with a resounding crash that brought heads sticking out of every window in downtown Jacksonville. It was as if a low-yield nuke had gone off in their midst. Needless to say, even going slowly, a thousand-ton ship can do considerable damage to a dock, and it did. As captain I was in trouble, since the ship was my responsibility, even though there was nothing I could have done to prevent this disaster.

I gathered all our rejected work order requests, the ship's log book, and a helpful statement from the pilot and reported to the Senior Officer Present Afloat (SOPA), who had the rank of captain and was captain of a sizeable Navy amphibious operations cargo ship. When I came to his cabin, he greeted me with, "Well, captain, what can I do for you?" (At that time I didn't look much over nineteen, albeit a haggard nineteen, which might have been the real reason I was carded at the Top of the Mark.) I was flattered and relieved to see that we were going to have a conversation one captain to another. I described what had happened and displayed all the evidence I had brought along in my defense. He then asked me if I was regular or reserve. Reserve, I told him. Next, when will you be getting out of the service? I guessed by the end of summer and added that I planned to go to Europe to graduate school.

The good SOPA, bless his heart, then conspired with the local Navy port director to pass my case back and forth for comments until I was a civilian and hopefully on my way to Europe before they finally followed the correct procedure of sending my case to the commandant of this naval district for a decision. When it finally reached the commandant, two things must have been obvious. One, a general court martial would undoubtedly result in finding me not guilty of negligence or of anything else. Two, it would have been politically inadvisable to recall a civilian, who had served his country well in combat, for a court martial that had no real purpose, since it was an open-and-shut case.

We next steamed up the St. John River to Green Cove Springs where we finally delivered our steel piling. While there, I happened to meet for the first time my sister's fiancé (and husband since 1946) Hugh Carr, who was an officer on a small Navy ship there. While we were anchored in the river, I went ashore and came back at late at night to find the sailor on anchor watch asleep. This is a very serious offense, since it can endanger the ship and everyone in it. I told him to report for captain's mast the next morning. As he stood at attention in the wardroom, I read from the *For the Government of the Navy*, popularly known as the "Rocks and Shoals," that falling asleep on anchor watch was punishable by death, upon which he understandably turned ashen. When I sentenced him to only a week's solitary confinement on bread and water (popularly known as "piss and punk") he teared up, and I was afraid he'd kiss my hand in gratitude. He had learned his lesson, which was all I cared for. He had to serve his sentence in a Navy brig on land because we had no brig on board.

Next we headed for our final destination, Charleston, South Carolina. By then, our crew had dwindled down to a single watch capability. As we approached Charleston Harbor, my one remaining (out of three) signalman fell ill. This meant that I had to get on the signal light myself and request harbor entrance instructions. I hadn't worked a signal light since I was a midshipman, but enough somehow came back to me for us to know where to tie up for the last time at the Charleston Navy Yard. So the poor old *67* reached her last berth, and I prepared to leave her at long last. I had taken a jeep from the Army in the Philippines in which I had hoped to drive off, but before I could someone in the Charleston Navy Yard stole it. I finally handed over the permanently immobile ship to one of the remaining officers. By the time I left this ship, I felt like a fatigued old man and was smoking up to five packs of cigarettes a day. (Shortly thereafter I went back to pipe smoking.) I must say this about my ordeal as the *67*'s last captain: since then everything else has been a piece of cake by comparison. There is nothing in civilian or military life that quite matches the degree of responsibility entailed in being a ship captain. Everything and everybody on board depends on the captain when you're out to sea. This responsibility was especially burdensome when skippering an ailing and worn-out ship like the poor old *Fighting 67*.

I was not due to sail to Europe for graduate school until the fall, so I decided to take the Navy up on the offer of a dream billet: as watch officer at the Navy barracks (now long gone) overlooking Columbia Pike in Arlington, Virginia, just across the Potomac from Washington. I was on duty only one day a week and had a nice suite in the officers' section. The rest of the time I hitched rides on military aircraft to visit friends and places I wanted to see. For example, I visited a former officer of ours, Joe Crudup, whose father headed a small women's college in Georgia that I greatly enjoyed visiting. I was rapidly recovering from the ordeal of skippering the ailing *67*. The Washington area was still teeming with women who had come to work in the government during the war days and still had jobs, and I thoroughly enjoyed being whistled at by groups of pretty young women. One of my favorite dating activities was attending the Watergate concerts. The Watergate consisted of concrete seats built into the rather high bank that looked like a white stairway from across the Potomac. The musicians performed on a floating stage. Most performances were band concerts. It was fun to take a date there in a rented rowboat with sandwiches and beer on hand. The concerts were discontinued with the advent of noisy airline flights over the Potomac. Later the whole area was redeveloped, and Watergate became an office, apartment, and hotel complex made notorious by the 1972 break-in at a Democratic headquarters.

By fall, my assignment was coming to an end, as was my time on active duty. I was demobilized out of Navy active duty (I remained in the reserve) with a month's terminal leave. During the whole leave I continued to wear my uniform, which I had found to be of great advantage: for example, I often found it hard to pick up the tab in bars and restaurants—others were always happy to do so for their returning "war heroes."

Chapter 10

Postwar Move to Europe

I N EARLY FALL 1946, I BOARDED IN NEW YORK the SS *John Ericsson*, a merchant ship that had been converted to a troop ship during the war and was still in that configuration when I came on board. We all slept in bunks, the men and women in separate compartments. I had the impression that most of the passengers were students like me. This ship was the least-expensive way to cross the Atlantic that most of us could find at that time. In fact, some of the most famous ocean liners had been turned into troop ships and hadn't yet been converted back to passenger ships. I believe it took us more than a week to reach France. We docked at Le Havre, and I took a train through Paris to Geneva where I would be going to school. Since it was only about sixteen months since the war had ended in Europe, there was still a great deal of war destruction visible en route. Switzerland, however, had completely escaped the war and was among the very few completely normal-looking countries in Europe at the time.

I checked in at a nice modest hotel near the Gare Cornavin train station in Geneva and caught a streetcar for the site of my future studies, the Graduate Institute of International Studies, part of the University of Geneva, which had been founded in 1559. I hadn't been able to find a suitable graduate program in the United States and, in any case, wanted to go to Europe, which I had been keen on seeing since I was a teenager. I was hoping to join the U.S. Foreign Service, which I eventually did. Having studied mostly engineering, math, and science, I needed a foreign affairs–related course of studies; this school was probably the best in the world for this purpose. It was located in a large old villa in a park overlooking Lake Geneva. The site could not have been more attractive. I soon located a room to rent in the nearby apartment of the Herzberg family, Germans who had been forced to leave their native Latvia when the Soviets took over the country in 1940 in a deal brokered with Hitler. The husband, wife, and little boy were agreeable, and the apartment was nice and located in a solid building on the Avenue Blanc that had been built around the turn of the century. For my board I found a small café where I could eat for little money.

I was on the GI Bill of Rights and received $75 (about $900 today) a month to live on, which wasn't bad at that time, especially in Europe. My tuition and books were all paid for. I believe that it is generally accepted that this post–World War II program was one of the wisest investments of taxpayers' money in history. It provided training for a whole generation of veterans, an investment that paid off royally for the country. It paid off well, too, for the veterans themselves, who were given the chance to receive professional training that most—certainly including me—could have ill afforded. The ability to study in Europe was especially beneficial to Jewish vets who wanted to study medicine, but who often were blocked from U.S. medical schools because of quota limitations for Jews, as incredible as this may sound today.

It wasn't long before I realized how much I was going to learn from my fellow students who came from all over Europe, East and West. For example, early on my eyes were opened by a seminar on Yugoslavia attended by former Partisans, Ustachis, and Chetniks, all of whom had been trying to kill each other in Yugoslavia's bloody civil war less than a year and a half earlier. When the professor was about to lose control of the bitter debate that ensued during a class, he threatened to call the police. This quickly quieted all of them, each of whom had his own reasons for not wanting to be expelled from the protection of Switzerland, including the prospect of a possible death sentence awaiting some of them in their native land.

The professors were outstanding and internationally known. The most impressive of the lot to me was economics professor Wilhelm Röpke. He was a leading proponent of a free market economy at a time when most European countries and Great Britain were resorting to government planning in trying to cope with postwar economic dislocations. This was total anathema to Röpke, whose idol and role model was his contemporary, famed Austrian economist and 1974 Nobel Prize winner Friedrich von Hayek, the world's leading free market advocate. The future West German economic leaders, notably future Economics Minister Ludwig Erhard, were being coached by Röpke in preparation for taking over the West German economy. One of the classes he taught consisted almost entirely of advice he was giving the Germans at that time.

His plan for West German economic recovery, at a time when cigarettes were a primary means of exchange, was to begin with a currency reform introducing the new "West Mark." He then described exactly what would follow this move. Frankly we were all skeptical and enjoyed making up limericks and jokes about his

West Mark. Then, in June 1948, West Germany (the Federal Republic of Germany) introduced the Deutsche Mark (that is, the German mark). What followed tracked exactly with what Röpke had been describing to us for a semester. For example, all sorts of wares began magically appearing in West German shops and stores, just as he had predicted. Prior to this, I remember buying a first-class train ticket from a German city on the Swiss border to Prague with a pack of cigarettes. The Deutsche Mark ended all that.

In no time at all this economic recovery was being referred to as the (West) German *Wirtschaftswunder* ("economic miracle"). Röpke deserves a very large amount of the credit for this remarkable recovery, especially since the vast majority of European economists advocated the state planning that kept most European economies lagging well behind that of West Germany. In four semesters of Röpke lectures I never once saw him use an equation or even a graph. He knew all that, of course, but chose to describe his theories in plain language, which he could do in English, German, and French. As a math major I still believe it is fraudulent to use an equals sign in any economic equation. (It's all right, however, to use a variables sign instead.) Too many factors in these formulas are guesses at best, like, for example, those affected by mass psychology and by unforeseen incompetence or dishonesty. Most cannot be precisely or even approximately measured, unlike physical sciences where in a formula like V (or E) equals R times I, volts, ohms, and amperes can be precisely measured. Just think how uncertain it is to game the stock market with mathematical formulas or models. One of Röpke's axioms, which I shall never forget, in effect sets in simple terms the criteria essential to preserving the free enterprise economic system: In the game of economics, governments are obliged to establish equitable and effective rules, but must then let private entrepreneurs play the game. It is by no means an exaggeration to say that Wilhelm Röpke was undoubtedly one of the most successful practicing economists of the twentieth century. Proof of this, inter alia, is the remarkable continuing economic success of first West and now united Germany, which can largely be traced to the initial direction Röpke gave it early on, as noted above. I have long believed that the secret of his success lay in his unusually broad knowledge, especially of history and of societies, increasingly rare in an era of narrow specialists.

One thing we especially welcomed was Röpke opposition to exchange control. This gave us a moral justification for smuggling currencies from Switzerland to various European countries. As I recall, all European countries except Switzerland practiced exchange control. That is, they pegged their currency's exchange rate vis-à-vis the dollar—for instance, keeping their currency artificially high. In Geneva, however, we could buy all these currencies at their true value. Let's say, for example, the French franc was officially pegged ten to the dollar whereas in the free market rate it was actually twenty to the dollar. Since most exchange control countries banned the import of their own currency, we had to smuggle currency if we were to benefit from significant exchange rate disparities. Since we were next door to France, we mostly smuggled francs. The French were soon on to us students. When we took a train to France (hardly any of us had cars) we had to go through French customs at the Gare Cornavin before we even left Switzerland. The French customs people sometimes strip-searched us; female customs agents on occasion made female students even remove their sanitary napkins, searching for contraband francs. They also made us remove the film from our cameras. However, the French customs officials never discovered our ultimate smuggling secret: we would take tubes of toothpaste or shaving cream, unclip the metal strip at the base, then stuff high-denomination bills wrapped in wax paper into the tubes. Then we reclipped the strips and went our merry ways loaded with cheap currency.

Smuggling currency got me into a truly scary situation later. The father of one of my classmates, Agnes Kemeny, was the state secretary of finance for Hungary and had engineered the currency reform that exchanged the old Hungarian pengö for the new forint, which is still Hungary's currency. Once when I was in Budapest I was invited to dinner at the Kemenys' home. During the dinner I asked Mr. Kemeny if there were problems with people smuggling in forints, which I had just done. He said that shouldn't be too much of a problem, since such smuggling was a capital offense in Hungary. He must have noticed that I turned as white as the tablecloth, but he didn't let on. Not long thereafter, the Kemeny family for political reasons "escaped" to London, where the father got a prestigious job in London's financial center.

The summer of 1947 three fellow students and I prepared for a tour of northern Europe and the Scandinavian countries by loading up with thirteen different currencies. Some we declared and changed at a favorable official exchange rate, others we smuggled and exchanged at a favorable free market rate. We lived like kings, eating at the best restaurants and staying in first-class hotels. At the end of the trip, we actually had more money than we began with. We were learning to be real currency operators.

Another source of unearned income for us was the anomaly resulting from Nazi Germany's having deposited a great deal of money and other assets in Swiss banks with their secrecy rules protecting the identity of depositors. The United States was well aware that these deposits included substantial assets stolen from occupied countries or taken from Jews and other victims. For this reason, the United States moved to try to freeze these assets until their ownership could be determined. In this connection, we moved to block the Swiss from using their francs to acquire U.S. dollars. To circumvent this, the Swiss hit upon acquiring U.S. travelers' checks as liquid dollar instruments. We students unwittingly or uncaringly helped them in this endeavor. We would go to the American Express office in Geneva where at one window we would buy travelers' checks at three and a half francs to the dollar and then go to the next window where we would sell the checks for four and a half francs on the dollar. At first we could exchange several hundred dollars a month and were making out like bandits. By student standards we were getting rich. Eventually the whole German asset situation was somehow sorted out and this deal was reduced and then discontinued.

The winter of 1946–47 was the coldest in the twentieth century. Coal mines in Germany and elsewhere suffered war damage and production was way down. Also, transportation was a problem. (Throughout Europe hot water and soap, among other necessities, were scarce, creating obvious problems in crowded situations. I eventually got used to the odors.) The result was that even in relatively prosperous Switzerland we froze that winter. All winter long one could touch the radiators where I was staying and feel no heat. I was told that men and women students were sleeping together just to keep warm, and I can believe it. There were times when I just stayed in bed instead of venturing out to attend classes. At least, however, unlike in much of Europe, we had enough to eat. Bread, and I believe other things, were rationed, but we did well by eating vegetables, rolls, and dairy products. I believe we had meat once a week where I boarded. It was paradoxical that when much food, especially meat, was scarce in the immediate postwar years, Europeans, unless they were actually starving—as for example, in Vienna— were really healthier than in later, more prosperous years. Before long, things had improved in Geneva to the point where one could get really good meals in restaurants and bistros. I became especially fond of the great local cheese dishes such as cheese fondue, especially when served with truffles, and other cheese dishes such as raclette and *biftek au fromage.* I also developed a lifelong fondness for snails, which I never dreamed I would eventually learn to like.

On the pretext of doing a study of the Spanish Civil War, I decided to go to Spain. At that time, Spain was a pariah state in Europe because of the key assistance Spain's dictator Francisco Franco had received from Germany and Italy during the 1936–39 civil war. For that reason, there were almost no tourists in Spain. Before I left Geneva, I, like a number of other students, worked out an arrangement with the Universal Watch Company whereby we could get all the pesetas we needed at the free market rate from the company's branch in Barcelona. When we returned to Geneva we would pay for the pesetas we had actually used. (Eventually this arrangement broke down when some students failed to settle up.) This enabled me to live very well indeed in Spain. There was no direct rail connection between Spain and France, which had built barriers in the tunnels under the Pyrenees, which divides the two countries. So I took a train as far as the border town of Cerbere, France, from which I took a taxi to the border with Spain. There a Spanish official noted in my passport my parents' address in Dos Palos whereupon he sternly declared that, "Dos Palos once belonged to Spain." And he wasn't being funny. From the border I took another taxi down to Spanish Portbou, from whence I took a train to Barcelona.

In Barcelona, where I drew all the pesetas I could possibly spend, I decided to take in a bullfight. It turned out that Franco had the same idea, and he and his entourage passed me on the way to the stadium. I was impressed by how quiet his BMW mounted motorcycle escort was. At the stadium, all sang the Falangist hymn "Face to the Sun" in Franco's honor, and then the action began. The star was Manuel Manolete, the world's greatest matador. He was spectacular, taking one risk after the other. At one point when a huge bull was charging him, he nonchalantly turned his back, facing the bull only at the very last moment for the kill. Amid thunderous shouts of olé and the strains of the band's *paso doble*, Manolete had triumphed again. Later I heard that the thirty-year-old Manolete was taking these chances because he was being challenged by an up-and-coming matador, twenty-one-year-old Luis Dominguín. All the pageantry and drama of the stadium made me an instant bullfight "aficionado" (fan), although I suppose I shouldn't admit it. A few months later, in August 1947, the great Manolete took one chance too many and was gored to death.

After Barcelona, I took a train along the Costa Brava, in Catalonia. I then thought the whole area with its somewhat poor-looking villages would someday make a great tourist spot, and I was right. I was struck that in all the villages I visited in the former leftist "Loyalist-held" areas the Catholic churches had been desecrated. For example, all the statues had been decapitated, and stained glass windows had been knocked out. This was, after all, only eight years after the civil war. Down on the Costa del Sol the city of Málaga and other towns and cities still showed a fair amount of destruction. Heading inland from Alicante en route to Málaga, the train was so slow I repeatedly got out and walked alongside it. The people in the train insisted on feeding me and couldn't have been more hospitable and kind. The Spaniards then struck me as a serious, if not somber, people of great character. I was impressed that in those days no one would ever take a tip, including waiters and cab drivers. I have always been struck by how similar the scenery was to that in the southwestern part of the United States where nearly every kind of scenery in Spain could be replicated. Spain even has cactus. I could see that the Spaniards must have felt at home in the areas they occupied in America. I quickly decided not to discuss the civil war in which virtually every Spanish family had lost someone. The whole trip, in any case, was unforgettable.

I had taken a job as a stringer (part-time correspondent) for the Mutual Broadcasting System (MBS) and was writing a column for a group of small papers in California. For a month I was substitute Switzerland correspondent for the *New York Times*. I also wrote advertising copy. I remember an ad I wrote for Atmos, a clock that ran on changes in barometric pressure. For this one I coined the term, "Atmos. The Clock That Breathes." I later saw this in a U.S. magazine. For this gem I received about $25. I began to cover Eastern Europe to some extent for MBS. At this point, the reader must be asking, when does this guy ever study? To which I would reply that most of my extracurricular activities, especially travel, took place during vacation periods. I was actually a fairly conscientious student, because I believed that my future success depended in good part on what I learned at the Institute.

For years I had longed to see Vienna, "City of My Dreams," as the song goes. Using the press card I used in covering the United Nations in Geneva I somehow bluffed my way past the Soviet guards who checked train passengers proceeding through the Soviet Zone to Vienna. When I arrived I managed to find lodging in a small hotel near the city's center. Unlike correspondents who were locally accredited, I could get no support from U.S. Army facilities because I was not supposed to be there.

The city had suffered some bombing destruction, but nothing compared to the rubble heaps to which major German cities had been reduced. For example, the main opera house had been mistaken for a train station and was bombed out. The roof of St. Stephen's Cathedral had collapsed after being hit by Soviet artillery during the attack on the city, but most of the city remained fairly intact. I had memorized a map of Vienna when I was in college and knew my way around fairly well. Everything was so sad there that I should have been disappointed, but I wasn't. Indeed I was thrilled just to be there after all these years. Food was very scarce and a number of people had been starving; some had even starved to death in the bitter cold winter just past. I had no military support and no Austrian ration cards, so for a day and half I found nothing to eat. Finally, I discovered a kind of black market restaurant where I could get a passable goulash for several times the legal price with ration cards. In another two years I would be moving to Vienna where I would be in the heart of the then-budding Cold War.

Norman Friedman in his masterful book *The Fifty-Year War* wrote that the Cold War actually started in 1937 with Stalin's attempt to take control of Spain, then in the throes of a civil war. (See p. 35 of Friedman's book.) Most, however, would put the start of that war later, when tensions began building between the USSR and the Western powers immediately after the end of World War II. Then, as Friedman put it, "On February 9, 1946, Stalin declared cold war." This referred to his speech clearly implying that there could be no peace between the Soviet Union and the capitalist world. In this speech he also called for tripling Soviet steel production, a sure sign of a military buildup. Liberal Supreme Court justice William O. Douglas found the speech "a declaration of World War III." The badly shaken State Department then queried our chargé d'affaires in Moscow, leading Soviet expert George F. Kennan, who replied in his classic "Long Telegram" (the bulk of which appeared in the July 1947 *Foreign Affairs*). This document explained Stalin's belief in permanent warfare with capitalism and emphasized the essential importance of containing Soviet expansion. He correctly predicted that this policy of "containment" would eventually prevail. Indeed it led to the dissolution of the Soviet empire. The world became aware of the Cold War with the Communist takeovers in Eastern Europe. U.S. media, including MBS, were becoming interested in this development.

This led me to both Budapest and Prague. Hungary became Communist dominated in 1947. When I first visited Prague in 1947, the city was outwardly free, but behind the scenes the Communists were beginning to gain control in initially subtle ways. I became very fond of Prague, which I still regard as one of the world's most beautiful cities. I also became much taken with Olga, a lovely young Czech woman who spoke very good English. When the Communists seized complete control of Czechoslovakia in February 1948, it was some time before Western journalists were able to enter the country. I finally received permission to enter the country to cover the Sokol Festival. The Sokol was a nationalistic Czech gymnastic society formed in the late nineteenth century. This year's festival was to be its last gasp. It came at a very interesting time, however, just after Yugoslav dictator Marshal Tito had been expelled from the COMINFORM (Communist Information Bureau), a Soviet-dominated association of European Communist parties formed in 1947 to combat the U.S. Marshal Plan for European economic recovery. There were a number of Yugoslav youth brigades visiting Prague, and everywhere they appeared they were cheered by the populace as symbols of resistance to the Soviets.

I observed the Sokol parade through the city's central Wenceslas Square from my hotel room. When the participants began to chant "Long live the Republic of Masaryk and Benes" (the first and then-present elected presidents of Czechoslovakia), I could see plainclothes police pulling participants out of the parade, and no doubt arresting them. Prague had been transformed. Previously one could buy all kinds of publications, for example. Now there were only Communist publications for sale. Now one needed to be guarded in speech and contacts. As much as I would have liked to, I didn't try to contact Olga for fear of getting both her and her family in trouble. The same held for everybody else with whom I was acquainted.

One evening I went to a concert given by the superb Czech Philharmonic Orchestra. When they played Dvorak's "Slavonic Dances" we all were crying, brought to tears by these deeply moving national treasures. What happened here epitomizes what happens when Communists take control.

Ever since the war ended, tension had been building between the Soviet Union and the Western powers. To me, however, the Cold War (first mentioned in 1948) officially began on October 5, 1947, when the newly created COMINFORM declared war on the Marshall Plan, which was just beginning to take form and that would prove to be *the* pivotal development in postwar Europe. Secretary of State George Marshall, in a June 5, 1947, address, proposed a cooperative economic recovery plan for Europe. The French and British foreign ministers quickly invited twenty-two European states to send representatives to Paris to meet on July 12 in order to formulate Europe's economic needs. Those invited included the Soviet Union and Eastern European countries. Soviet Foreign Minister Molotov turned it down, but the Czechoslovaks had already accepted and were ordered to follow the Soviet suit. This revealed to the population the degree of control Moscow already had in their country. I was in Prague just after this became known, and it jolted everyone. Stalin could see that the economic progress in Europe would thwart Soviet ambitions there. Moscow then ordered the large French and Italian Communist parties to bodily oppose the Marshall Plan by fomenting strikes and disorders, but this effort fizzled out by year's end due to lack of popular support. The next move was the Communist takeover of Czechoslovakia and increased pressure on Finland. Moscow felt compelled to force Eastern Europe to resist the American blandishments represented by the Plan.

Since we students at the Institute were immersed in international affairs, we followed European developments with acute interest. One notable example was the upcoming parliamentary elections in Italy, scheduled for April 18–19, 1948. A number of students actually went to Rome and elsewhere in Italy to observe the process. A great deal was at stake. All of us, as well as the U.S. and Allied governments, were greatly concerned that the powerful Communist Party, well financed and guided by Moscow, might win. Its main opponent was the Christian Democratic Party headed by one of the greatest postwar European leaders, Alcide de Gasperi, whose party the United States quietly help finance through the CIA. Amazingly, de Gasperi's party won the first absolute majority in Italian parliamentary history, to our collective enormous relief.

A welcome respite for me from international politics was the 1948 Winter Olympics at St. Moritz, Switzerland; at the very last minute, MBS decided I should cover the games. I went to the games already behind a journalistic eight ball, since I had no time to arrange anything or get any technical assistance. I did manage to interview some stars, however, notably popular top skaters Dick Button (United States) and Barbara Ann Scott (Canada), but I never saw a single event. I later wondered if that didn't make me unique in the field of sports journalism, a journalist covering a major sports event that he never laid eyes on.

At any rate, my purpose for being in Geneva was not journalistic, but to acquire a knowledge of foreign affairs, and this I did. The several international law courses were later to prove especially valuable. I also gained a great deal of knowledge of and insight in the conduct of international relations and very considerable knowledge of international economics. I have always treasured this experience. For the master's degree I spent four semesters on courses that, in essence, required a thesis on each major subject, which was quite demanding. Of course, a good knowledge of French was essential, because some lectures were in French, as were some required readings. Later, in defending my doctoral dissertation, I had to be able to field questions in both French and English. My having gotten the equivalent of As in all my courses absolved me of much class work while I pursued my doctorate, which I began after receiving the *licence* (or master's) degree at the end of the 1948 spring semester. This gave me a good deal of freedom, since I only had to show up at the Institute from time to time to give seminar papers. For the doctorate, the Institute placed considerably more emphasis on the dissertation and less on class work than is usually the case in U.S. universities.

The demands for the dissertation were exacting. First, the dissertation had to pass the academic scrutiny of an international mixed committee of experienced professors from leading universities in continental Europe, the United Kingdom, and the United States; then the dissertation had to be commercially published, with 250 paperback copies going to the university, before it could be defended. This meant that it not only had to survive the steely eyed scrutiny of trained academics, but also had to be interesting enough to be sold to a commercial publisher, unless one had enough money to finance this costly requirement, which none of us did. I had heard that a rich student had hired another student to write his dissertation that he subsequently paid to have published. During the dissertation defense it became clear that he had not written it, and he failed. I got this story second hand, but I can believe it. One advantage of the publishing requirement was the elimination of highly specialized dissertations that were of little or no interest to anybody outside limited academic circles, as is so often the case in the United States. The university sent the 250 copies to leading universities throughout the world. In fact, years later I discovered one such copy in Georgetown University's library when I taught there.

I do have a few remarks to make about Switzerland and the Swiss. They are basically good folks, but epitomize petit bourgeois values and characteristics. I recall in traveling across the country that Swiss men armed with a timetable and a good Swiss watch checked the time of arrival at each station. Once when I was traveling clear across the country I arrived at my destination at precisely when the minute hand was on twelve. We had arrived on the second at the correct time. This helped make me decide to move to Vienna where the trains never arrived on time, and some didn't arrive at all, having been hijacked by the Soviets. During my last year or so in Geneva, three other American students and I rented the second-floor apartment in a villa overlooking Geneva. On the night of May 8, 1948, we had a particularly noisy and boozy party singing not only good old American songs, but also

Nazi, fascist, and Communist songs. The next morning I encountered our landlady, Madame Wahl, and sheepishly apologized for our rowdy behavior. She replied that she and all the neighbors "understood why you American veterans would be celebrating V-E Day." Of course, we hadn't a clue as to what we were celebrating.

One of my fellow students, a Swiss, invited me to his room for a drink one day. I noticed on his table a gold-plated model of one of the standard Luftwaffe fighter planes, the Messerschmidt 109. I asked him what that was all about. He replied that he got it because he had been an ace in the Swiss Air Force. I said, "An ace? That means you shot down five enemy aircraft. How did that happen?" When I saw his embarrassment, I realized that, in fact, he had probably downed five crippled American B-17 bombers that had strayed over Switzerland—perhaps in the belief that it would be better to be downed in Switzerland than over Germany. The treatment of American Air Force personnel interned in Switzerland actually left something to be desired until it was clear that Germany was losing the war. On the one hand, the Swiss had to be very careful in order to stay clear of the war, for which one could hardly blame them. Their armed forces were truly formidable, since nearly all adult Swiss men were in the reserve and armed, ready to fight. Also, there were impressive mountain fortifications to further discourage any German invasion. On the other hand, the Swiss did make some concessions that were helpful to the Germans, giving them other incentives not to invade. One facet of Swiss wartime defense was extensive wiretapping of all foreigners and a number of Swiss. This continued for some time after the war, no doubt due to bureaucratic inertia, and was still in full swing for some time after I arrived.

One thing that fascinated me about Switzerland was how well its four language groups—German, French, Italian, and Romansch—get along and how all enrich the country. I attribute this to their federal system and the semiautonomy of the cantons that neatly solves the problem of being a multilingual country. I was always intrigued that I could cycle in the countryside near adjacent German and French cantons. One could just cross a field and everything would change: the architecture, the language, the customs, and even the mentality. I thought that was just great. Also, I very much admired the Swiss ancient democratic traditions. Their faults are trivial compared to their deeply embedded principles and virtues. In the future, there would be times when I missed the predictable normality and security of Switzerland.

Chapter 11

Vienna

THERE WERE PRACTICAL AS WELL AS SENTIMENTAL REASONS for moving to Vienna. First, my dissertation was to be on Soviet policy toward Austria and most of the material I needed was in Vienna. I found that commuting between Geneva and Vienna simply didn't work. Then there was my secondary occupation: reporting on Eastern Europe. By 1949 American and most other Western journalists were banned from what was by then solidly Communist Eastern Europe. This region was being largely covered from Vienna, which itself was a hundred miles behind the "Iron Curtain" since it was located in the Soviet zone of Austria. In Vienna one could gather information on neighboring and other Communist countries from travelers, diplomats, refugees, and others. In 1945 Austria had been divided into four occupation zones: the Soviet zone in the east, the U.S. and French zones in the west, and the British zone in the south. Vienna was divided into four sectors with the central part, the "Inner City," coming under the jurisdiction of the Allied Council chair, which rotated monthly among the four occupying powers.

This raises the question of why Austria was occupied in the first place. At war's end, Austria found itself in an ambiguous position. In 1943 in Moscow, Soviet, U.S., and British foreign ministers declared Austria to be "the first country to fall a victim to Hitlerite aggression," but, at Soviet insistence, this Moscow Declaration added that Austria had responsibility for fighting on the side of Germany. Never mind that Germany had occupied and annexed Austria in March 1938, after which Austria ceased to exist as a sovereign country and could not fairly be made responsible for anything. Of course, this also held true for the German-annexed Alsace-Lorraine that had been taken from France, and for Luxemburg. To be sure, many individual Austrians willingly cooperated with the German occupiers and many Austrians fought and fought well in the German Wehrmacht. In any event, that is why Austria, like Germany, was occupied and divided into zones. In point of fact, the most the Nazi party ever gained in any free election in a free Austria was less than 17 percent of the vote. Under massive pressure from Hitler, the Austrian government in March 1938 sought to protect the country by calling for a plebiscite on an Anschluss (annexation) with Germany. Hitler, no doubt knowing that an Anschluss would decisively lose in a vote, invaded Austria and took it over. Then he called for another plebiscite that he couldn't lose, since only "*ja*" was on the ballot. During the course of the Nazi occupation, more than 1 percent of the total population was arrested by the Gestapo for *political* reasons. (That would be the equivalent of more than 3 million Americans today.) While anti-Semitism always had been rife in Austria, especially in Vienna, it is very doubtful that any Jew would ever have been harmed had Nazi Germany not taken over the country.

My move to Vienna in 1949 took place during a period of considerable tension dramatized by the Soviet blockade of West Berlin beginning June 24, 1948, and ending May 12, 1949. During the subsequent airlift, U.S. and British aircraft delivered an average of five thousand tons of food and other necessities every day to sustain some 2.5 million West Berliners. This was, to say the least, a dramatic earnest of the Western Allied support for West Berlin. Vienna was in a similar position, and there was considerable concern that it, too, could be blockaded. In this case, there would be little chance of a successful Berlin-type airlift since all the Western Allied airports were in the Soviet zone. At one point, the Soviet sought to block the movement of British troops from their zone to their sector of Vienna because the British soldiers didn't have the right kind of identification cards. The British then moved in a convoy of trucks with soldiers in battle dress with fixed bayonets on their rifles. The officer in charge flipped up the crossbar barrier and the convoy went through without incident. End of threat.

Earlier we had had a more deadly confrontation with the Soviets over transit rights through their zone. In early 1946 Soviet soldiers had taken to boarding the U.S. Army "Mozart" train from the U.S. zone to the U.S. sector of Vienna. U.S. high commissioner Gen. Mark Clark notified his Soviet opposite number in no uncertain terms that this no longer would be tolerated. Nevertheless, on January 16, 1946, several armed Soviet officers and soldiers boarded the train. They were confronted by military policeman T/Sgt Shirley B. Dixon of Toledo, Ohio, who ordered them off the train. The officers made the mistake of drawing their pistols, whereupon Dixon shot and killed the senior officer, a captain, and wounded a senior lieutenant. The Soviets never boarded that train again. Unrelated, of course, but shortly thereafter, on March 5, 1946, Winston Churchill anticipated the Cold War in his famous "Iron Curtain" speech in Fulton, Missouri.

The 1949 film, *The Third Man*, masterfully captured the atmosphere in Vienna in the early postwar years, except that what was really going on was far more dramatic. For example, hundreds of Austrians, including a number of officials, had been "arrested" by the Soviets in all sectors of the city. These arrests more closely resembled gangster-like abductions, the victims often being nabbed on a sidewalk and then dragged into a waiting car. Here are just a few causes célèbres. (All of those arrested were accused of being American spies, no doubt resulting from Austrian officials working with their principal source of assistance and support, American officials.)

- Leading Austrian railroad expert Paul Katscher was going to an Inter-European Freight Car conference in Geneva, reportedly to raise the question of the fourteen thousand Austrian freight cars that had disappeared into Eastern Europe. On the eve of his departure on December 4, 1947, he was arrested. He died in a Soviet prison in 1949.

- Anton Marek, a very senior Vienna police official who had been investigating the disappearance of Austrian citizens, was arrested on June 17, 1948. Incidentally, Marek had been instrumental in thwarting a Nazi antigovernment plot in 1934.

- Dr. Margarethe Ottilinger, chief of the Planning Section of the Ministry of Property Control and Economic Planning, was arrested on November 5, 1948. She was finally released after the occupation ended in 1955.

- Irving Ross, a senior member of the U.S. Economic Recovery Plan mission in Vienna, was clubbed to death in Vienna by Soviet soldiers in what appeared to be a planned murder during the night of October 30–31, 1948. I covered this as a correspondent and none of us could figure out what prompted this atrocity.

- A U.S. Navy captain naval attaché in Sofia, Bulgaria, was murdered when he was thrown out of an Orient Express window in the U.S. zone.

So you can see that Orson Welles's sinister machinations with medications were innocent compared to what was really going on.

In Vienna, I was duly accredited as a correspondent by U.S. Army authorities, which had a number of advantages. I found lodgings in the apartment of a middle-aged midwife whose specialty was delivering the babies of aristocrats. This was located in an apartment house in the Alserstrasse that had been built in 1848. The toilet was in a corridor and was shared by other apartments. There was a bathtub in the kitchen, which was next to my small room. It was at least comfortable and clean and suited my modest bachelor's needs. With my GI Bill stipend I was able to make out all right.

Not long after I moved to Vienna, my humble abode became a way station for Hungarians escaping their country. An "underground railroad" operation had been organized by junior Foreign Service officers (FSOs) at our legation in Budapest; they would first smuggle an escapee's luggage and deposit it in my room. The owners who were successfully smuggled out picked up their luggage from me and went on their way. The Budapest legation smugglers couldn't easily involve their colleagues at our legation in Vienna, so they turned to me. Finally, the ringleader in Budapest was PNGed (declared persona non grata) and expelled. I later learned that as he was leaving he smuggled out one last person. He deliberately arrived just before midnight and told the Hungarian border guard that he had to be out of the country by midnight and, if that were interfered with, there would be trouble for him in Budapest. It worked. His car was not searched. Some twenty-five years later, I ran into this daring officer walking along Washington's C & O canal towpath with a woman. After hearty greetings I asked him who that last person was. He turned to his companion and said to me, "You haven't met my wife, have you?"

In Vienna I gained a great deal of knowledge of what life was like under Communism. One incident especially brought home to me its insecurity. A well-educated Hungarian professional, whom I had come to know in Vienna, explained why he had to escape: For years, he had been meeting once a week with three of his oldest and best friends to play bridge. One evening in winter after the weekly bridge game he went into his hallway to gather up the coats of his three friends. As he draped them over his arm, out of one of the coats—he didn't know which one—there tumbled an AVO (secret police) badge, which he put in his pocket. During bridge that evening, all four had been especially uninhibited in condemning the government and Communism in general. As soon as his company had left, he packed a small suitcase and headed for the Austrian border—I suppose most of the way by train. (This was still before extensive barriers of barbed wire and mines had been erected on the Austrian border.) He always felt guilty that he couldn't warn his two innocent friends—but he didn't know which were innocent.

Just prior to my permanent move to Vienna, I was on the famed Orient Express going to Geneva when a very attractive young lady came into my compartment. I helped her place her suitcase in the rack overhead and was immediately smitten. Her name was Eva Dolenz and she was on her way to a job near Innsbruck. On my way back to Vienna, I stopped off to visit her to discover she was about to leave since her employer was making unwanted advances, so we went back to Vienna together. Eva came from an upper-class, partly aristocratic family that lived in the small town of Mödling south of Vienna in the Soviet zone. Her father was from Trieste in the Italian part of the old Austrian empire. He had been a naval officer in the Imperial Navy in World War I, and his ship had been sunk. He had recently retired as the director of a local factory. Her mother was a direct descendent of Andreas Osiander, a leading figure in Martin Luther's reformation. She and Eva were among the few Protestants in Austria. Eva was going to the University of Vienna medical school and spoke perfect British English, having had an English governess. She was eleven when the war broke out and she went to her grave with American bomb fragments still in her leg. When the Soviets took Mödling, her family had hidden her in the attic to keep her from being raped. In the dreadful 1946–47 winter, her family subsisted largely on wormy dried peas and frozen potatoes stolen from some local farmer's field, and they were constantly cold.

I tried to spend every weekend in Mödling, which was somewhat tricky, since as an American I was not supposed to be in the Soviet zone. Her parents were very understanding and always made me feel welcome. I went down there disguised as a Swiss journalist. On Sunday mornings as I lay in bed in Mödling I could hear Soviet troops marching from their barracks to the local swimming pool for their weekly bath. En route they would always break out in song, which was musically great but otherwise scary. This weekend commute did have its unsettling moments. Once in the winter, when I planned to ski on a nearby hillside, for some reason instead of my own skis I took along a pair of white Army mountain troop skis with "U.S." plainly marked on them. I got into a train car at the Südbahnhof ("south station") that was entirely empty. I welcomed the room, but thought it strange, since the other cars were more or less full. When we reached the first stop in the Soviet zone I found out why when Soviet soldiers poured into it. All I could think of was getting those Army skis out of the car. I grabbed them and ran to another car, forgetting my rucksack on the luggage rack. When I showed up at the Dolenz house, Eva asked where my rucksack was. Fortunately I was able to get the nice people at the station to call the next stop to retrieve my rucksack, which was back in Mödling in forty minutes, not having been stolen or even plundered by the soldiers.

One Sunday in early January 1950 Eva and I were standing in the back of a thirteenth-century Gothic chapel, attending mass. Usually we were careful not to speak English, but for some reason we had a brief exchange in English, after which Eva instinctively looked over her shoulder and was shocked to see standing behind us a known local *Spitzel* (informer) for the Soviets. As it turned out, there was good reason for her to be shocked.

The following Saturday, Eva was in Vienna at a friend's apartment across town getting ready to go to a ball with me that evening. That afternoon I got a frantic call from her mother telling me that Eva couldn't come home because a Soviet officer and an enlisted man had come to arrest her. I can't remember whether or not we went to the ball, but one thing was clear: she couldn't go home or she would wind up in a gulag in Siberia. She didn't want to impose on the friend she was with, since she had a small apartment, and moving in with me was out of the question. Since we planned to get married later that year, there was only one good solution: get married right away. In the meanwhile, it was important to get her out of Vienna where she could be abducted by the Soviets. Our top Army brass were very understanding and arranged to have us flown out to Salzburg in the U.S. zone. Since our regular airport was in the Soviet zone, which we did not want to risk entering, we had to fly in a small Piper Cub that took off from a curved landing strip in the U.S. sector next to the Danube Canal.

When we arrived in Salzburg, we went to the Mirabeau Palace to be married. After a brief honeymoon, we returned to Vienna, again by small plane, to live in my little room. I got an automatic handgun and shoulder holster from the Army that I wore everywhere when we were out together to prevent the Soviets from snatching her on the street and pulling her into a waiting car, a not-uncommon occurrence even in the U.S. sector. The Soviets, meanwhile, thwarted in their attempt to arrest Eva and send her to Siberia, had arrested her father. With great presence of mind, he feigned a heart attack just before being taken into the Soviet *Kommandatura* (local headquarters) just off Mödling's main street, so that a number of people gathered around and witnessed the scene. The Soviets quickly took him home and thereafter left him alone.

I was at that time not in a very good position to support a wife. Even in Vienna, my GI Bill would go only so far, and my journalist income was hit or miss. Fortunately, a good acquaintance, Halvor Ekern, came to our rescue with an offer for me to work for the Army. Hal managed the U.S. element of the Allied Commission for Austria, which came under the Army. He also made me a part of the Quadripartite Political Directorate, which he also headed: he made me the U.S. representative on a subcommittee charged with what Americans would call "First Amendment issues." In that capacity, for the next four and a half years I would be negotiating with the Soviets, always allied with my British colleagues and generally also with my French colleagues. One very big advantage of this position was that Eva was no longer in danger, since the Soviets were now colleagues. I could give my pistol and holster back to the Army. We could now safely go to Mödling, and we could move into a nice Army leased apartment in an upscale residential part of town.

Hal Ekern, incidentally, became a colonel in the Army and was one of the officers that were key to forming the famed Army 10th Mountain Division, leading some of those troops in the bloody Italian Campaign. We remained friends until his death in 2006; I am eternally in his debt for getting me into U.S. government service, which has made for a fascinating and fulfilling career and life. If ever there was a fine American, Hal was one. In 1951 the State Department took over the U.S. Element of the Allied Commission from the Army and, after passing a required examination, I became a Foreign Service Staff officer (FSSO), which then was a big step toward my goal of becoming a FSO, which is a fully commissioned officer.

The other part of my responsibilities was rather amorphous and seemingly public relations oriented. The previous incumbent, Theodore (Ted) Kaghan, had left on his way onward and upward. He will come up later in this chapter as the victim of a political scandal. One of my first acts was to get the Army to abolish separate restrooms for Austrian employees. This practice reminded me of the Panama Canal zone where the Panamanian employees used facilities marked "silver," whereas the Americans used facilities marked "gold," apparently originally based on how one was paid. At some point I began to transform this office into a prime source of unclassified information about Eastern Europe, initially to serve the Voice of America and other official entities, then later to serve the locally based foreign correspondents, who had to cover this region from Vienna, being effectively banned from those countries. I began soliciting publications from our missions in Eastern Europe; I had a couple of my staffers, who knew the languages, select and translate items of interest. Later we even did some radio monitoring. Actually these "open sources" can be a goldmine of information, indeed a goldmine of intelligence, as I was later to discover. We carefully filed all these items by subject matter and sent copies of some items to those interested.

Before long, I hit on a fantastic source of information. In compliance with a Four-Power agreement, the four occupying powers each received copies of letters and telegrams, and transcripts of telephone conversations to and from those in foreign countries. I collected those from Eastern Europe, "sanitized" them by removing identifying information, and disseminated them to our "customers." We added to that "sanitized" interrogation reports based on interviews with those escaping from or traveling in Eastern Europe. When journalists from a wire service wanted to do a piece on, say, mine disasters in Hungary, they would send over a messenger, and we would lend them our file on mine disasters in Hungary. We soon became the correspondents' prime source of information. Reuters filed something on its worldwide service based on our information nearly every day. I can safely say that for some time a substantial percentage of all that appeared in Western media on Eastern Europe came from our little, inexpensive operation. Not unexpectedly, we became anathema to Eastern European regimes, who labeled us the Stearman Dienst ("service"). When correspondents began to go to East European countries they were admonished not to be believe what they had gotten from the notorious Stearman Dienst.

I actually most liked the political directorate subcommittee part of my employment. It was never dull dealing with the Soviet representatives who, under instruction of course, were trying to limit media freedom and other freedoms in Austria through accusations of Nazism and militarism. Agreements on these issues had to be very carefully worded to eliminate later Soviet exploitation of sloppy language, which happened all too often in our general dealings with the Soviets. I always wondered why so often American negotiators agreed to things that were replete with loopholes that the Soviets could exploit. Years later I got my answer when I made a bid on a townhouse near Georgetown in Washington, DC. I looked over the standard contract and viewed it as if I were dealing with the Soviets, which resulted in my rewriting the whole document to eliminate the loopholes. The result was that the owner refused to deal with me. When I discussed this with a lawyer friend of mine, he pointed out that in the Common Law the concept of *equity* takes care of the problems that troubled me in the sales contract. Then it all became clear how we were going wrong in negotiating with the Soviets and later with the North Vietnamese Communists: State Department lawyers were all beholden to equity, an alien concept to the case-hardened types with whom we were dealing.

I can recall once arguing with my Soviet opposite number for three hours over whether there should be a comma or a dash between two words in something we were negotiating, because one version could be used to put a newspaper out of business. I won out, strongly supported by my British colleague and somewhat by my French opposite number. As a pipe smoker, I would come into those meetings armed with several pipes, a tin of tobacco, and a large bottle of water. The Soviets knew that I was, to paraphrase General Grant, prepared to fight it out on this front if it took all day and into the next one. My formula for negotiating with the Soviets was to be precise, patient, perseverant, and powerful. (This formula could apply to dealing with today's antagonists.) One member of the Soviet element in our meetings, Loginov, was obviously the KGB watchdog, and probably outranked the Soviet representative. Sometimes he had to be called to order for getting involved in the negotiations since he was just a support participant. He used to doodle a lot, and once left his doodle behind when he left the conference table. I couldn't resist picking it up: Loginov had doodled a gallows with a stick figure hanging from it. I always wondered if he had deliberately left this behind.

At parties KGB agents loved to ask us Americans about our colleagues who were really CIA people with a diplomatic cover. The Soviets' task in this regard was made easy by the State Department's published Biographic Register, which listed all Foreign Service personnel with brief biographies. (The single female secretaries in the Foreign Service gave it the popular name of "Stud Book" because it revealed whether or not a new male arrival was married or single.) The CIA personnel were always listed with obviously atypical Washington assignments, usually with the Department of the Army. This flaw led to the Register's permanent demise later in the 1970s. I thought it would have made more sense to give the CIA people made-up State Department assignments as we did overseas.

After our meetings we would always have a nice reception hosted by whoever was in the chair that rotated for the whole Allied Commission every month. They were best when the Soviets were in the chair. They always had plenty of caviar, smoked salmon, great cheeses, and very good vodka. In their initial social encounters with the Soviets, Americans used to wonder how they managed to drink so much and still hold it. The secret was that, unlike average Americans, the Soviets ate a great deal of rich, fatty foods such as caviar and cheese, which coated their stomachs. I had little trouble emulating them in this regard and to this day I still eat fatty things as I drink. Even during the Korean War when relations with Moscow were strained, to say the least, we had fairly convivial postmeeting receptions.

After the death of Stalin and the subsequent end of hostilities in Korea, there began to slowly blossom a sort of détente with Moscow. In this spirit, a newly arrived young Soviet member of our subcommittee got into the spirit of things and suggested we have interelement volleyball games. The next meeting he was gone, never to return. Not long thereafter, there arrived a new Soviet representative named Gurov who had been badly wounded in the war. His teeth had mostly been shot out and he had all-steel teeth. He was great, and we really hit it off. We both had baby girls the same age. Betsy had been born March 11, 1953. Both babies had colic and other problems of that age, and after every meeting we got together to compare notes on baby care.

In the new spirit, Eva and I received an invitation from the Soviet Embassy to attend a reception. When we arrived at the Soviet Embassy for the reception, we noticed that the whole embassy seemed dark. We again checked our invitation and determined that this was the correct date and time. We asked the Austrian police officer on duty on front of the embassy if he had seen anybody go into the embassy. He said he had just come on duty and wouldn't know if others had preceded us—we *were* running a bit late. I then told him that if we didn't come out of the embassy by midnight, he should call the American Embassy duty officer (I gave him the number) and tell him that we went into the embassy at this time and had not appeared again by midnight. He agreed, so we went to the main entrance of the embassy. The door opened and we entered a large half-darkened room guarded by a couple of Soviet goon-like guards. We then went into another room and encountered the same thing. By then, we were getting more than nervous. Finally we went into still another room and there was the party in full swing. Invited were only political directorate members and their wives, which was why there was no outward appearance of a social event at the embassy. Actually, everybody there was in a jolly mood and having a good time. Our hosts had not in any way stinted with regard to drinks, food, and music. Eva and I were having such a good time we almost forgot we had to leave before midnight to avoid an embarrassing diplomatic misunderstanding. When the police officer on the beat saw us come out just before midnight, he was visibly relieved.

My joy in hunting led to one of the most fascinating evenings I have ever spent. In Europe, especially in Austria and West Germany, hunting is only for landed nobility and, in general, the well-to-do. I had the privilege of hunting on the large estate of Count Rudolph Hoyos in Gutenstein, south of Vienna. The Hoyos family was famous in Austrian history and had been brought to Austria from Spain by Empress Maria Theresa. Count Hoyos was a fine gentleman and had a great hunting preserve. Once, when I was down there to do some hunting, Hoyos had invited a number of somewhat impecunious old friends who were aging counts and princes. After a very successful hunt, we changed for dinner and gathered for a marvelous meal served by liveried servants wearing white gloves. When dinner was over, we retired to the castle's library for cigars and brandy. At some point, the conversation turned to speculation about whether World War I could have been avoided when, in June 1914, the crowned heads of Europe and other European leaders or their representatives were in Vienna to attend the funeral for the recently assassinated Archduke Franz Ferdinand, next in line to succeed Emperor Franz Josef I. His assassination started a chain of events resulting in World War I and the loss of more than 10 million lives.

All present, through family connections in one capacity or the other, had been close to the Imperial Court or were in the upper reaches of the imperial bureaucracy. In short, they had a good firsthand idea of what had been going on in Vienna at the decision-making level. The discussion produced facts and a quality of speculation that would have delighted if not astounded any professional historian. These aging noblemen were almost evenly divided. One group believed that the European leaders gathered in Vienna, had they realized the danger of war they faced, could have put their heads together and come up with a plan to head off war. The other group insisted that a number of external factors, such as the alliances that had formed, the recent Balkan Wars, developing tensions, and the preparation for war that was consuming leading powers in Europe created a situation too far advanced to be headed off by anything decided in Vienna. Being the only non-aristocrat and non-Austrian present, I sat quietly like a fly on the wall taking all this in. I would give anything to have a transcript of this unforgettable exchange. As an inveterate history buff, I was in seventh heaven. I tended to side with the latter group, given Austria's determination, no matter what, to punish Serbia, which it held responsible for the assassination and which was allied with Russia. (More than ninety years later, Russia still supports Serbia politically.)

I also had the privilege of meeting some unforgettable people in Vienna. I met composer Oscar Straus who, in 1908, had composed the classical, popular operetta *The Chocolate Soldier*. I also met Robert Stolz, who composed a favorite musical *Two Hearts in Three-Quarters Time,* the film version of which reportedly played longer in New York than probably any other film ever made. I sat next to and escorted composer Gian Carlos Menotti at the European premier of his opera, *The Consul.* The U.S. Embassy was touting Menotti as an American composer, but he confided in me that he had never become a U.S. citizen because his mother wanted him to remain Italian. One unforgettable character was writer Joseph Wechsberg who wrote *Blue Trout and Black Truffles,* long a great favorite of international gourmets. Wechsberg was born in Czechoslovakia and spoke with a very heavy accent and wasn't all that articulate. I once came up to him at a party and began, "Mr. Wechsberg, I have a question." Whereupon he said, "Stop. I know what you're going to ask. How can it be that I write so well and speak so poorly?"

During my stay in Vienna, the world crisis that most affected us was the Korean War. When it began, many believed that this was simply the gambit in a worldwide Soviet offensive and that Western Europe would soon be invaded. The West, especially the United States, had effectively disarmed to the point where there was not one combat-ready Allied infantry division in West Germany. As the wags were wont to say, "All the Soviet Army needs to march to the English Channel are shoes." Not long after the war started, I went on active duty as a naval reserve officer in the leading German seaport of Bremerhaven, where our training exercise was how to destroy the port facilities there before this area was evacuated and captured. We then had no idea of how severely the Soviet Union had suffered in the war: its loss of more than 20 million lives was long a well-guarded Soviet secret. Had we known, I believe we would have been a bit more relaxed about an imminent Soviet military attack. Conventional wisdom attributes the North Korean invasion of South Korea to a January 1950 speech by Secretary of State Dean Acheson who, in defining our defense perimeter in the Western Pacific, excluded South Korea and Formosa (now Taiwan). Actually, Gen. Douglas MacArthur made the same point in March 1949. I believe that the development that made the Korean War inevitable was the withdrawal of American troops from South Korea by June 1949. The following year Stalin approved the invasion, which was launched in June 1950.

The Korean War transformed our defense establishment. The United States had precipitously disarmed after World War II, so that by 1947 the United States had no combat-ready infantry division or combat-ready Air Force wing. Moreover, it turns out that we also had no atomic bombs, only parts that could eventually be assembled. In short, we had so effectively unilaterally disarmed that little Switzerland could have fielded more ground forces in twenty-four hours than could the mighty United States. This began to change somewhat after the Soviets exploded their atomic bomb in August 1949, but still our defense recovery was proceeding slowly. This prompted a landmark document, NSC-68, which in alarmist terms called for a very substantial military buildup both conventional and atomic.

I was wont to explain this document's turgid language to my Georgetown students as not really necessary to convince Truman, but needed to energize public opinion. Once, at a university social function, I spotted Paul Nitze who had drafted NSC-68 some thirty years before. I suggested to one of my students present that he ask Nitze to explain the turgid language and then tell the class the next day. The next day the student said that, according to Nitze, he had so written this document to shake up President Truman, hang public opinion. Once the Korean War began, our defense buildup proceeded apace, effectively implementing NSC-68 after all.

Before I had joined the U.S. Foreign Service, Senator Joseph McCarthy had begun to pillory it and the State Department in general. In February 1950 McCarthy, in a speech to the Republican Women's Club of Wheeling, West Virginia, stated, "I have here in my hand a list of 205 Communists in the State Department." The number would change when he later repeated this baseless charge. In the face of this and other outrageous allegations, everybody seemed to roll over and play dead, I suppose because attacking the senator could get one labeled a Communist, which was political poison. This was especially galling to those State Department officers in my generation, since all the ones I knew were, like me, combat veterans of World War II and highly patriotic Americans. McCarthy never proved that anybody in the State Department or anywhere else in government was a Communist. There certainly were Communists infiltrated as Soviet agents in government positions, however, as we learned convincingly from our Venona program that broke Soviet codes beginning in World War II, but that was not declassified until 1995. McCarthy's nefarious campaign against State was no doubt inspired by the 1949 trial of Alger Hiss for having been a Soviet agent while in the State Department in the 1930s. Hiss was rightly convicted in a 1950 retrial. (He was one of those exposed by Venona.) The most outrageous of McCarthy's charges came in June 1951 when he called then–Secretary of Defense Gen. George C. Marshall a Communist. This accusation was based on this well-intentioned if misguided and unsuccessful effort to bring about a Nationalist–Communist coalition to end China's civil war. President Truman had commissioned him to try to accomplish this in 1945. The great irony here is that Stalin had to have considered Marshall his archenemy, since his plan as secretary of state was instrumental in thwarting Soviet designs on Western Europe. Marshall, as Army chief of staff in World War II and as secretary of defense in 1950–51, had a heavy responsibility for the conduct of U.S. operations in the Korean War. In short, McCarthy sought to discredit our secretary of defense while we engaged in a bloody conflict to counter Communist aggression in Korea. What should that have told us? Marshall was, in fact, a greatly admired and patriotic American. I could never forgive Eisenhower's refusal to stand up for this fine man. (Eisenhower later admitted that his position had been a mistake.)

McCarthy sent two aides, Roy Cohn and David Shine, to Europe to investigate U.S. cultural and information operations, primarily those in West Germany. These two sounded like a vaudeville act and sometimes acted like one. They were especially keen on finding Communist-leaning books in our libraries. As I vaguely recall, even some of Mark Twain's works were suspect. Of course Howard Fast's *Citizen Tom Paine* about the Revolutionary War superpatriot was banned because Fast was a known Communist. Finding this one was always a triumph for them. In any case, their antics were a major embarrassment to us in Germany. At one point, Ted Kaghan, whom I had replaced in Vienna and who then headed our large information and cultural program in West Germany and Berlin, labeled Cohn and Shine "junketeering gumshoes" in remarks to the press. McCarthy then had Kaghan investigated and found out that when he had been a freshman at the University of Michigan he had signed a petition urging that a Communist be allowed to run for mayor of Ypsilanti. On the basis of only this, he got Ted fired, even though he was unquestionably a dedicated *anti-Communist*, which I could verify based on the files of his that I inherited and on his actions on the job in Germany. The only employment he could subsequently get was working for the *New York Post* as night police reporter covering the lower east side of Manhattan. Eventually his career recovered and he became the public affairs director for the UN's Food and Agriculture Organization in Rome.

The next caper of Cohn and Shine was a real shocker. They had come to Vienna to investigate *me*, among others, even though I had been an ardent anti-Communist since the 1936–39 Spanish Civil War. The Stearman *Dienst* clearly was regarded by East European Communist regimes as a first-class bane of their existence. Fortunately the two had my name spelled wrong on their paperwork so our ambassador could honestly say that no one of that name worked for him. I later found out from one of our journalist clients that an unreconstructed Austrian Nazi had told the two that I distributed Communist propaganda to journalists in Vienna. Of course he was referring to the Eastern European media excerpts we disseminated that helped shed light on what was going on in those countries. The purpose of our operation was to discredit the regimes in those countries, and everybody knew this.

When Stalin died on March 5, 1953, the Voice of America should have been at the top of its game to take advantage of this momentous development. Instead, McCarthyism had cowed its staff into a state of near paralysis, according to some State colleagues of mine who were in Washington at the time.

By now, I had begun to detect what I considered a highly suspicious pattern in McCarthy's antics. He was not exposing any real Communist agents in government, but he was attacking dedicated anti-Communists like Secretary Marshall and lesser lights like Ted Kaghan and me. Moreover, he was drawing attention away from the very real and highly menacing Communist threat embodied in the Soviet Union and its satellites. The Communist ideological threat he seemed concerned about was hardly of any great moment in the United States. Indeed, Communism never was able to take root even among the most put-upon Americans, our black population. Norman Friedman in his masterful *The Fifty-Year War* noted,

> In the wake of McCarthyism, anti-Communism was linked in many American minds to a sort of wild reaction to liberal ideas . . . by the end of the 1950s it had become almost impossible to label anyone as a Communist. One consequence of that was that pro-Soviet propaganda could not be discredited. . . . The gradual change in perception undermined the moral basis for the Cold War. If domestic Communists were not a real threat, it became difficult to believe that the foreign variety was any more menacing. . . . Stalin's thrust into Europe did threaten American national existence, but it was at least as important that many Americans perceived him—and, by extension, Communism—as an unalloyed evil, worth staving off.

Most importantly, as Friedman noted, McCarthy was discrediting anti-Communism, which was a major victory for the Soviet Union and for Communism in general. His baleful influence is still felt today. For example, when referring to countries with Communist governments, most—and not just liberals—use Soviet terminology by calling them "Socialist" countries. I have long lamented that democratic socialists never objected to this misuse of their party's name. I suppose they didn't want to be considered McCarthyites. All this was actually causing me to begin wondering whose side Senator Joseph McCarthy was on, because I know of no other American, apart from the atomic spies, who rendered a greater service to the Soviet Union and to Communism in general than did he. As it turned out, though, he simply was motivated by perceived political gain. He was fairly safe in going after those of us at State and abroad because we had no popular constituency. His big mistake was going after the Army, which had a broad popular constituency. His false charges against a member of this organization in televised hearings in the spring of 1954 ultimately led to a sixty-seven to twenty-two Senate vote condemning him for misconduct. This took the pressure off State and its minions who had been largely abandoned to their fate by incoming Secretary of State John Foster Dulles and President Eisenhower, neither of whom were ever great favorites of mine, for a variety of reasons. I devoted this much space to McCarthy in reaction to current efforts to rehabilitate him.

Another unhappy development about this time, and one that directly affected me for much of my career, was the creation of the U.S. Information Agency (USIA) and its overseas operation the U.S. Information Service (USIS), thus removing the information function from State. The origin of this move, as told to me by those presumably in the know, was Dulles's initial desire to turn over management of State to his deputy and set up an office and small staff in the White House complex, presumably in the Old Executive Office Building (OEOB), where he could be close to and so better influence newly elected President Dwight D. Eisenhower. Eisenhower would have none of it, but did allow Dulles to divest himself of "operations" then under State. These included the foreign aid and information functions. I have never seen this documented, but I can believe it. The result was an extended body blow to the effectiveness of our overseas information program. Highly capable FSOs of real substance—for example, Soviet expert Foy Kohler who headed the Voice of America—were replaced in large measure by former media types, with a fair share of has-beens. There were some talented exceptions, but they were exceptions. The result was a general switch from emphasis on substance to an emphasis on technique, with exceptions here and there, which plagued USIA to its merciful end in the George W. Bush administration.

To my chagrin, the advance party from USIA honed in on my modest operation with the clear intent to acquire it and me. The fact that I came under the political section of the embassy apparently made no difference. Prior to this, I had made plans to take advantage of State's new "lateral entry" program that would have allowed me to become an FSO, which was my career goal. This new move trumped my goal, to my utter dismay. I spent the rest of my Foreign Service career trying to rectify this sad situation with a number of near successes but ultimate failure. I did manage never to serve at USIA and only in highly atypical USIS positions that turned out to be far more interesting than positions I would generally have held as a State FSO. In the long run, my being assigned to USIA redounded to my ultimate benefit, as I eventually recognized. My constant attempts to distance myself from an organization for which I had little respect posed obvious career problems that I somehow managed to overcome, at least partially. I worked in the State Department and later the White House, but it was up to USIA to promote me, not exactly a prescription for success. After I left Vienna in early 1955, the budget of my operation was at least doubled at a time when it was no longer as needed or potentially as effective as before because Eastern Europe was opening up to Western correspondents.

For years, the Four Powers had been negotiating a State Treaty to end the occupation of Austria. (It was a "state" treaty instead of a "peace" treaty, since we had not been at war with Austria.) The Soviets had effectively blocked progress in this direction because it did not really want to give Austria the freedom it deserved.

By the time we left for my new assignment in Berlin, some were actually speculating that Moscow would seek to divide Austria the same way it had divided Germany. This belief was being actively encouraged by the Soviets and their Communist underlings in Austria. Then, in April 1955, an Austrian delegation that had been invited to Moscow by the Soviets was informed that the USSR was ready to sign a state treaty that provided for Austria's neutrality and contained a number of economic and other stipulations. This was followed by Four Power negotiations to improve the deal in Austria's favor; surprisingly, the Soviets made key concessions they had balked at for some eight or nine years. The treaty was signed on May 15, 1955, and by October 21, 1955, the last occupation troops had left Austria, which had now become completely free for the first time since March 1938.

Why did the Soviets suddenly become so interested in quickly concluding the treaty? I analyzed possible Soviet motives in my doctoral dissertation, which was published as a book. In brief I posited three reasons for this Soviet move. First, Austria's becoming neutral split NATO by creating a neutral wedge reaching from Bratislava (then in Czechoslovakia) and Geneva. This severed the north–south lines of communication that had linked West Germany and Italy. This move also created a military near vacuum, given the vast numerical military superiority of Austria's eastern neighbors, Czechoslovakia and Hungary, versus the projected paucity of Austrian troops. Second, the Soviets' move was designed to encourage a neutral West Germany, but this was a lesser reason and in any case was a long shot. The third reason was of fundamental importance to the Kremlin: the promotion of a spirit of détente that would encourage the West, especially the United States, to reduce its superior military strength resulting from the Korean War buildup and continuing afterwards. To kick off this détente, the Soviets needed a summit conference with the United States. President Eisenhower had set a number of individual preconditions for a summit, one of which was the conclusion of an Austrian treaty. The summit took place in July 1955 in Geneva and was touted by the Soviets as creating a happy "Spirit of Geneva."

A number of other Soviet measures and moves reinforced this détente spirit: the much publicized "reductions" in Soviet and Eastern European armed forces; the Adenauer visit to Moscow, followed by establishment of diplomatic relations with West Germany; the release of the last German POWs still held; the return of the Porkkala naval base to Finland; the India trip of Soviet leaders Bulganin and Khrushchev; the 1956 attempt at the Moscow Twentieth Party Congress to blame the evils of Soviet Communism on Stalin; and the dissolution of the COMINFORM and the Bulganin trip to Great Britain. In April 1956 U.S. Chief of Staff General Omar Bradley stated, "I am concerned also because Russia propaganda is having an effect on the integrity of NATO." In other words, the Soviet détente policy was

My grandmother Icie May Stearman and grandfather Fred Carlton Stearman in the early 1900s. (*Author's collection*)

The "Sweet Shop" in Harper, Kansas, where my father worked as a soda jerk, c. 1914. *(Author's collection)*

The first Stearman, the C-1, at the first Stearman factory, in Santa Monica, California, 1927. *(Author's collection)*

The wreck of Stearman stalwart Fred Hoyt's plane in southern Idaho, January 1928. He had bailed out and then froze to death. (*Author's collection*)

My sister Marilyn, 1933.
(Author's collection)

With my pal Ching and my mother, 1933. *(Author's collection)*

When I was in military school, 1934. *(Author's collection)*

Aviation pioneer Wiley Post was a familiar face at Lockheed Aircraft Corporation. Here he is visiting in 1934, the year after he became the first pilot to fly solo—in a Lockheed Vega—around the world and the year before his fatal crash with Will Rogers in Alaska. *(Author's collection)*

As a cowboy on the Lazy S Ranch in northern California, 1940. I had shot the raccoon and made a hat out of it. *(Author's collection)*

An apprentice seaman in the Navy, in the V-12 program at the University of California, Berkeley, 1943. *(Author's collection)*

A brand new ensign, April 1944. *(Author's collection)*

The "Fighting 67" returns to San Francisco Bay, January 11, 1946. USS *LSM 67* served in commission only twenty-one months, including nine months in the Pacific war zone, but earned four battle stars for operations in the Philippine Islands and Borneo during a five-month period in 1945. *(U.S. Naval Institute Photo Archive)*

As gunnery officer in *LSM 67* checking our destination, White Beach, as we advance in the first assault wave of the Lingayen Gulf landing, the less bloody "Normandy" of the Pacific War, January 9, 1945. The mountain range in the background hid a number of gun emplacements. *(Author's collection)*

Enjoying a glass of tuba in La Paz, Luzon, just after it was liberated, January 29, 1945. *(Author's collection)*

Finally back in the United States and reunited with my parents at the Hewitt home in San Francisco, California, January 11, 1946. *(Author's collection)*

With Eva in Salzburg, Austria, twenty-five minutes after our wedding on February 6, 1950. *(Author's collection)*

"Stalin Smiles at Vienna," outside the parliament buildings, Vienna, during the communist May Day parade in 1950. *(Author's collection)*

On Austria's famous Wolfgangsee, during the 1950s. *(Author's collection)*

My mother-in-law Hilde Dolenz, Betsy, and Eva in Berlin, 1955. *(Author's collection)*

At the stern of the Navy river patrol boat (PBR) that may have saved my life, on the Saigon River in 1966, with its skipper, a chief boatswain's mate. *(Author's collection)*

Armed with a .45 pistol and camera, I escorted a journalist to a village in the Mekong Delta area, 1967. *(Author's collection)*

On July 14, 1969, a unique "Old Timers Luncheon" for pioneers of aviation met at
the International Hotel in Inglewood, California. Seated, left to right, are Claude Ryan,
Charles F. Willard, Donald W. Douglas, and William A. Patterson. Standing, left to right, are
"unidentified," Hall L. Hibbard, Reuben H. Fleet, Lloyd C. Stearman, and John K. Northrup.
(Author's collection)

With Tom Lowe, president of the Stearman Restorers Association and co-founder of
the National Stearman Fly-in, at an early fly-in. Stearman owners and enthusiasts have met
annually at Galesburg, Illinois, since 1972. *(Author's collection)*

Accompanying Vice President Gerald Ford to his swearing-in as president on August 9, 1974.
To my left in a light suit is my deputy, Kenneth Quinn. Others are Betty Ford, the military aide,
and several Secret Service agents. *(Author's collection)*

With Joan on the quarterdeck of the newly recommissioned USS *New Jersey* at Long Beach, California, December 28, 1982. President Ronald Reagan spoke at the recommissioning ceremony. At that night's formal dinner, Secretary of the Navy John Lehman recognized me especially for my role in bringing back the battleships. *(Author's collection)*

Standing in Moscow's Red Square, with the Kremlin wall in the background and Lenin's Tomb behind me, to my left, during the eventful year of 1983. (*Author's collection*)

On my right Ambassador Jack Matlock and on my left Georgy Arbatov, top Soviet expert on America, and his deputy. *(Author's collection)*

I look like the proverbial Cheshire Cat.
Joan's and my wedding day, May 5, 1984.
(Author's collection)

Best Man Oliver North lifts a toast to Joan and me at our wedding reception.
(Author's collection)

Joan with Pat and Julie Nixon and fellow First Lady staffers about to board the presidential yacht *Sequoia*. (*Author's collection*)

Saying good-bye to President Ronald Reagan in the Oval Office, January 19, 1989. (*Author's collection*)

Saying good-bye to President George H. W. Bush in the Oval Office, January 14, 1993. (*Author's collection*)

Being dubbed a knight by Cardinal Hickey in the church of the Franciscan Monastery in Washington, D.C., 1997. *(Author's collection)*

beginning to pay off. However, this became all for naught when, in November 1956, the Soviet Army crushed the Hungarian Revolution.

I greatly regretted leaving Vienna, my second home and the only city for which I have ever been homesick. This city especially fed two of my greatest passions: history and music. Up to late 1918, Vienna was the capital of an empire that was long a world power. Austria and Hungary were home to eleven different nationalities, the influence of most of which was still felt in Austria when I lived there. This was especially true of Austria's cuisine, which combined Hungarian, Slavic, Italian, and Germanic influences. Even today in Vienna there is a church representing each of the leading nationalities of the empire. When the Austro-Hungarian empire was dismantled by the victorious Allies in 1918–19, Austria emerged as roughly the equivalent of the United States reduced to its thirteen original colonies. This was a devastating blow to its remaining citizens who doubted that this new rump country was viable.

The empire, especially the Austrian part, was ruled with considerable benevolence, which generally took into consideration local customs and language. However, having eleven nationalities under its wing made for considerable problems in its armed forces. The officers mostly spoke only German, but the enlisted men spoke a variety of languages. This didn't exactly make for an efficient, cohesive fighting force, as had become clear early in World War I. The tolerance of the empire was exemplified by the life sentence given to Gavrilo Princip, the Serbian terrorist who murdered Archduke Franz Ferdinand, setting off World War I. Princip was not executed because he was only nineteen at the time. (He died in prison of tuberculosis when he was twenty-three.)

Czechoslovakian leaders convinced the Allies during the 1919 Versailles Conference that their people had been oppressed under the empire. The Allies, who were determined to dismantle the old empire, were only too ready to believe this. In point of fact, the Czechs, especially, were anything but oppressed. In fact, they made up a good bit of the empire's Vienna-based bureaucracy and played an important role in many aspects of Viennese life. Their large presence in Vienna can still be seen today in the Vienna telephone book, which is loaded with Czech names. I talked to many residents of countries that were in the empire and which had been taken over by Communists after World War II, and all of them thought that it had been a mistake to have dismantled the old empire. The pre–World War I internal pressures that were pulling apart the empire were well described in Joseph Roth's masterpiece novel *Radetsky March*. For centuries Vienna had played a lead role in Europe, and this is apparent to this day. Its castle (Hofburg), palaces, and old public buildings, not to speak of its museums and other cultural sites, are those of a major world capital, and not one of a country with a population of only some 8 million people.

Music was literally in the air in Vienna, especially in good weather on the northern and northwestern edges of town. There, the hills are covered with vineyards producing a white wine that is called a Heuriger when it's new and that is served in nearby wine houses also called Heurigers. In the Heurigers, one sits at long tables with others inside in bad weather and outside in a courtyard in fair and warmer weather. The new wine is served with food accompanied by a music group (a *Schrammel*) made up of an accordion, a violin, and a double-necked guitar, with one of the group singing beloved old Viennese songs. A number of guests usually sing along; I was always one of those singing guests. When guests are outside in Heuriger courtyards there is literally music in the air. My favorite Heuriger was the Eroica Haus in Heiligenstadt, which is where Beethoven composed his Eroica Third Symphony. I remember one smaller Heuriger in the middle of a vineyard dissected by a path up the hill to the Kahlenberg, which overlooks Vienna from the north. It was along such a path that Beethoven was inspired to compose his great Sixth Symphony, known as the Pastoral. It was easy to imagine how this came about. And then there was the opera, great concerts, and excellent theater. We had a subscription to the opera and we went about three times a month for ten months of the year. The opera and the theater were then affordable so that even working-class people could attend. This, alas, is no longer true. The major churches had full orchestras and featured the great classic masses of Mozart, Hayden, Schubert, and others. At the old Imperial Palace Chapel (*Burgkapelle*) one could hear the famed Vienna Choir Boys sing every Sunday.

I loved to explore the narrow streets of Vienna's original medieval core, the Inner City. My favorite restaurant Zum weissen Rauchfangkehrer is located there, as well as another favorite, the fifteenth-century Griechen Beisel. And there is that great Viennese tradition, tea at Demels, which features wonderful canapés and the best pastry ever. . . . To this day I cannot hear that beloved old Viennese song, "Vienna City of My Dreams," without tearing up.

Chapter 12

German Interlude: Berlin, Then Bonn

FLYING INTO TEMPELHOF AIRPORT in the heart of Berlin has been, for many, a bit of a white-knuckle experience, since the flight path was over a cemetery with buildings looming on both sides of the plane. Just as we were coming in, two-year-old Betsy comes out with, "Schau, Mama, Budapest!" (Look, Mama, Budapest!). She said this with such authority that I am sure some who had never flown to Berlin might have wondered if we weren't victims of yet another hijacking.

I had been transferred to West Berlin to be the political officer for RIAS, the American-run Radio in the American Sector, which broadcast to East Germany. This position was created in the wake of a massive workers' demonstration in East Berlin on June 17, 1953, protesting against an increase in production quotas. Radio broadcasts describing this unprecedented event resulted in uprisings all over East Germany that, as in East Berlin, were quickly put down by Soviet troops. Official Washington, both impressed and concerned about the potential of RIAS to stir up trouble in East Germany, decided that RIAS needed an officer to vet political broadcasts, since Berlin was the only trouble spot in the world that had the ongoing potential of triggering World War III, and throughout the Cold War was thus a perennial worry. There was no great desire in Washington to help foment uprisings that we would not risk supporting.

Actually, there was really not that much need for me, since RIAS's highly intelligent American director, Gordon Ewing, was unlike most USIS officers in that he was a man of considerable substance and political savvy. Moreover, he had the confidence and respect of the very impressive and highly talented German staff, which did the work, including both planning and implementation. For me it turned out that this assignment was primarily an opportunity to learn a great deal about East Germany, usually referred to by the staff as "die Zone" (the Soviet zone of Germany) or DDR (Deutsche Demokratische Republik, or German Democratic Republic). RIAS was exceptionally well informed about almost everything that transpired in the zone because there was a constant stream of East Germans coming to RIAS to tell us what was going on in their locales. Prior to construction in 1961 of the wall dividing Berlin, there was easy access between the two parts of the city and thus with East Germany. This is why the Soviet Union and its East German satraps were always so keen to get rid of the Western Allied presence in West Berlin: as long as we were there and remained in effective contact with East Germans, it remained difficult for the Soviets to consolidate control over them.

Because of its ties to East Germany, RIAS broadcasts were very effective. I was especially impressed by the *Schulfunk* (school broadcasts) that tracked the daily East German lesson plans, first grade through *Gymnasium* (high school plus) and that provided non-Communist correctives for social study lessons. We also had an excellent program that targeted university students, pointing out the political and philosophic fallacies to which their professors exposed them. For the farm population we offered down-to-earth advice on farming methods and opportunities; most important, though, we also gave farmers detailed instructions on how to avoid traps that would lead to their farms being collectivized. This kind of advice was a special burr under the regime's saddle. We also told people what to do when they were summoned for police or *Stasi* (secret police) interviews. Among other things, we told them to inform as many people as possible when and where they were going for these potentially treacherous encounters. This was based on the practical theory that the regime liked to keep arrests as quiet and secret as possible. The much-put-upon population was enormously grateful for such advice and counsel.

Of course, we provided our listeners with a great deal of news and news-related features and commentaries. We also had excellent music programs, usually featuring the well-regarded RIAS Symphony Orchestra for classic programs. In addition, we had great *Unterhaltungsmusik* (popular music) programs and an excellent satirical comedy team. RIAS was without exception far and away the most effective of all our public affairs endeavors. The American taxpayers more than got their money's worth from this outstanding institution. I have always been proud of having been associated with RIAS. The Soviets and East German leaders hated RIAS, of course, and in 1959 made a strong push to get rid of it, as we will see later.

Berlin still showed signs of having been pulverized in the war, but in the ten years since the war had made consider progress in building up and modernizing West Berlin. East Berlin, however, provided a depressing contrast, being far less prosperous and very run down. We used to go over to East Berlin, and with cheap East German marks (*Ostmark*) bought on the open market, got some great bargains, especially in books and records. We used to buy all our flowers there, and had our pictures framed in a small framing shop that, alas, was slowly squeezed out of business by being denied supplies. The regime had little tolerance for any form of free enterprise. Once a year we received permission to visit the annual Leipzig *Messe* (fair) where one could get great bargains in antiques. In terms of area covered, I always thought of Berlin as the Los Angeles of Europe. It was huge in area and even included farms within its borders. It had a very large park, the Gruenewald, that had once been a royal hunting preserve. Within the city was an unusually large lake, the Wannsee; many seagoing yachts had come down from the Baltic and North Seas through rivers and canals to seek refuge in the Wannsee and wound up stuck there, their owners not wanting to risk having them confiscated by transiting the zone en route to an open sea. I always enjoyed sailing on the Wannsee, although it was a tricky spot for sailing, since the wind would frequently and radically change direction, keeping us all on our toes.

We lived in a four-bedroom house in the residential district of Zehlendorf, which had largely escaped bombing damage, and we led a fairly enjoyable life, even though we were a hundred plus miles behind the "Iron Curtain." Little Betsy's vocabulary had expanded to include "sector border," "tank," "soldier," and "Russians." If we went anywhere through the zone, we had to be cleared at Soviet checkpoints. Usually this routine operation didn't take much time. Once, before Christmas 1955, we were going west on the autobahn and stopped at the Soviet checkpoint on the edge of Berlin. It seemed to take the guard forever to return our ID cards, and we were beginning to worry. Then the guard opened his little window and handed back our IDs and a handwritten note with a carefully lettered "I wish you a Merry Christmas." Apparently the "Spirit of Geneva" filtered down to the guard's level.

Here is a good spot to explain how Berlin wound up more than one hundred miles behind the Iron Curtain in the heart of the Soviet zone of Germany, a situation that evolved into one of the most serious East–West bones of contention in the Cold War. At times it even posed the threat of a possible World War III and the nuclear holocaust such a war would create. The discussion of how postwar Germany would be divided among the victorious Allies began in earnest in early 1943 when Deputy Prime Minister Clement Atlee proposed a Soviet zone that was largely the one that finally emerged, with Berlin in the middle of this zone. He proposed a U.S. zone in southern Germany and a British zone in northwestern Germany. In November 1943 Roosevelt boarded the battleship *Iowa* in which he would travel to Oran, Algeria, on his way to the upcoming British, U.S., Soviet summit conference in Teheran, Iran.

While under way on the Atlantic, Roosevelt took out a National Geographic Society map of Germany and heavily penciled in a U.S. zone that covered all of northwestern Germany and extended east to *include* Berlin. Very unlike the Atlee

Plan, this left the Soviets with a much smaller zone and the British with a zone in southern Germany. Roosevelt wanted the northwestern German ports for supplying U.S. troops in Germany and for redeploying them to the Pacific after the war in Europe ended. Unfortunately and foolishly, no one from the State Department was on board, with the result that State was unaware of Roosevelt's very favorable plan; through Roosevelt's bureaucratic carelessness, they remained unaware of it. Unfortunately, the actual negotiating of the division of Germany in London became a diplomatic exercise involving the U.S. ambassador to Britain, John Winant, backed by State Department personnel, all of them clueless with respect to Roosevelt's wishes. When the original Atlee plan was proposed by the British, the U.S. delegation, without instructions, said little. Then, in February 1944, the Soviet ambassador in London accepted the Atlee proposal on behalf of this country. Faced with this turn of events, Roosevelt caved and agreed, thus unwittingly ensuring the creation of what turned out to be one of world's most dangerous trouble spots. In all fairness to FDR, once the Soviets had occupied Berlin and all of eastern Germany, it might have been very hard to get them to leave, agreement or no agreement.

In the fall of 1956, I received orders transferring me to our embassy in Bonn to be assistant press attaché because the new press attaché didn't speak German. I much looked forward to this move and we packed up and moved. No sooner had I arrived in Bonn than I was told to be ready to go to Vienna should the Soviets move back into Budapest to crush the Hungarian Revolution which had begun on October 23. I was convinced that the Soviets could not let the Hungarians get away with evicting their army and were bound to come back. I flew to Vienna on November 3, 1956, and the very next day at 4:00 AM the Soviet Army charged back in full strength.

I believe the Hungarian Revolution actually had its origins in Poland. No doubt encouraged by Khrushchev's "secret speech" denouncing Stalin at the Twentieth Party Congress in February 1956, the Polish Communist Party decided on October 19, 1956, without consulting Moscow, to restore the leadership of Wladyslaw Gomulka. In 1951 Gomulka, at Moscow's behest, had been expelled from the Party and then jailed for three years for "nationalist deviations." Khrushchev was outraged and flew to Warsaw with other Soviet leaders to bully the Poles into reversing their decision on Gomulka and to back off on other things that irked the Soviets. When threatened with Soviet armed intervention, the Poles made it clear that they would resist with force of arms, if necessary. The Soviets knew that the Poles were capable of putting up a good fight. Indeed, in 1920 the Polish Army had defeated Moscow's Red Army. For this and other reasons, Khrushchev and company backed off, and the Poles prevailed in their attempt to show some independence from Moscow.

This greatly encouraged Hungarians in Budapest. On October 23 they demonstrated in large numbers their solidarity with the Poles and in support of their own demands for more freedom. The demonstrators assembled at Petöefi Tér (Petöefi Square) with its statue of Sándor Petöefi, the national hero and poet who did much to inspire Hungarians to revolt against Vienna's rule in that year of European revolutions, 1848. To demonstrate their solidarity with their historic friends, the Poles, the Hungarians then marched to Bem Tér (Bem Square) with its statue of Polish general Józef Bem who had come to the rescue of the 1848 Hungarian revolutionaries—such has been the influence of history on many Europeans. On the following day the demonstration largely moved to Parliament Square, which filled up with demonstrators. The Soviets sent tanks into the square to keep an eye on things, but the Soviet tank crews fraternized with the good-natured demonstrators, some of whom actually rode into the square on their tanks. All this I have from eyewitnesses. What followed was unclear to most present.

Evidently, some of the crowd tried to push into the Parliament's main entrance, at which point, some individuals, believed to be AVH (secret police, previously AVO) agents, who were on the roof of the opposite building, apparently opened fire on this part of the crowd. The Soviet soldiers, not knowing what was going on and evidently fearing they had been lured into an ambush, opened fire on the demonstrators, killing or wounding many. Thus began the war between the demonstrators and the Soviets. The Hungarian army, largely under the leadership of senior officer Pal Maleter, either remained neutral or aided the demonstrators. In any case, many of them received weapons from their army. A number of the Freedom Fighters, as they were called, successfully attacked Soviet tanks with Molotov cocktails. (These were wine bottles filled with gasoline and plugged with a cloth. When the cloth was ignited, the bottle was thrown at a tank, shattering and bursting into flames. They were devastatingly effective.) In due course, the Soviet Army retreated from Budapest, leaving the populace believing they had actually won the fight. According to documents revealed after the fall of Soviet power, there was considerable disagreement within the ruling Soviet Party Presidium about what to do next. The Hungarians, in the meantime, had emulated the Poles by bringing back their own "Gomulka," Imre Nagy, who soon made the mistake of declaring that he would take Hungary out of the Warsaw Pact, which was Moscow's 1955 answer to NATO.

Taking back Hungary with force would effectively end the highly successful Soviet détente campaign described in the last chapter. On the other hand, failure to take control of the situation could result in an unraveling of Soviet power in Eastern Europe and in trouble at home. For the United States the whole situation was considerably complicated by the concomitant British, French, and Israeli attack on the Suez Canal that came as an unwelcome surprise to us and that severely strained the Western Alliance, to the extent that even our personal British and French colleagues and friends wouldn't speak to us. To further complicate things for us, it was an election year in the United States.

Our ambassador in Vienna, longtime Soviet expert Llewellyn "Tommy" Thompson, had forbidden all American officials in Austria from going to the Hungarian border in order to avoid unwanted incidents. Pretending that I didn't get the word, I checked out an embassy car and headed for the border to find where Freedom Fighters were still in control. I did this in large measure because, due to technical difficulties, we apparently had no communications with our legation in Budapest and therefore had very incomplete knowledge as to what was going on in Hungary. U.S. officials had access only to those in refugee camps who had left Hungary days before. I was going to try to rectify this situation and, to a substantial extent, I did. In retrospect I wondered if I had not been subconsciously inspired by the old empire's highest award, the Order of Maria Theresa, which was bestowed on those in the military who carried out a successful operation in defiance of orders. Even years later after both Ambassador Thompson and I had retired, I still didn't have the heart to tell him that I had disobeyed his orders back in 1956.

Probing the border area I discovered where the Freedom Fighters were still in control, an area in the vicinity of the village of Nagycenk (Deutschkreuz, in German) due south of Hungary's westernmost city of Sopron and due west from the town of Kőszeg. These Fighters primarily consisted of young workers from the nearby Brennbergbánya mines and college students from Sopron, some of them led by their professors. This was one of the few remaining areas through which refugees could escape into Austria without interference. My primary, indeed sole, mission was to find out from these refugees what was going on in Hungary, some of whom had been in Budapest only hours before reaching the Austrian border. The Austrian gendarmes and customs officials on the border were extremely cooperative and rounded up groups of refugees in what I took to be local schoolrooms for interrogation. This went on for three days or more, sometimes well into the night. It was an extremely trying and stressful experience. All of the Austrian officials, gendarmes, and customs personnel were locals who were bilingual in Hungarian and German, so they could all interpret for me. (This province of Austria, Burgenland, belonged to Hungary until 1920, when it was ceded to Austria by the Treaty of Trianon.)

The gatherings of refugees would be from six or seven to nearly twenty. At the beginning of each session, the refugees would vent their spleen at the United States for not having gone to Hungary's assistance in its hour of need. It has become conventional wisdom that our Radio Free Europe (RFE) broadcasts to Hungary encouraged revolt. After the Revolution was suppressed, the West German government conducted a thorough study of RFE broadcasts before and during the Revolution and concluded they did not urge Hungarians to revolt, as has so often been alleged. Of the many dozens of refugees with whom I spoke, none said that he or she had heard such instigating broadcasts. One charge has been that RFE instructed Hungarians on how to make Molotov cocktails. This is absurd, since such knowledge was already widespread in Hungary. I am sure that some broadcasts that mentioned that such weapons were being used described them, but that is a different story. The refugees did state, however, that the very fact that we broadcast to Hungary *implied* that we would help them when the time came. Most, if not all, refugees agreed that the main reason why so many Hungarians believed we would help them when they revolted were the promises by John Foster Dulles and other Republicans, during the 1952 presidential election campaign, to "roll back the Iron Curtain." Some actually believed that President Eisenhower would ride into Budapest on a white horse, as Adm. Nikolaus Horthy reportedly had done in 1919 when he liberated Hungary from Béla Kun's Communist rule.

I tried to explain why the United States could not risk going to war with the Soviets over Hungary. Once, after I had said that our intervention could have led to World War III, a middle-aged man rose and said, "As far as we're concerned, this is World War III." I didn't try to argue much with these good people. I just listened to their complaints until they were ready to relate what they knew about the current situation in Hungary. Much of what they told me was very current information. As noted above, some had left Budapest only hours before they met with me. What I learned from them I passed on to a former colleague acquaintance in the embassy who had it transmitted it to the State Department and to our UN Mission in New York. He promised to cover for me and attributed what I told him to a "very reliable source." I wouldn't rule out that I was probably the only reliable source of firsthand information on the situation in Hungary that our government had, at least for a few days.

Most of the Freedom Fighters in the area anticipated a Soviet attack at any moment, and set up roadblocks along the highway between Sopron and Budapest. Accompanied by two Austrian gendarmes stationed on the border—Austrian army units being kept well inside the country to avoid clashes with Soviet troops—I was taken to an Austrian exclave (land island) well inside Hungary, where we climbed up on a haystack to await the attack. Before long, a column of Soviet T-34 tanks stretching as far as the eye could see came barreling down the highway about three hundred to five hundred yards away, making a roar so loud we could hardly converse. The gendarmes, both of whom had fought on the Eastern Front, were lamenting the fact that they had no *Panzerfäuste* (World War II German antitank rocket launchers) to take on all those tempting targets.

With binoculars we observed the deployment of Soviet troops throughout the area. (I later heard that the Soviets had sent two armored regiments to this area.) The troops seemed very nervous to us. I later learned that most were raw recruits who had just come from Ukraine and who may have had no idea where they were. At one point a Soviet plane flew over us dropping leaflets in Hungarian ordering us to surrender, which both gendarmes read. Soviet patrols were approaching, so we thought it best to make our way back to Austria. Had the patrols spotted our little group with two of us carrying rifles they probably would have opened up on us. The two gendarmes were armed with World War I Mannlicher bolt-action carbines made in 1917, whereas the Soviet troops had the latest fully automatic AK-47s, so we could hardly risk a firefight.

When we got back to Austria, we learned that the lightly armed students and workers manning roadblocks understandably lost their nerve when faced with the Soviet tank onslaught and came over into Austria where they were disarmed and fed. Many then resolved to go back and take on the Soviets and asked that their weapons be returned. Austrian officials at the border refused and counseled them to stay put to avoid being wiped out. They became refugees. Refugees from all over Hungary had been coming into Austria to escape the Soviets. This was greatly facilitated by the spirit of détente's leading to the May 1956 removal of all physical barriers along Hungary's border with Austria. The Soviet occupation of this area had largely stemmed the flow of refugees through it. In all the time I spent on the Hungarian border, I have no recollection of ever sleeping or eating, although obviously I must have been doing both.

Austria's performance during the Revolution was magnificent and put the rest of the West to shame by comparison. Austria and Hungary had long been like two brothers who could never really get along with each other. But when its Hungarian brother was attacked by an outsider, Austria instinctively came to the rescue, as would be the case with most brothers. In other words, Austrians and Hungarians instinctively came together in this hour of need. Some thought of it as a kind of restoration of the old dual monarchy that died in 1918. Austria had only regained its freedom for about a year and was a neutral country with an army of only thirty thousand, most of them raw recruits. So it took nerve for the Austrian Chancellor, Julius Raab, on October 28, 1956, to tell the Soviet Union to stop fighting the Hungarians and restore freedom in Hungary. There is no evidence that any military supplies ever came from Austria, although the Soviets repeatedly made this accusation; however, the Austrians provided every other kind of assistance possible, which the Hungarians enormously appreciated. In addition, Austria took in one hundred and seventy thousand Hungarian refugees. For some time, there were many thousands of Soviet troops with tanks on Austria's eastern border, and Austria had to endure continuous Soviet invective accusing it of aiding and abetting the Revolution. Nevertheless, the Austrians held firm. The Revolution was finally completely quashed, and courageous Imre Nagy and his associates were executed by the Soviets.

With the Revolution completely suppressed and the flow of refugees largely stemmed, there was little point in remaining in Austria, so I returned to my assignment at the embassy in Bonn. Eva and Betsy were established in a nice unit in the two- and three-story garden apartment complex in Plittersdorf southeast of Bonn where embassy personnel were housed. Top embassy officers had detached houses, and the ambassador had his residence near the embassy in Bad Godesburg south of Plittersdorf. No sooner had I reached our new home than I fell ill with a severe case of hepatitis, which my attending physician thought was stress induced. Unable to eat any solid food, I had to be fed intravenously for more than a week. Fortunately German doctors made house calls. For more than a year, I couldn't drink even a sip of any alcoholic beverage without getting sick. So at the numerous cocktail parties, receptions, and dinners I drank tonic water for well over a year. The whole Hungarian experience also left me decidedly down in the dumps psychologically. Eva was effectively playing the role of a diplomat's wife. She had a remarkable and very useful gift of being able to hone in on a conversation across the room, and of course being completely bilingual in English and German with a knowledge of French was a big help. Betsy was going to our nearby American school. Early on, she showed remarkable artistic talent. At seven she was carving realistic little animals from bars of soap, and one of her early paintings could have passed as a work of renowned painter Paul Klee. (She later graduated with a Master's degree in fine arts from the California College of Arts and Crafts and became very skilled in turning out etchings, that most difficult form of graphic art.)

I spent a good bit of my time in the embassy's branch office in Bonn, established to be accessible to the local press corps members, who were to be my special clients. My German was fairly good and greatly facilitated making connections with German members of the Fourth Estate. The press attaché, Bill Bell, a former newsman who had come down from our mission in The Hague (Netherlands), spoke no German, which he (and others) quickly realized put him at a distinct disadvantage. In about a year I had replaced him. The embassy itself was a very large establishment originally built to house the U.S. High Commission at a time when we had substantial responsibilities in the newly established Federal Republic of Germany. By 1955 the High Commission had shrunk and that year became the American Embassy. By the time I got to Bonn, our mission had been reduced to the extent that its complex not only housed the embassy but also one German ministry and part of another. The wags were saying that we had the only diplomatic mission in the world large enough to house the government to which we were accredited.

Our ambassador at the time of my arrival was renowned scientist and former Harvard president Dr. James B. Conant. At my level in the embassy, I had almost no contact with him, but always held him in high esteem. Some months after my arrival, in March 1957, he was replaced by David K. E. Bruce, the only personal acquaintance whom I have ever idolized. (My other idols, like George Washington and Robert E. Lee, were most long dead and none was anyone I had ever known.) Ambassador Bruce was a witty, urbane, highly intelligent, exceedingly competent, and sophisticated (in the true sense) patrician. Although he was not a career FSO, he was no doubt the most professional of all our ambassadors: he had been ambassador to France, Germany, Great Britain, and China, and had headed our (Marshall Plan) Economic Cooperation Administration in Europe. He had served in the Army in World War I and World War II, the latter in a senior position with the OSS (Office of Strategic Services, forerunner of the CIA). I got to know him quite well since we went hunting and fishing together; on occasion I acted as his interpreter. He was an excellent dry fly fisherman and the best wing shot I had ever seen. He simply never missed. He was helped a little bit by having a beautiful pair of matched English Purdy shotguns, the world's best.

After one of our outdoors activities, we would usually have tailgate stiff drinks of Jack Daniels (we always had a driver) and he would entertain me with tales of the prominent people he had known—for example, Ernest Hemingway, whom he knew quite well. He obviously had no need to impress anyone at my level and most certainly was not the namedropper type. He just simply enjoyed relating anecdotes involving notables. His telegrams back to the State Department were masterpieces of insight and wit. I remember one sent at a time when West German Chancellor Konrad Adenauer, for some reason that slips my mind, was persisting in giving his highly competent economics minister, Ludwig Erhard, a hard time of it. Bruce's reporting telegram on this stated, "Adenauer is not content with just making Erhard eat crow. He wants to make crow Erhard's permanent diet." When he was informed by State that ambassadors would be given Cadillac limousines that had been first used by cabinet members, Bruce replied, "In days of yore, ambassadors had to make do with castoff courtesans. If now they must make do with castoff Cadillacs, at least send me the one used by 'Engine Charlie' [Secretary of Defense Charles Wilson, former CEO of General Motors]." Once when he addressed a ladies' luncheon at the Embassy Club in Plittersdorf he noted that wags have often claimed that diplomats are "sent abroad to lie for their countries." He then stressed that diplomats who lie about substance are making a grave mistake. He added, "I do not, however, include the small social lies one is obliged to use from time to time. After all, in this regard, one has to lie to live." (For more on this outstanding personality, read *The Last American Aristocrat* by Nelson D. Lankford [1996]. Bruce died in 1977.)

I soon took up my favorite sport of hunting. With the right connections, there were great possibilities for an enthusiastic hunter like me. I somehow got myself appointed Embassy Master of the Hunt and gained control of the issuance of hunting licenses for embassy personnel. To get a hunting license, the average

German had to pass a rigorous theoretical and practical exam covering gun safety and shooting, game habits and habitats, traditional hunting customs, dressing game, and a host of other subjects. This required some months of intense preparation. Diplomats, however, could forgo all of this in getting a license. As a result, they were often clueless as to how to conduct themselves at a German hunt. Before I issued anyone a license, he had to demonstrate at least a knowledge of gun safety and German customs and terminology, as well as correct conduct at a hunt. Word about this soon got around the hunting community with the result that we soon were receiving all kinds of hunting invitations that I distributed as fairly as possible to those deemed eligible for a license.

Hunting rights went to those who could afford to lease a *Revier* (preserve) that had to be at least a certain size to facilitate game management. A *Revier* could spread out over several farms; the owners of those farms were compensated for the use of their land, but did not have the right to hunt on their own property, a situation of course unthinkable in the United States. For game management, those who leased a *Revier* were required to shoot a certain number of game each year, but no more. A large German hunt was quite an experience. The stages of the hunt were signaled by calls on the hunting horns (after which French horns have been fashioned), the sound of which I dearly loved, especially when it echoed through small valleys. When the horn sounded the beginning of the hunt, beaters, usually local farm boys, began driving the game toward the hunters who had to be prepared to cope with anything from a partridge to a stag or wild boar. We usually had a rifled slug in one barrel of our shotguns and birdshot in the other. (Single barrel repeating shotguns were frowned on.) Some fortunate ones carried Drillings, a double-barreled shotgun with a rifle barrel underneath.

When the horn at last sounded *Jagd vorbei*, "the hunt is over," there followed the ritualistic finale with the game laid out in order of rank, with stags at the head and birds at the bottom before a large bonfire, at which time tribute was paid to all these dead animals ending with another *Jagd vorbei* on the horn. The hunters went home with some of the game, most of which was sold to special game shops that were all over the country. At the end of each hunting season we gave a special hunters' dinner at our club to which we invited all those who had invited us to hunt. From U.S. sporting goods firms we received some great films about hunting in America, which the Germans much enjoyed; we also offered the best eats and drinks we could provide. This became an occasion to which German hunters in our area began to look forward all year.

Hunting brought me in contact with some interesting people in our general area whom I would never have otherwise had a chance to know. One, Count Fery Strasoldo, had a moated castle not far from Bonn, which intrigued an old history buff like me. The rooms abutting the moat were always damp and plagued with mildew, so the family and help lived in the castle's keep. (The keep is the strongest part of a castle and is usually a large sturdy tower located away from the main gate. When the rest of the castle fell to a foe, the keep was where a last stand was made. It was supposed to be self-sufficient in water and food.) Another castle owner who became a good friend was Baron Philipp von Boeselager who had a small castle on a hill west of Bonn. When I hunted there I would usually spend the night at the top room of the keep. I was intrigued by looking up at the maze of medieval beams and rafters holding up the roof. Philipp had been a cavalry officer (horse) with the German Wehrmacht on the Eastern Front and had fascinating war stories to tell. He said that horse cavalry made the very best reconnaissance units since the horses were quiet and could negotiate terrain impassable for wheeled vehicles. Moreover they didn't require fuel, since they could live on grass, even when it was under the snow in winter.

Philipp told the story of how once his squadron was going west when they had spotted a long column of infantry headed east; he assumed they were German. Too late he discovered that they were retreating Russian troops, not advancing German ones. All the soldiers on both sides were so bundled up against the bitter cold they could not be identified as to which side they were on. Philipp just prayed that all his troops realized what was going on and wouldn't say a word. For some hours Philipp's squadron silently shared the road with the Russians with his cavalry going west and the Russians going east. They were never discovered and successfully made their way back to German lines.

One thing I never learned about Philipp until I read his obituary in the *Washington Post* in 2008 was that he was heavily involved in the July 20, 1944, plot, code-named Valkyrie, to assassinate Hitler and seize power. He had written a book, *Valkyrie*, about the plot, which was made into a film starring Tom Cruise (2008). The plot leader, Col. Count Claus von Stauffenberg, attended a meeting at Hitler's eastern "Wolf's Lair" headquarters, during which he placed a briefcase with a powerful explosive charge and timer under the table where it would certainly have killed Hitler. After von Stauffenberg left the meeting, the briefcase tipped over and an aide leaned it up on the other side of one of the thick oak slabs supporting the table. When it exploded, Hitler was largely shielded from the blast and the plot failed, thus eliminating a possible chance to end the war. Many, including of course von Stauffenberg, were arrested, tried, and executed. One of the plotters was none other than famed Field Marshal Erwin Rommel; he was given the choice of suicide and a hero's funeral or trial and execution with attendant hardships for his family. Not surprisingly, he chose the former, and took poison. A later acquaintance of mine told me he had been asked to participate in this plot, but decided against it because he wasn't all that sure the plotters knew what they were doing.

By late 1957 I had become the embassy press attaché, which, for anyone substantively oriented as was I, is the most interesting position in a large embassy like the one at Bonn. I had direct access to the ambassador and his deputy chief of mission and a license to get involved in everybody's affairs on the theory that one can never know what will interest the media. I attended the weekly staff meetings of all the embassy's sections, including the CIA (which had an anodyne title that I have forgotten). I acquired as much knowledge as possible on issues that were causing us public relations problems, one of which was the issue of vested German external assets, which involved untangling Nazi regime foreign deposits and investments. I got to know this issue well enough that I could sometimes substitute for the embassy treasury attaché who normally handled it.

Always of prime interest was our policy toward the Soviet Union in respect to German issues. This was especially true in periods of crisis or during East–West negotiations. I also was involved with contingency plans for Soviet actions against West Berlin. My background in Soviet and Eastern European matters served me especially well in one of my most interesting and perhaps fruitful encounters during my tour in West Germany or, as we usually called it, the FRG (Federal Republic of Germany).

On October 4, 1957, the West, especially the United States, was shocked and surprised by Soviet success in placing Sputnik in orbit, soon followed by another much heavier Sputnik II carrying a dog. This meant that the USSR possessed a rocket that could be converted to an intercontinental ballistic missile (ICBM), which could reach the United States; we had no comparable weapon. This created a national inferiority complex in the United States with respect to our science and technological capabilities and launched a major campaign to promote science and math in our schools. (Today's school science fairs are one result of this campaign.) It also triggered an extensive civil defense effort in the United States. More worrisome was that this gave Moscow political and diplomatic leverage that could be used against the West. This would be manifested about a year later.

The FRG's leading print media magnate was Axel Springer, who owned a number of publications, from the somewhat tabloid, large-circulation *Bild Zeitung* to the serious daily *Die Welt*. He came across as somewhat standoffish toward Americans, and he seemed somewhat open-minded when it came to the Soviets. In 1958 he went to Moscow to meet with Khrushchev. When he came back he was more than vexed at the reception he received in Moscow. I would guess that Khrushchev took a particularly tough line with him on Berlin during a period in which he was preparing a major political assault on that city, which he launched in November 1958. Adam Vollhardt, the Bonn correspondent of Springer's Hamburg daily, *Hamburger Abendblatt*, who had gotten to know me well, thought the time was ripe for me to have a talk with his disgruntled if not somewhat disillusioned boss. He arranged for me to spend a long afternoon with Springer in the garden of his home in upscale Blankenese just outside Hamburg. The two of us had a good talk about the Soviets, about Soviet–FRG and Soviet–U.S. relations, and about *Weltpolitik* in general. Afterwards, Springer seemed to have become decidedly friendlier toward the United States. People at the embassy and others gave me credit for this turnaround. While I am not overly modest when it comes to touting my accomplishments, I believe my encounter with Springer was something akin to an auto dealer selling a car to someone who had already decided to buy it.

As noted earlier, Moscow regarded a free West Berlin as a constant obstacle to consolidating its control over East Germany, since East Germans could see for themselves the enormous contrast between life under Communism and life in a free democracy. Moreover, radio broadcasts, especially from RIAS, were a constant irritant and a major obstacle to the East German regime's gaining popular support and cooperation. Of course, West Berlin also was ideally suited for basing intelligence operations against East Germany: East Germans could escape to West Germany through West Berlin, and many did. Stalin tried to eliminate this troublesome Western presence and freedom in West Berlin by ordering a blockade of the city. The dramatic Berlin Airlift broke the blockade, which had lasted nearly a year, from June 1948 to May 1949. Later, emboldened by Soviet space successes and the potential military prowess they represented, Khrushchev, on November 27, 1958, sent identical notes to the United States, Great Britain, and France that demanded the end of the occupation of West Berlin so that it would become a demilitarized "free city." If this were not accomplished within six months, Moscow would sign a separate peace treaty with East Germany and end the occupation that way. This was aimed at severing West Berlin's lifeline to the West and bringing it under Communist control, of course.

To cope with this new assault against West Berlin, the United States, Great Britain, and France agreed that their foreign ministers would meet with the Soviet foreign minister in Geneva on May 11, 1959. At Soviet insistence, the "two Germanys" would also be represented at the conference, thus bestowing on the East German puppet regime a degree of recognition it did not deserve. I was present at this conference and was struck by the insistence of a senior member of our delegation that we were negotiating from a position of weakness, given the existence of a "missile gap" resulting from the Soviets having an ICBM capability whereas we did not. Indeed, it seemed to me that the "missile gap" was like a sword of Damocles suspended over the Western foreign ministers, although I never saw this presumed threat spelled out anywhere in writing. It was at this conference that I first realized that strategic weapon systems were in fact actually the "blue chips" in potentially deadly diplomatic poker.

Secretary of State John Foster Dulles, long a stalwart defender of a strong U.S.–Berlin policy, was terminally ill with cancer. Even after he was hospitalized he continued to be pilloried by influential Democratic Senators Mike Mansfield and William Fulbright for refusing to appease the Soviets on Berlin. No longer capable of carrying on, Dulles resigned on April 15 and was replaced by Under Secretary of State Christian Herter, who was hardly the tower of strength and determination Dulles had always been. I remember seeing Herter descend from his plane in Geneva appearing frail and partially crippled. (During the conference, our delegation received many medications and prescriptions from numerous private individuals [mostly European] concerned with his Herter's health. For some reason, they all were turned over to me.) The French were represented by Couve de Murville and the British by Selwyn Lloyd. None of the three Western foreign ministers came across as a tower of strength. The Soviets were well represented by a highly skilled and case-hardened pro, Andrei Gromyko.

Before the conference could begin, the modalities involving German participation had to be worked out. It was finally agreed that these two foreign ministers would not sit at the main circular conference table, but at two adjoining tables, one pencil's width from the main table. On May 14 the Western foreign ministers presented a complicated package calling for the reunification of Berlin followed by the reunification of Germany through democratic processes. The Soviets, however, were really only interested in Berlin, so naturally Gromyko immediately and categorically rejected this proposal. For the next four weeks, the Western side made no progress in selling its complex plans. Late in this period the U.S. delegation spokesperson somehow let slip that our side would be willing to negotiate only on Berlin. On May 26 Dulles died and some days later the foreign ministers flew to Washington for his funeral.

Well into June, Gromyko came up with the Soviet proposal on Berlin that allowed the Allied occupation to continue for one year, but called for the reduction of Western troops to "symbolic contingents" with no atomic or missile installations (that in any case were never planned) and the elimination from West Berlin of "hostile propaganda against the GDR [East Germany] and other Socialist countries" and "espionage and subversive activities directed against the GDR, the USSR and other Socialist countries." During the one-year period, both Germanys would set up an all-German committee to reach unification and a peace treaty. If no agreement were reached in one year, the Soviet Union would conclude a peace treaty with the GDR and future Berlin negotiations would be based on this reality.

Incredibly, instead of adhering to their original game plan, the evidently weak-kneed Western foreign ministers began negotiating on the basis of Gromyko's outrageous proposal. The West's position, first delineated on June 16 and made in final form on June 19, agreed to limit the Western garrison to eleven thousand men, armed only with conventional weapons, with consideration of a reduction of their troop strength; to the establishment of a quadripartite commission for the purpose of eliminating "subversion and espionage" in both parts of Berlin; and to the acceptance of East German control as "agents" for the Soviet Union for Allied access to Berlin. Unbelievably, no mention was made of the Allied rights of occupation that we had been using all along to justify a continued Allied presence in Berlin. Agreement to curtail "propaganda activities" would clearly eliminate RIAS, a prime Soviet target, and probably all other non-Communist media. Moreover, the quadripartite commission would provide the Soviets with a voice on what occurred in West Berlin. Of course, letting the East Germans substitute for Soviets on access control was another step down a slippery slope.

In short, this posed a potential disaster for the continued freedom of West Berlin. It was immediately recognized as a threat, especially by those in West Berlin and by the FRG. Since my primary purpose in being in Geneva was to service West German correspondents covering the conference, I was placed in an impossible situation. I could in no way defend what was happening, but could also not go against our own delegation's unfortunate position. The conference recessed from June 20 to July 13. On June 25 Herter made a quick trip to Berlin and was told by our senior general there that eleven thousand troops were the absolute minimum needed to control possible Communist organized riots and disturbances in West Berlin. In our final proposal made on July 28 there was no longer mention of reducing Western troop strength. Added, however, was a five-year limitation on the agreement. When I asked a senior member of our delegation to explain the five-year proposal, he said that it was our estimate that it would take five years to close the missile gap, but that I shouldn't repeat what he said.

It was our salvation that the Soviets did not accept our final offer, which would have undoubtedly doomed the freedom of West Berlin. I soon learned why they did not accept our offer. In early July 1959 Khrushchev received an invitation from President Eisenhower to come to the United States for a meeting. Khrushchev immediately accepted. I learned much later from a knowledgeable source that the invitation was sent by mistake by a senior White House official who had misunderstood something the president had said about meeting his Soviet opposite number. Eisenhower was furious, but could not retract the invitation after it had been accepted with such alacrity by Khrushchev. I have never heard this story confirmed, but it may well be true. In any case, this invitation was a godsend for Berlin because Khrushchev was convinced he could cut a better deal with Eisenhower than Gromyko could with the Western foreign ministers in Geneva. And, for a time, it began to look as if he were right. In final analysis, however, although no doubt inadvertent in intent, the invitation turned out to be a diplomatic master stroke that saved the day in Geneva.

Khrushchev arrived in the United States on September 15, 1959, and began a highly publicized tour of the country during which he oozed friendliness and down-to-earth demeanor, all the while touting the virtues of "peaceful coexistence." On September 25 he met with Eisenhower at Camp David, the presidential retreat in the Maryland hills near Washington. There the discussion not surprisingly centered on Germany, especially Berlin. They agreed to a Big Four summit meeting in the following year, which was eventually scheduled for Paris on May 15. Khrushchev for his part removed the Soviet deadline for a settlement. At an Eisenhower press conference on September 28, it appeared that Khrushchev had read Eisenhower correctly. When asked if we would "guarantee Allied rights there [in Berlin] and protect the freedom of the West Berliners," Eisenhower replied, "I don't guarantee anything of this kind for the simple reason, I don't know what kind of solution may finally prove acceptable, as I say, but you must start with this. The situation is abnormal." "Abnormal" is how Khrushchev had been characterizing Berlin. This signaled a clearly weak stance on Berlin by the president, which must have greatly encouraged Khrushchev since it had disturbed those who wanted a strong defense of West Berlin.

Ambassador Bruce left Bonn in early November 1959 to become ambassador to the Court of St. James in London; he was replaced by Walter C. "Red" Dowling, who had been my deputy chief of mission in Vienna.

As noted earlier, I was told that our policy on Berlin was greatly influenced by our belief in the "missile gap." In September 1959 this was certainly still the case. However, by mid-January 1960 our intelligence had concluded that there was no strategic delivery systems gap and not much of a missile gap. As one analyst explained to me, we had assumed that the Soviets could produce a large number of their basic ICBM, the SS-6 Saperwood. Since it used a cryogenic fuel, it would be fueled by rail. Our high-altitude U-2 reconnaissance flights over Soviet rail lines failed to uncover any missiles. I believe we may also have had some humint (human intelligence) source who confirmed this. As we now know, the Soviets were dissatisfied with the SS-6 and chose to save their missile assets for the next generation ICBM. By mid-January 1960 we were convinced that there was no "deterrent gap." Based on this intelligence, our position on Berlin began to increasingly toughen. This position culminated in a very tough speech by Under Secretary of State C. Douglas Dillon in early April 1960, which concluded, "We will not accept any arrangement which might become the first step toward the abandonment of West Berlin." When asked about his position on Berlin at an April 27 press conference, Eisenhower stated that the administration's position had been fully covered in Dillon's speech and added, "We are not going to give up the judicial rights we have."

Based on these increasingly tough U.S. statements, Khrushchev must have realized that the jig was up as far as Berlin was concerned and that he was going to leave the upcoming Four Power summit empty-handed. Then he had the great fortune to have delivered to him the perfect excuse for blowing up the summit: the May 1 shoot-down of a U-2 spy plane conducting espionage over the Soviet Union. (Incidentally, the capture of the intact U-2 informed Soviet intelligence of how effective this type of reconnaissance was and how much we knew about their defense weaknesses.) When the summit participants arrived on May 14, Khrushchev announced that the meeting could not begin until President Eisenhower had apologized and agreed to dismiss all those who had anything to do with the U-2 incursion. Of course, he knew full that these were impossible conditions and that he was off the hook as far as the summit was concerned. I was in Paris for the summit and was struck by how my fellow U.S. delegation members were relieved that the meeting was off, at least in part because they had discovered that Eisenhower, who was flying in from India, hadn't read any of the position papers prepared for him, but instead had read a detective novel the whole trip.

After sabotaging the meeting, Khrushchev called what turned out to be a monster press conference in the old Palais de Chaillot conference hall with what seemed like thousands of correspondents present. Seated next to barrel-chested, bemedaled, grim-faced, and intimidating Minister of Defense Marshal Rodion Malinovsky, Khrushchev treated his huge audience to unrelieved invective. I was seated about a third of the way from the front with a few dozen West German correspondents and Foreign Office types, some of whom started to heckle. Then suddenly Khrushchev paused, pointed his figure directly at us and declared, "We buried you at Stalingrad and we could bury you again." From then on silence reigned in our group. I could never figure out how he knew his hecklers were German; maybe it was because some used German or German-accented insults. I simply don't recall that they did. After this tirade Khrushchev proposed that the summit was not cancelled but only postponed, awaiting a more auspicious time. (Since this was an election year in the United States he was clearly waiting to deal with the next president.) Not long thereafter the Soviet Embassy in Paris announced that the Soviet Union would make no unilateral moves toward concluding a separate peace treaty with East Germany. This was subsequently confirmed by Khrushchev himself. For the time being things definitely cooled off a bit.

It was always a special treat to attend a conference in Paris, a city I dearly love. Until 1966, when President de Gaulle in effect withdrew France from NATO, that organization had its annual meeting every December in Paris. I went to all of them while I was stationed in Bonn. At one point I learned a valuable secret from an admin type: I could get "conference orders" with half per diem that let me stay at a hotel of my choice. My choice was always the magnificent, elegant old Hôtel de Crillon on the Place de la Concorde, across the street from the American Embassy. It was not far from the Louvre Museum and was close to the Orangerie Museum, with its great collection of impressionist art, which is my favorite style of art after the art of Rembrandt. And, of course, eating in Paris is always a special treat. While spending time in France, I came upon an interesting and somewhat surprising phenomenon: the French had actually become fond of the Germans, their old traditional enemy with whom they had gone to war three times in seventy years (1870, 1914, and 1939). I wondered why the French always seemed so friendly toward an American like me until someone told me I spoke French with a German accent. I would go to a restaurant with a group of Germans and we would get extra special service. The next evening I would go there with a group of Americans, and the service was mediocre at best.

I became very curious to discover the origins of this unexpected relationship and came up with several thoughts. Young Germans and French men of my generation had suffered inordinately, especially the Germans, in fighting each other while having had no influence on the events that led to war. There was a postwar sentiment among them to foster mutual friendship in order to banish this tragic old enmity. Also, many French peasants were conscripted to work on German farms, to the extent that by war's end a large percentage of German farms were being run by French peasants. Having a common background and interests fostered a certain bond among the peasants of both countries that survived the war. (After the war German POWs wound up working on French farms.) Also, the French and Germans got along better during the occupation than is generally realized. On the whole, most French would have characterized the behavior of German troops in Occupied France as "correct." On the other hand, many French Jews were being picked up for transport to death camps, and there were brutal reprisals for attacks against Germans by the Resistance, which didn't really go all out until it was certain that our 1944 landings were going to succeed. The most odious example of reprisal that I know of was in June 1944, when an SS division herded the inhabitants of the French village of Oradour sur Glane into structures, including the church, then set them on fire, killing 642; only ten inhabitants escaped.

It turned out that there was a fair amount of French fraternization, cooperation, and outright collaboration with their German occupiers. In 1971, French film producer Marcel Ophuls released a four-hour documentary about French behavior during the German occupation that created a sensation and garnered worldwide acclaim. I sat through the whole thing, fascinated from beginning to end. It was titled *Le chagrin et la pitié* (The Sorrow and the Pity) and was devastating. I was especially disappointed to learn that two of my favorite actors, Danielle Darrieux and Maurice Chevalier, had collaborated. It was jolting to learn that more French fought in German SS divisions than in the Resistance. On the other side of the coin, I had much earlier learned that some of France's finest actors, including the greatest of all pantomimists, Jean-Louis Barrault, the fabulous Arletty, and Pierre

Brassins, joined together to spend more than three years making a film in order to avoid working for the Germans. The result was what many film critics and I regard as the greatest film ever made, *Les enfants du paradis* (The Children of Paradise). I have seen that film more than a dozen times, and each time it's been like seeing it for the first time.

While Soviet threats against West Berlin abated, at Soviet behest the East German regime sought with some success to erode Western rights in Berlin until that regime was threatened with a potentially damaging trade embargo that forced it to cease and desist. In the meantime, a new administration had come to power in Washington. One of President Kennedy's first foreign policy objectives was to meet with Soviet leader Nikita Khrushchev, which he thought could lead to reducing the chances of a deadly East–West conflict. To this end, in February 1961 he instructed our ambassador in Moscow, veteran Soviet expert Foy Kohler, to hand-deliver to Khrushchev an invitation to meet. This involved chasing after the peripatetic Khrushchev until Kohler finally caught up with him in the Siberian city of Novosibirsk on March 9. (One of the reasons given for Krushchev's 1964 ouster was his frequent absence from Moscow.) Weeks went by with no word from Khrushchev—then came the disastrous April 17, 1961, Bay of Pigs invasion by Cuban émigrés seeking to overthrow Fidel Castro.

This whole operation was essentially organized by the CIA although it was designed to be seen as a strictly Cuban affair, a farfetched assumption if ever there was one. This operation, in any case, was foredoomed when the landing site was changed from a beach that provided essential ready exits to nearby cover, to a landing site that guaranteed most would be trapped on the beach. Kennedy also ordered a last-minute 80 percent reduction in air support. The resulting total absence of air superiority cost the invaders their supply ships and ensured defeat. A U.S. Navy carrier and escorts were standing by, but did not intervene. Upon coming into office, Kennedy had virtually eliminated the NSC system that had been systematically developed under Eisenhower, and that could have provided expert vetting of this enterprise before it kicked off, a precaution that logically could well have resulted in its cancellation.

It is puzzling that Eisenhower's NSC system ever allowed this half-baked scheme to get off the ground in the first place, however, since history tells us that such ventures only succeed when their victory is all but guaranteed. For example, in 1944 the French Resistance only took off when the success of the Normandy landings was ensured. Moreover, Castro enjoyed widespread support (especially among the poor)—as did those other tyrants Hitler and Stalin—and the country was hardly ripe for revolt. Moreover, according to Alexis de Tocqueville's theory of revolution, which has been proven by history, revolts against unpopular or tyrannical regimes usually only occur when such regimes begin to loosen controls.

Castro was tightening them. After the Bay of Pigs disaster, Khrushchev no doubt concluded that this evidently feckless Kennedy "is my pigeon." It should be added that Kennedy was suffering from recent U.S. setbacks in Laos, then in the forefront of our problems in Southeast Asia. Not long after the Bay of Pigs and nearly two months after receiving Kennedy's February invitation, on May 4 the Kremlin indicated an interest in the meeting; Khrushchev formally accepted Kennedy's invitation on May 18. It was agreed that this summit would take place in Vienna on June 3 and 4, 1961.

Kennedy, who was used to dealing with rational, reasonably well-behaved interlocutors, was ill-prepared for an encounter with a thuggish type like Khrushchev. As I much later described this meeting to my students at Georgetown University, "This was Little Boy Blue meets Al Capone." In addition, Kennedy entered these talks with diminished self-confidence and egg on his vest. Twice a day, I received a rundown on each morning and afternoon session from the U.S. note-taker, Martin Hillenbrand, the U.S. State Department's leading Germany expert, who was also my friend. Since this was a "principals only" meeting, the only Americans present were Marty and our interpreter. The interpreter and I must be the only Americans still alive who at the time were completely privy to what went on in these ill-fated sessions.

The first meeting, on June 3, was in the Music Room of the U.S. Embassy. I was soon appalled by the direction things were taking. Khrushchev was tough, hard, and ruthless, while Kennedy was apologetic and defensive, the worst possible stance under these circumstances. Kennedy sought hard to defend U.S. positions, but with little effect. On the second and final day, June 4, at the Soviet Embassy, Khrushchev repeated his November 27, 1958, threat to turn over control of access to Berlin to the East Germans who would most certainly block all escape routes to West Berlin and then on to West Germany. Kennedy left this last session visibly shaken. John O. Koehler, who was covering the summit for Associated Press, later told me that Kennedy "looked green" when he left that session, uncharacteristically brushing by the waiting reporters.

Defending Four Power Control of Berlin and access thereto was an issue of gravest importance to the three Western Powers. Then, about the only way World War III could have been triggered would have been a Western Allies clash with the Soviet Union over Berlin access or in inadvertent involvement in a greatly feared widespread revolt in East Germany. Thus, this threat was serious business, indeed. Kennedy, who genuinely feared the possibility of an armed conflict over Berlin, reported to the American people that these were "a very sober two days" and that "our most somber talks were on . . . Berlin." Kennedy reportedly revealed to *New York Times* correspondent James "Scotty" Reston that he had been treated by Khrushchev like a little boy and that this was "the worst thing in my life. He savaged me" (Friedman, *The Fifty-Year War*, p. 272). The most pernicious result of the disastrous Vienna summit is that the weak impression made by Kennedy most probably emboldened Khrushchev to install offensive missiles in Cuba in 1962, thus bringing the world to the brink of a thermonuclear war.

Khrushchev's Vienna ultimatum was not mentioned by us, by design; however, the Soviets chose to release its text on June 10. Khrushchev publicly repeated his threats against the Western position in Berlin with a disturbing lack of rebuttal from Washington. To make matters worse, Democratic Senate Majority Leader Mike Mansfield proposed turning Berlin over to a totally unprepared United Nations, a disastrous and demoralizing proposal. Finally, after considerable unsettling vacillation, Kennedy got his act together and on July 25 delivered an exceedingly strong defense of maintaining the Western position in Berlin, and coupled it with details of a very substantial planned U.S. defense buildup. In the meanwhile, Khrushchev's threats to turn over access to Berlin to the East German regime had been interpreted by East Germans as foreclosing any chance to flee to the West, and that it was now or never for those who wanted out—and there were thousands of those. In July alone a record 30,444 had fled to West Berlin from whence they could fly to West Germany to begin a new life free of stifling Communism. (By then a total of 2 million East Germans had fled the country since 1945.)

Most important, these were people East Germany simply could not afford to lose: physicians, scientists, engineers, and skilled professionals in all fields. For example, one district (*Bezirk*) lost its last obstetrician. One cause of this mass flight was brought home to me on a July flight from Berlin to West Germany. I had a window seat; next to me sat a well-dressed man in his mid-thirties. At one point, over East Germany, I looked out the window and murmured aloud to myself, "*Lauter LPGs*" ("Nothing but collective farms," for which I had used the East German term) My neighbor turned to me and asked, in German, "Are you also from the [refugee] camp?" I replied, also in German, "Don't tell me you're a refugee?" He explained that he, his wife, and their two children had escaped to West Berlin two days before and that he was an engineer who had a very good job in Leipzig heading the *Vermessungsamt*, a bureau of weights and measures. He had a car, a nice house, and a maid, and was not unsatisfied with his material life. He was leaving all this to become an ordinary worker at the Semperit Tire Factory in Braunschweig, West Germany, because he didn't want his children to grow up under Communism, and it seemed like the last chance to escape.

In short, East Germany was suffering a potentially crippling hemorrhage. The question was, "Where will the tourniquet be applied?" Conventional wisdom was that all of Berlin would be encircled by barriers to stop the refugee flow. I insisted that Berlin would be divided right down the middle by barriers separating the Soviet sector from the three Western sectors. As far as I know, I was the only person in the U.S. government to hold this view. My reasoning was that cutting off all of Berlin from surrounding East Germany made little sense, since this would sever it from its capital and would permit more than 1.25 million East Berliners to escape to the West; many of these Berliners were key government and other personnel East Germany could ill afford to lose. This seemed to me reasonable and logical enough, but my arguments were always met with, "It's technically impossible to split a major metropolis like Berlin right down the middle." Berlin did indeed cover a very large area.

I would counter that I had observed in 1950 how British troops in Vienna were prepared to cordon off the center of Vienna (another city under Four Power control) in coping with an ongoing and deeply disturbing Soviet-encouraged Communist effort to foment a crippling general strike. The British troops had a number of trucks stacked high with concertina wire, great rolls of barbed wire that could rapidly be stretched out considerable distances in very short time to form formidable barriers. I suggested that is exactly what the East Germans, backed by Soviet troops, would do, and that they would do it in the middle of the night. This was pooh-poohed every time I raised the issue in embassy staff meetings, which was frequent. In other words, I gained zero support for my views in our embassy in Bonn. I then went to the Western Foreign Ministers' Conference in Paris, August 5–7, where I presented my views to senior U.S. State Department and British Foreign Office officials with the same dismal results as in Bonn.

Very early in the morning of August 13, 1961, East German Peoples Police (Volkspolizei) began sealing off the border between the Soviet sector of Berlin and the three Western sectors with numerous rolls of concertina wire. Nearby, as a backup, were East German troops (Volksarmee), in turn backed up by more distant Soviet troops who had recently come under the command of renowned Marshal Ivan Konev of World War II fame. Thus the Berlin Wall was born, and the wire was soon replaced by a solid wall. Not one soul ever acknowledged that I had been right when everyone else was wrong. As far as I was concerned that was all to the good. In any bureaucracy the one unpardonable sin is to be right when everyone else was wrong. I subsequently learned that erecting the Wall must have been greeted in Washington with considerable, if well-concealed, relief, since it defused a very tense and potentially dangerous confrontation.

U.S. News and World Report correspondent James O'Donnell told his colleague John Koehler that on August 13 he had contacted senior State Department official George C. McGhee (who became ambassador to West Germany in 1963) and was told, "Thank God they solved our problem." The main fear in Washington was most probably the prospect that the situation in East Germany could lead to widespread uprisings that could spill over and lead to a conflict between the USSR and the three Western Allies. Isolating the population of East Germany and bringing it under control eliminated this danger. Incidentally, the night that East Berlin was sealed off, our embassy duty officer (who was not an FSO) neglected to inform the ambassador of the development. The next day the ambassador attended a Little League baseball game in Plittersdorf.

I attribute my being right and the others wrong about the Berlin Wall to the fact that my undergraduate work was concentrated on math, science, and engineering, whereas my Foreign Service colleagues and others were all liberal arts majors. They used deductive reasoning while I used inductive reasoning, reaching my conclusion by mustering all the facts in the case. Some twenty years later, history repeated itself when I was the only one I knew in government or elsewhere who insisted that the Soviets were not going to invade Poland during the 1980–81 crisis. On the other hand, I have subsequently been spectacularly wrong. In 1990, I confidently informed my boss, National Security Advisor Brent Scowcroft, that the Soviets would never permit Germany to be reunified. Not too long thereafter that reunification happened without Soviet interference. Even worse was that I could not make myself believe that Gorbachev was really serious about his "Sinatra Doctrine" of letting each Eastern European leader adopt a "I did it my way" approach without fear of Soviet interference. Even when this doctrine was ratified by the Soviets at a Warsaw Pact meeting in 1989, I didn't believe it. It was precisely this guarantee of Soviet noninterference in Eastern Europe that led to the collapse of the Soviet empire, and I didn't see it coming. Neither did Gorbachev who had made a profound miscalculation, as it turned out. (See Chapter 16.)

To reassure the badly shaken and demoralized West Berliners, many of whom had friends or family cut off in East Berlin, President Kennedy decided to honor requests by courageous Berlin Lord Mayor Willy Brandt to send a high official to Berlin and to reinforce our garrison there. The president opted to send both Vice President Lyndon B. Johnson and a fifteen-hundred–man battle group to Berlin, the latter by autobahn through East Germany. For some reason, I was asked to go to Berlin to assist with Johnson's visit. Since Brandt and his staff were in charge of arrangements, I concentrated on security, although this was already well under control. On August 19 the vice president arrived and proceeded with Brandt, in the lead car of a motorcade, to City Hall, with four hundred thousand Berliners lining the route. At one point, LBJ decided that he and Brandt should proceed on foot. Ever the consummate politician, Johnson simply could not resist "pressing the flesh" (and passing out ballpoint pens) with such an emotional and receptive crowd.

I became extremely concerned about the safety of the vice president in the midst of such a crowd that was closing in on him. When I expressed my fears to members of his Secret Service detail, they assured me that this was a situation they could handle. Interestingly, they said they mainly concentrated on watching peoples' feet: that evidently best signaled the onset of an nearby assassination attempt. They said there was one thing they constantly feared because they could not prevent it, however: a determined assassin equipped with a high-power rifle with a telescopic sight firing from some building along the motorcade route. This Secret Service nightmare became reality when Lee Harvey Oswald, firing a surplus Italian Army rifle with a scoped sight in Dallas on November 22, 1963, killed President Kennedy from a window overlooking his motorcade route.

The following day, Johnson went out to greet the battle group as it entered West Berlin on the autobahn. Again, there was a large crowd around him whom he happily greeted. When the troops arrived, they were greeted like conquering heroes. There had been some fear that Soviet checkpoint troops might prevent their transiting East Germany. That would have been extremely embarrassing, at a minimum, as well as a cause célèbre. I later learned that the anxious battle group commander, in order to avoid any problems with the Soviets, agreed to some inspection of his vehicles, which we had always refused to do; this had caused several tense incidents in the recent past. Actually, the Soviets obviously had little to fear from the safe arrival of just fifteen hundred U.S. troops, since Berlin had long been surrounded by up to thirty divisions of Soviet troops in East Germany. But their arrival greatly cheered and reassured the Berliners who viewed it as an earnest of our intention to preserve West Berlin's freedom.

In his July 25 speech, referred to above, Kennedy called for a $3.25 billion (1961 dollars) increase in the defense budget and a substantial increase in our armed forces' strength by calling up reserves and increasing draft calls. Perhaps as a delayed response, Khrushchev ordered the October 30, 1961, detonation of a "don't-ever-mess-with-me" 57-megaton weapon, which was actually a shielded 100-megaton weapon. That was the greatest manmade explosion in all history, equivalent to nearly three thousand Hiroshima bombs.

On November 7, however, he dropped the ultimatum on Berlin he had delivered in Vienna, thus substantially ameliorating Soviet threats to Berlin access. In March 1962, however, the Soviets attempted to interfere with Allied air access, leading to a flurry of indeterminate diplomatic activity to find a solution to this troublesome problem. It took the demolishing of the Wall in November 1989 and the subsequent end of the East German regime to definitively resolve the longstanding nettlesome access issue that, since the 1948–49 Soviet blockade, had repeatedly resulted in potentially dangerous, hair-raising, and nail-biting crises conjuring up the threat of a disastrous World War III.

In the midst of all our trials and tribulations with the Soviets, life went on in the American settlement in Plittersdorf. This settlement was originally built to accommodate the personnel of a much larger mission, so we had a fair amount of surplus housing. This was wisely opened up to families from other diplomatic missions who made our settlement considerably more interesting, since we had been somewhat isolated from other diplomatic families. Among the new arrivals was a delightful Indian embassy couple, Wadshoo and Leila Khanna, who became among our best friends. They brought an excellent cook from New Delhi who prepared memorable Indian dinners that were always followed by wide-ranging and usually scintillating conversations. The Khannas were an example of a very happy, but traditionally arranged, marriage. Our other best friends were British correspondent Gerald Long and his wonderful wife, Anne. Gerry eventually headed the Reuters News Agency. Both were enjoyable company and great conversationalists. My crowning personal achievement was finally completing my doctorate in 1961, which I had begun in 1948. I had worked nearly every day on the dissertation, often after coming back from some formal dinner or late reception.

As I mentioned earlier, I figured the Institute had to be the most difficult school in the world when it came to getting a doctorate. The final manuscript had to first pass the steely-eyed academic muster of the Mixed Committee, consisting of professors from leading universities in Europe, the United Kingdom, and the United States. Since one could not even defend the dissertation until the Institute had been given 250 commercially printed and bound copies (to be sent to leading universities all over the world), one next had to sell the manuscript to a publisher, since few, if any, of us could afford to have it printed on our own. This has one big advantage: it discouraged the writing of dissertations so specialized as to be of interest only to a limited number of academics and nobody else, as is often the case in this and other countries. I found a publisher to whom I gave all rights in exchange for my 250 copies. As a book entitled *The Soviet Union and the Occupation of Austria*, it did quite well. It came out in hardback and paperback and in a German edition, which I edited. It is in colleges all over the United States and has been used by the White House, the U.S. State Department, and the CIA. To this day, it is still one of principal reference works on Soviet policy toward Austria. I successfully defended my dissertation in a public university forum in Geneva.

Toward the end of my Bonn tour an incident reminded us all that our embassy and its personnel were prime targets of East German and other Communist intelligence agencies. The head of our political section had a rather mousy, nondescript maid whom I had often seen at cocktail parties passing around the hors d'oeuvres. I don't remember her name so I'll call her Anna. Immediately after FRG counterintelligence arrested the top East German intelligence agent operating in West Germany, Anna fled to East Germany, which clearly indicated she must have been a quite senior agent to have gotten word of her boss's arrest so soon. When her hurriedly abandoned quarters were examined, all manner of spycraft equipment was found, even disappearing ink. We all got to thinking about all the conversations she must have overheard at receptions and dinners, especially those where all present were embassy personnel who would be much less cautious among their own than would be the case if non-Americans were present.

In March 1962 I received orders to report to the Armed Forces Staff College in Norfolk, Virginia. This is exactly the kind of assignment I hoped I would get when I finally returned to the United States. Eva and Betsy moved to Vienna where Eva's mother lived. Eva preferred to remain in Vienna, and eventually we had an amicable parting of the ways. Betsy later came to the United States to go to college.

chapter 13

Return to the United States

As I indicated in the Preface, coming back to the United States in 1962 after having been away for most of the previous eighteen years was a Rip Van Winkle experience. You will recall that this famed Washington Irving character fell into a deep sleep before the American Revolution and when Rip finally awoke after the Revolution he discovered a transformed country. I, too, discovered that my country had been totally transformed in many respects, some of them good and some not so good. I had never seen a modern postwar suburb, nor a supermarket. I found the latter profoundly depressing and impersonal after having shopped in small specialized grocery stores in Europe. I was overwhelmed by the variety, like the variety of soap powder. In Germany there had only been Persil on the shelves. Since my return I have grown to appreciate some of the differences: for instance, I love the variety offered in supermarkets. Also, here customers can handle the fruit and vegetables without being reprimanded by the shop owner. (Those small green grocers operated on a slim profit margin and couldn't afford having customers bruise produce by handling them.)

Rock music was coming into vogue, epitomized by a highly successful new group from Liverpool, the Beatles, whose music was really musical and a far cry from today's rock music, which is a nerve-jarring, primitive assault on the ear drums. Actually I liked early rock music much better than the jazz I had grown up with. John F. Kennedy was our president, and a popular one he was; the civil rights movement in the South was beginning to gain traction with a push toward eliminating racial segregation in the schools, public facilities, and restaurants. Children seemed to be losing their childhoods to adult-sponsored activities, such as Little League baseball, and families were becoming more child-oriented. My generation, since the late forties, had been raising the children of the Baby Boomer generation, which became characterized, not always fairly, as being essentially self-centered and overindulged. The solid, conventional wholesome family life, especially as depicted in television in such idealistic shows as *Leave it to Beaver*, was giving way to a different set of mores and morals, not always with felicitous results.

The Armed Forces Staff College (AFSC) to which I had been assigned was located in Norfolk, Virginia, a city I had gotten to know during the war. It seemed quite different from what it had been, and had a surprisingly rich cultural life. I grew to know some very nice families there. It was in Norfolk that I acquired one of my favorite pastimes, catching crabs with a hand-line.

I was very much taken with the AFSC. The program was well organized and interesting, and the officers selected for this course were those considered among the most promising. We had all the same lecturers as did the more advanced and prestigious National War College in Washington, DC. We also had more hands-on experiences, visiting Army and Air Force installations and going on board submarines and aircraft carriers. Among my favorite friends at the school were Pete Mongilardi and his lovely wife. Pete was a naval aviator and among those first shot down and killed over North Vietnam. When we played war games, I was usually the POLAD, or political adviser. I was generally politely tolerated as a required participant until we had a game in the Middle East centered on northern Iraq and Iran. When I suggested "cranking in the Kurds" as an important factor in this area, I was not taken seriously until the next day's newspapers reported a Kurdish revolt in the very area where our game was taking place. After that, my fellow players never made a move without consulting me.

After about six months, my course was finished. How it happened I never knew, but I wound up getting a dream assignment at the State Department as the public affairs adviser for the Soviet Union, a position then held by very capable FSO Dick Davies, who later went on the become our ambassador to Poland. All the other positions at my level in the Office of Soviet Union Affairs (SOV, the Soviet Desk) were fairly specialized, whereas my position got me involved in everybody's business, something like being the press attaché in Bonn. I was involved in all our problems with the Soviets, from crab-pot confrontations off Alaska to the Cuban Missile Crisis. Before long, the powers that be decided to add Eastern Europe to my title and responsibilities. This made things even more interesting, and I began attending the Eastern Europe (EE) as well as SOV staff meetings. One of my primary responsibilities was preparing briefing papers on issues in my countries for presidential press conferences. These would contain a hypothetical question with a suggested reply as well as background on the issue involved. This was a delight with Kennedy because, within limits, he would read anything we prepared for him, in contrast to Eisenhower who reportedly would never read more than one page.

(Like most military officers, Eisenhower would sit still for "dog and pony show" briefings with pointers charts, graphs, and so on, however.)

Another thing we all liked about Kennedy was actually a result of his basic lack of organizational sense that had resulted in the virtual dismantling of the extensive NSC organization Eisenhower's NSC staff had developed. When Kennedy wanted to know about something related to foreign affairs, he wouldn't call the secretary of state, which would be the normal practice, but he would instead call middle-level desk officers directly. I was told that when this first started, the unaware officer he called thought the call was a joke and gave a flippant reply something like, "If you're the president, then I'm Little Orphan Annie." Then the officer recognized Kennedy's distinctive voice and apologized profusely. Fortunately, the president took it in good humor, and we all came to love the idea that he would directly call us underlings for information. Kennedy's penchant for reading everything saved the career of a talented fellow officer I knew, David Manbey. At this time, the European African colonies were becoming independent countries. Dave had been assigned to open our mission in Kigali, the capital of the newly independent country of Rwanda, in the summer of 1962. He was living over a butcher shop and was experiencing all manner of surprises and problems in coping with the primitive conditions and disorganization he found. He described all his trials and tribulations in a highly humorous as well as informative reporting telegram to the State Department that was numbered "Kigali 14." The assistant secretary for African affairs at that time was the fifty-one-year-old ex–Michigan governor Mennen Williams, nicknamed "Soapy" after Mennen's line of products. (His mother was a Mennen.) Soapy's constant refrain was, "Africa for the Africans." He was very solicitous of all his new countries and believed that my colleague was being unduly condescending and critical, as well as frivolous, in his observations in Kigali 14. In fact, Soapy was outraged and determined to put its author in his place, if not end his Foreign Service career with a bad efficiency rating. Then he got a call from the president: "Soapy, have you read Kigali 14?" "Indeed I have, Mr. President," Soapy reportedly replied. Kennedy continued by praising Kigali 14 to the sky as a great piece of reporting and insisted that its author be commended. Soapy said nothing, but obviously gave up his intention to do in Dave, who went on with his career. (I long wondered how, of the huge number of telegrams coming into Washington daily, Kennedy could have gotten hold of Kigali 14. I finally got my answer at a May 2010 gathering of retired FSOs when retired Ambassador Robert V. Keeley told me that he had been an Africa desk officer at the time, and had sent Kigali 14 to a friend on the White House NSC staff, who thought it would amuse the president.)

Kennedy held his major press conferences in the West Auditorium of the State Department, and many of us would attend these conferences and marvel at his wit and skill in fielding questions from the media correspondents, most of whom were very fond of the president. In this connection, most if not all of them knew all about Kennedy's affairs and other peccadilloes, but never filed a word about them. In fact, a wire service correspondent who covered State once described to me in detail where Kennedy's current girlfriends lived, when he had visited them, and how Secret Service agents stood guard outside their apartment doors while the president amused himself. I can't imagine such solicitude on the part of the media today in protecting the reputation of any public figure.

I always believed that Kennedy quite unintentionally did American men a great disservice by showing up at his inauguration on a wintry January day in 1961 bareheaded and without an overcoat. (He was wearing long johns, as it turned out.) This macho exhibition prompted American men to stop wearing hats, which throughout our history American men had worn the year around, protecting them from the sun in summer and keeping them warm in winter. The American hat industry was dealt a devastating blow, needless to say.

Kennedy's great moment came in October 1962, with the Cuban Missile Crisis, for which he was, in my opinion, in large measure to blame. As I mentioned in Chapter 12, I am not the only one who believes that the weak impression Kennedy made on Khrushchev in their June 1961 Vienna summit encouraged the latter to create this crisis. It wasn't until Kennedy's speech on October 22, 1962, that the world learned that the Soviet Union was deploying offensive missiles and aircraft to Cuba. Most of us on the Soviet desk learned about this just before the speech. Khrushchev had two salient reasons for making this exceedingly risky move. The United States had forged far ahead in the deployment of ICBMs that could reach the Soviet Union from bases in the United States. By that time we had 240 ICBMs to the Soviets' 36. This created a huge missile gap for the Soviets that they sought to rectify, just as we coped with our own earlier ICBM gap by deploying shorter-range missiles to Great Britain, Italy, and Turkey, from whence they could reach the Soviet Union.

The shorter-range missiles the Soviets were installing in Cuba could reach a good bit of the United States. For the Soviets, this would help to some extent to rectify the strategic imbalance that had developed as the result of the considerable missile buildup in the United States. The other reason for the Soviet move was to protect this outpost of Communism from a U.S. attack. Kennedy wisely ignored the advice of some of his close advisers in the ad hoc executive committee set up to cope with this crisis to launch a military strike against the Soviet presence in Cuba and instead opted for a naval blockade of Cuba to prevent Soviet ships from reaching the island. After some very tense moments, his scheme worked.

This potentially dangerous situation ultimately was defanged by a backstage agreement with the Soviets to withdraw our missiles in Turkey and a promise not to invade Cuba if the Soviets withdrew their forces and weapons. When Kennedy heard that the Soviets had mentioned a quid pro quo involving U.S. missiles in Turkey he became enraged that the order he gave the previous May to withdraw those missiles had not been carried out. In fact, he was so enraged that he went out and paced around the White House Rose Garden until he regained control of himself. In the end, leaders in both the United States and the USSR were sobered by this movement toward the brink of a thermonuclear holocaust. What actually was decided in resolving this crisis is still an open question despite drawers of documents we have covering the agreements, which I have inspected. Incidentally, not long ago we learned that Soviet submarines off Cuba then had nuclear-armed torpedoes, but through an oversight were given no rules of engagement on when to use them. Fortunately, none of the submarine captains whose boats had been forced by U.S. Navy destroyers to surface opted to use these torpedoes.

In the spring of 1963, the Soviets moved to another détente campaign, to lull the West into believing that the Soviet Union had reformed and that the West could relax its vigilance and cease its military buildup, among other activities. Khrushchev also was no doubt becoming increasingly concerned about the growing truculence emerging from Mao's China and wanted peace and quiet on his Western Front. The détente was actually initially encouraged by President Kennedy's June 10, 1963, American University commencement address, which was highly conciliatory in its approach to U.S.–Soviet relations. The détente that followed resulted in the cessation of Soviet jamming of the Voice of America; the institution of a "Hot Line" between Moscow and Washington to provide rapid, uninterrupted communications between Soviet and U.S. leaders in times of crisis; and the conclusion of a limited nuclear test ban treaty.

The highlight of this tour of mine in State was a very interesting and instructive "familiarization" visit to Eastern Europe and the Soviet Union. I can't remember too much of my visits to Belgrade, Bucharest, and Sofia apart from the usual briefings I received in the embassies' "ice boxes": clear plastic rooms within a room that were protected against listening devices. In Prague I had an especially unnerving experience. In the downtown hotel where I was staying was a bar on the ground floor. Like most European bars, this one had dancing, with music provided by a small combo. I happen to love dancing, so I asked a young woman sitting at the bar for a dance. She was friendly and a good dancer so I bought us a round of Slivowitz (a potent clear plum brandy) with seltzer water chasers. Soon a table somehow magically became available for us, so, ever the cautious one, I picked up both glasses of Slivowitz and carried them to the table, ignoring the fact that the waiter had brought over the seltzer water. I tossed down the brandy and sipped a bit of the water, whereupon things started to go around and around. I excused myself to go to the restroom and then slipped out a side entrance that was close to the street on which the hotel had its entrance. I noticed a car with its engine running and a couple of obvious StB (Czech secret police) types in the usual long coats standing next to it. The side door exited into an alley that I took in the opposite direction to the rear of the hotel where I found an entrance, got to my room, barred the door with a chair and collapsed on my bed. I figured they were going to abduct and drug me and then take compromising photos of me in bed with some woman, or worse, with some man, which they could use to blackmail me into cooperation. We were always told that if we ever got caught in such a situation, we should admire the quality of the photos and order several sets to give to friends.

I had actually come up from Budapest, a city I dearly loved, especially my favorite restaurant Matyas Pinces with its great gypsy orchestra. One afternoon I was walking in Pest (the newer part of Budapest) and noticed that a tea dance was in progress at the great old Buda Hotel (now gone) on a side terrace. Always looking for a good dance, I went up to a comely young lady and asked her to dance. She was an excellent dancer, but I thought it would be nice to have a bit of conversation. Since I spoke only a few words of Hungarian, I had to try out other languages. Do you speak English? *Nem* (no), *Parlez-vous français? Nem. Sprechen Sie Deutsch? Nem.* Finally, *Gavareeti po Russki?* Whereupon she spat on the terrace and took off. I don't how she could have possibly thought I was Russian. Maybe it was bad enough to assume she would ever speak that hated language.

Warsaw was very interesting. I was enormously impressed how the Poles had completely and lovingly restored the old city that had been so badly destroyed that hardly any wall stood higher than four or five feet. On one of the restored building was a large banner that read (in Polish) "Confrontation 1963." I went inside to encounter the most far-out (and I must say hideous) modern abstract art one would find anywhere and at a time when Khrushchev had mounted a campaign against such art in the USSR. This was clearly in-your-face art if ever I saw it.

One evening I went for dinner by myself at the dining room of a nearby hotel that had been recommended to me. When I entered there was a sizeable party of happy Poles who clearly recognized me as an American. (Most Europeans have little trouble recognizing Americans.) They invited me to join them, which I happily did. They then began to repeatedly toast me and America, which made me fear for them in case someone from the UB (Polish secret police) might be lurking around. Obviously they didn't give a damn what anybody thought. They were going to toast anybody or anything that suited them. Unfortunately, at each toast I had to toss down a shot of vodka. Before long I was feeling no pain. In the end I had to be helped back to my hotel. It was a great and memorable evening. I have always admired the courage of the Poles. Just think: in 1920, the Polish Army defeated Moscow's Red Army, and the Poles were the first to successfully completely overthrow Communist rule with the ascendancy of their Solidarity Movement in June 1989.

Then it was on to the Soviet Union. The plane I was on first made a landing at Kiev and I was intrigued to see that the surroundings of the city were pock-marked with still-visible filled-in craters left over from World War II. Moscow was my destination and I was put up at the tall gingerbready Hotel Ukraina, fortu-nately on a lower floor because the elevators didn't always work. I spent a good bit of time being briefed at the embassy, but I noticed that we rarely went into an icebox for classified conversations. When I asked about this, I was told State's physical security people had thoroughly swept all the walls of the embassy and had pronounced the embassy free of bugs. Not long after I returned to Washington, we learned from a defector that the embassy was riddled with bugs buried deep in the walls with undetectable wooden tubes leading from the bugs to just inside the plaster. When we undertook a damage assessment we had to give up. Not only were all the numerous classified conversations outside the iceboxes compromised, but everything that had been typed, including highly classified telegrams, was com-promised, since the Soviets could acoustically read typing, because each key had a characteristic sound. After learning this highly distressing news, our embassy immediately had the walls torn apart and, sure enough, found scads of bugs with wooden tubes buried in the walls.

I happened to be in Moscow at the same time an American circus was there. One evening the Soviet cultural people gave a reception at the Ukraina for the cir-cus and some embassy people, so I joined the party. The performers were a some-what motley crew most of whom were, I suspected, not American. The interpreter provided to the circus was an attractive blonde university student majoring in English. Her name was Tanya, and she was obviously seconded to the KGB. In fact I quickly spotted her handler. Everything was going nicely until a couple of women trapeze artists began fighting over a circus man they both fancied. This was a classic foul-mouthing, dress-ripping, hair-pulling fracas. The Russians were shocked by this performance and everybody, including waiters and hotel personnel attracted by the fracas, who crowded around and began peering into the reception, muttered "*nie kulturny*" (uncivilized). Poor Tanya was beside herself with embarrassment, as if it all were somehow her fault. When things had settled down, I asked Tanya to have dinner with me the following evening. She promised to get back to me, and to my surprise, she later accepted my invitation, obviously after having cleared it with her handler.

We met at a well-known Georgian restaurant, Georgia being known for its good food and good wine. I ordered only bottled wine and water and dishes we both shared. I wasn't about to risk getting drugged this time. In addition to having attractive company I was especially interested in what young Russians were think-ing those days. Dinner went well and afterwards we took a taxi out to a new build-ing complex outside of Moscow. Even though she had a room at the Ukraina, she preferred to be back with her parents with whom she lived. When we got to where she lived, we sat on a pile of lumber and had a very interesting conversation for about two hours while the cabbie slept in his cab. Finally, noting the late hour, she got up, thanked me for the meal, and bid me good night. Where she lived was really out in the country on a piece of ground overlooking Moscow in the distance. On the way back to Moscow, the driver suddenly slammed on the brakes, ran out ahead of the taxi and threw his jacket down on the road. I thought, oh hell, I've been set up and the cabbie is signaling KGB agents lying in wait to come and take me. When the cabbie got back into the car, he opened up his jacket in which there was a little hedgehog he had just captured for his little boy. These little European animals look like small versions of porcupines and make great pets.

My visit to all the countries in my account was an extremely worthwhile experience which I shall never forget, but it was awfully nice to get back to Washington. I lived in Georgetown, the original English settlement that predated Washington and was ultimately absorbed by it. Until recently it had had a sizeable black population, but as it became increasingly popular, especially during the Kennedy administration, it became too pricey for most residents, some of whom had lived in Georgetown for generations. Georgetown had been a typical old southern town. All this was rapidly changing.

I shared an old brownstone with five nurses from the nearby Georgetown University Hospital. I lived on the ground floor, and they on the second and third floors. We had little social contact with each other. I marveled at how five women could live together, seemingly in harmony. After the house was sold and we all scattered, I asked one of the nurses how they all had managed to get along, and she said they were divided into two factions who didn't really like each other, but said little about it. I remember being shocked when I came down with a strep throat and a very high fever and none of the nurses could persuade a doctor to come and see me, even though I was less than a ten-minute walk from the hospital. They finally gave me penicillin. In Europe doctors routinely made house calls, and I gather they still do.

The legislature of the U.S. state of Georgia passed a law requiring the teaching of courses on Communism in state colleges, and, incredibly, it turned to the State Department to provide assistance in this endeavor. I was singled out to help Georgia in this effort, to which I much looked forward. When I got to Georgia, the bus stations were being desegregated, and state troopers were deployed to all stations to prevent protests from getting out of hand. They needn't have bothered, since Georgians clearly couldn't have cared less and all came off without incident. I have a strong hunch that this was going on all over the South and was simply ignored by the media to which any peaceful action is not news.

As noted before, columnist George Will cogently put it, "*Good* news is an oxymoron" to the media. I visited several state colleges and advised them on how to go about teaching Communism, a subject I knew very well. At one time in south Georgia I had the great pleasure of taking advantage of some of the best quail hunting in the country. Unfortunately, clouds of quail took off when flushed by the dogs, which made it difficult to focus on a single bird that, counterintuitively, in bird hunting is usually more productive than simply shooting at a bunch of birds.

The most interesting experience I had on this tour was while visiting the all-black Fort Valley State College. I was picked up by one of the professors after dinner and taken to an all-white motel on the outskirts of Fort Valley. Since it looked as if I were going to be deposited at the motel until morning, I asked if it wouldn't be possible to meet with a group of professors that evening. My host professor gave me a quizzical glance, then called one of his colleagues and said, "I have Dr. Stearman here and he seems kind of bohemian in that he wants to get together this evening with some of us. Can you call a few and meet at my place?" He then took me to his house where about four or five professors soon arrived. What followed was one of the most interesting evenings I have ever spent. The atmosphere was a bit stilted at first until I broke the ice and put everyone at ease by explaining that I came from a long line of Southerners and grew up in a Southern family, a slight stretch but not by too much. Northerners, especially liberals, expect whites and blacks in the South to be at daggers drawn and always mystified when I tell them that Southerners generally have a far better rapport with blacks than do Northerners, because, for centuries, the two races have lived cheek to jowl in a relationship that albeit long badly wounded by slavery, segregation, and discrimination, was still a relationship. In the South blacks and whites knew each other and largely understood one another to an extent that never existed in the North. Moreover, the two races to some extent shared a common culture.

The host broke out a quart of bourbon, and they all set about to educate me on what segregation meant in day-to-day practical terms. Travel was always an ordeal, especially for these well-educated, cultivated gentlemen and their families. En route they could only eat and overnight in "black" places, which generally left much to be desired. Usually they brought food and drink with them, but then there was always the problem of finding a place where they could go to the toilet. Husbands and wives took turns driving so they didn't have to overnight anywhere. I found it especially poignant to hear how difficult it was for one professor to explain to his little boy why he couldn't use the local swimming pool "like the other children did." The evening was certainly an eye-opener for me. We polished off the quart of bourbon and ended the evening in a spirit of bonhomie. The next day, I went to the college and was surprised to discover that it had the most modern and best-equipped plant of any of the several colleges I visited. It was explained to me that this was an attempt by Georgia to demonstrate that separate could not only be equal, it could actually be *better*. Although I was the only white person at the school, I felt quite at home.

I learned that a senior White House official hosted a poker game three or four times a month that was usually attended by a number of senior State and other officials, as well as always by a certain Soviet TASS correspondent. I was very disturbed by this and requested a profile on him from the CIA. Not in the least to my surprise, I discovered that he was not only a KGB agent, but a rather senior one, using a reporter cover, a common Soviet practice. I made sure that this file was passed around to those whom I knew to be regular attendees at the poker games. I personally handed a copy to one of them, an assistant secretary of state, who read a few sentences, turned pale, and collapsed on the couch in his office. Clearly, he must have recalled all the incautious and sometimes revealing comments that the TASS man had to have overheard as the result of the relaxed and unguarded atmosphere that characterized these games. The TASS correspondent immediately sensed a change of attitude toward him on the part of his former poker partners and, with his cover blown, soon departed for Moscow.

On November 22, 1963, I was having lunch with colleague John McGowan at Kitty and Al's, a popular greasy spoon restaurant near the State Department (long since demolished to make way for traffic developments). Halfway through lunch, we heard that the president had been shot, but for quite awhile nobody knew whether it was fatal. When the bad news finally came, everybody was in total shock. I remembered what the Secret Service people told me more than two years earlier in Berlin about their fear of exactly this sort of thing happening.

This tragic loss was compounded by Lyndon Johnson's becoming president. In my opinion, he was one of the worst the nation has ever had. Kennedy had his foreign policy failings, as I pointed out above, but had a major success in handling the perilous Cuban Missile Crisis. Perhaps his greatest contribution was building up our conventional forces so we were no longer totally dependent on using nuclear weapons in a major conflict; however, he also built up our strategic nuclear delivery capability. Another major achievement, establishment of the Peace Corps, was a great way to acquaint young and some not-so-young Americans with developing countries. In general, he created a rather optimistic spirit in the nation and was widely beloved by his fellow citizens. His approval rate, however, had fallen from 76 percent in January 1963 to 59 percent before he was assassinated. Nevertheless, he most certainly was assured of winning a second term in 1964.

There has been much speculation about what Kennedy would have done about Vietnam had he lived. By the time he died, Kennedy had sent some sixteen thousand troops to Vietnam as advisers. He certainly fully understood the consequences of a Chinese- and Soviet-backed Communist conquest of this country.

Kennedy's administration, however, definitely had encouraged the generals' coup that led to the overthrow of Vietnamese leader, Ngo Dinh Diem, who was murdered by coup plotters, on November 2, 1963, much to Kennedy's shock and chagrin. This coup destabilized Vietnam and thrust responsibility for Vietnam's fate on the United States. Encouraging the coup was thus a major blunder. Under these circumstances, it is highly unlikely that Kennedy would have abandoned Vietnam had he lived. Moreover, he most likely would not have made the basic mistakes the Johnson administration made.

Given the Soviet support of North Vietnam, especially from 1965 on, I took considerable interest in the Vietnam conflict, never realizing that Vietnam would be my destiny for more than ten years. When in early 1965 the Soviets began installing surface-to-air missiles (SAMs) in North Vietnam, which would be targeted at attacking U.S. aircraft, I met with people who were working the Vietnam account and strongly suggested that we take out these missiles with air strikes before they became operational. Everybody I talked to greatly feared killing Soviet personnel installing the SAMs because of a possible hostile Soviet reaction. I tried to convince them that the Soviets would never admit they were involved in this operation and, therefore, would not react to U.S. attacks on their people in North Vietnam. I pointed out that in the Korean War the Soviets had taken over the whole air defense task in North Korea and that nearly all North Korean fighter aircraft were manned by Soviet personnel. We shot down a great number of these Soviet-manned airplanes without a peep from the Soviets, who had dedicated up to eighty thousand personnel to the air defense of North Korea. (In 1991, Gen. Georgii Lobov stated in an interview that in his 64th Fighter Aviation Corps in Korea [during the war] approximately seventy thousand Soviet pilots, technicians, and gunners had served ["The Cold War in Asia," *Cold War Bulletin*, Winter 1995–96.]) In fact, on the eve of the Korean War, Stalin had all Soviet advisers withdrawn from North Korean forces to prevent any from being captured, thus revealing Soviet participation. It was not until a number of years after the war, however, that the Soviets ever admitted they had been directly involved in that war. I believed that the same would certainly hold true in the case of North Vietnam. My advice, of course, was ignored, later costing a number of American flyers their lives.

As a result of post-coup destabilization and demoralization in South Vietnam, the Communist side began substantially increasing its military action with considerable success. North Vietnam was sending regular units south, so that by March 1965 there were three North Vietnamese Army (NVA) regiments in the South and about 5,800 total troops. In that month we introduced the first U.S. combat troops into South Vietnam, a battalion of Marines with about three thousand men assigned to protect U.S. installations in the Danang area. That same month I asked my colleagues working on Vietnam how many U.S. troops would be in the South by the end of the year. Most agreed that it wouldn't exceed about thirty thousand. When I said that I would bet there will be quarter of million troops there by then, they all thought I had lost my mind. I was, indeed, wrong. By the end of 1965, we had just 184, 314 troops there. Also, by then I was also there.

Since my tour in the State Department was coming to an end, I had lined up the ideal next assignment. I was to be the deputy principal officer (in other words, the number two) and political officer at our consulate general in Hamburg, a mission larger than most of our embassies. I was also, at long last, about to transfer permanently to the State Department. This was just the job for me, since Hamburg was the media capital of the FRG and I was well connected there in this regard and knew nonmedia heavy hitters there as well. Moreover, the consul general, Coburn Kidd, was about to retire and I had visions (probably unrealistic) of succeeding him. Then, after I had been "front-paged" (confirmed) for that position, my world caved in. My assignment was changed to Saigon, where I was to be in charge of psychological warfare against North Vietnam and its army.

I was not opposed to our participation in Vietnam, but I was greatly opposed to losing my great job in Hamburg. At that time, Ambassador Bruce was in Washington and weighed in on my behalf, since I had accompanied him to Hamburg on occasion and he knew of my connections there and knew that my German was nearly bilingual. Despite the clout one would have suspected he had in Washington, nothing could be done. My choice was go or resign my commission, a solution I seriously considered. After I had officially received my orders, I was offered a dream job with a major defense contractor at triple my salary and with an unlimited expense account to travel around the world seeking good investment possibilities. Since I had my orders in hand, I considered it a form of desertion to resign from the Foreign Service at that juncture, even though I thought I had more than paid my patriotic dues in World War II. My decision to stay the course turned out to be a wise one and led to my having a far more interesting, if at times hair-raising, career than would have been the case had I gone to Hamburg and then fallen into a normal FSO career cycle. In fact my Foreign Service career became so unorthodox and atypical that I never once used the two titles the Foreign Service had, along the way, bestowed on me: consular officer, and secretary in the Diplomatic Service of the United States.

One great thing about returning home in 1962 was the chance to see more of my parents of whom I had seen little since 1946. During the war, my father had joined the Harvey Company in Los Angeles where, among other products, he designed and manufactured engine cowlings and other parts for military aircraft. He left Harvey soon after the war and went into agricultural aviation, in California's upper San Joaquin Valley, where he had a crop-dusting operation and where he modified war surplus Stearmans for that purpose. In that enterprise he invented agricultural equipment, including a revolutionary mower that used moving upper and lower blades, making it far more efficient and powerful than those in common use with just one set of blades moving over stationary teeth. For some reason, this very practical invention never was manufactured. Knowing my father, he probably didn't even patent it. In 1955 he had a yearning to go back to his old creation, Lockheed Aircraft Corporation. Although he knew the president, he typically did it the standard way by going to Lockheed's personnel office. There he filled out a form that had an entry "Prior position at Lockheed, if any" that he filled out "president." The personnel officer then called the front office noting that he may have a nut case on his hands who claims he was once president of Lockheed. He was told, "This could only be Lloyd Stearman. Send him up." He spent the next thirteen years having the time of his life doing what he liked doing best as a senior design specialist working on a wide variety of projects from an early version of VTOL (vertical take-off and landing) jet fighters, to space reentry vehicles. I even heard that he was a coinventor of the space program's weightless simulator.

When he retired from Lockheed in 1968, he formed another Stearman Aircraft Company in the hope of manufacturing his latest design, essentially an improved agricultural plane. He designed it to have three interchangeable modules, making it a small passenger plane and a small cargo plane, in addition to being a super crop duster. It was in essence mainly a larger version of the Stearman Hammond. Declining health unfortunately stymied his being able to carry his design to manufacturing. For years he had become very attached to a series of Siamese cats. I have always thought that cats were the pet of choice of thinking people. After a lingering illness, he died of prostate cancer in 1975. During his funeral service in Northridge, California, a flight of several Stearmans flew over in tribute. The *New York Times* ran a full-column obituary and *Time* magazine had one of its short "Milestones" obituaries. Later, my mother even received an obituary from a newspaper in a town in the extreme southern tip of South America. Here is what my father's full-column obituary in the *New York Times* (April 5, 1975) had to say about my father's time at Lockheed:

> In 1955, he returned to Lockheed, as a designer. "I'm happier than I ever was as president," he told an interviewer. He designed the swing wings for the F-111 fighter-bomber and worked on vertical take-off and landing rockets to loft men into space, ion-propelled craft that may one day orbit Jupiter and re-entry vehicles built of columbium to withstand high friction temperatures. In designing spacecraft, he found himself working with problems he foresaw

in 1930 [in a *Denver Post* interview]. He predicted that by 1980 Americans "will have rocket-shaped aircraft that will travel at such speed they will be able to circle the earth in an hour."

Differences Between Americans and Europeans

My knowledge of Europe and Europeans is obviously dated, since I left that continent forty-eight years ago, although I have subsequently returned a few times. I believe that, for the most part, my observations remain reasonably valid. I readily admit, however, that there are substantial risks in generalizing about more than seven hundred million Europeans from Russia west to Portugal, since each European country obviously has distinct and sometimes markedly different characteristics and backgrounds. As with any generalization I make in this book about people, I admit there could be millions of exceptions. (This also holds true for the some 300 million Americans about whom I make sweeping generalizations.) This does not discourage my penchant for making those sweeping generalizations, though. I best know the more developed countries of Central and Western Europe and of the United Kingdom, and my generalizations apply to them more than to other European countries.

Generally to a far greater extent than Americans, Europeans value security. My theory explaining this is that Europeans, with the exception of the Swiss and the Swedes, all have been subject to security-shattering economic dislocations and war or revolution on their soils in recent history. In the United States, this experience of violence generally applies only to our former Southern states in the Civil War as well as to the economic upheavals experienced by the nation during the Great Depression. Thus, security-minded Europeans are willing to pay taxes far higher than in the United States to ensure having adequate broad health care, a reliable pension, good unemployment insurance, and tuition-free education for their children through university (including graduate studies like law and medicine). Americans have generally been far more willing to take the chance of being able to afford these benefits in our free enterprise system with its relatively low tax rates. However, the generous European social benefits are, to some extent, bound to be reduced in many countries in light of global economic setbacks beginning in 2008. European countries are discovering their extensive social safety nets need reducing, that they are more generous than can be afforded. In the spring of 2010, Greece—where, for example, some are able to retire in their early fifties—provided a prime example of extravagant social benefits leading a country to financial ruin. (More-frugal Germany is helping bail out Greece.) Paring back social benefits has led to union-incited strikes in Greece, France, and elsewhere, which, along with popular opposition, doesn't make these needed changes easy. In France, for example, the proposal to raise the retirement age from sixty to sixty-two generated widespread strikes in that country. (In the United States, it is being proposed that the retirement age for our much-less-generous Social Security be raised from sixty-five to sixty-seven.)

One very distinct difference that I noticed immediately and still notice is that Americans, on the whole, seem more inscrutable than Europeans and others. Although, as noted in Chapter 1, my family has been in this country since the late seventeenth century, I usually find it difficult, if not impossible, to know what my fellow citizens are really thinking. When I am with Europeans and some others, though, I immediately get vibes that convey to me what that person is thinking of me. That rarely happens with native-born Americans. In one important respect, this is a great advantage, since it enables Americans to work and live more harmoniously together, since they relate to each other far less candidly or intimately and there are thus fewer points of friction. When I mention this phenomenon to Europeans, they all know exactly what I'm saying; however, frustratingly, my fellow citizens never seem to understand what I'm talking about.

In returning to this country, I was surprised and disturbed to discover the tension that seems to exist between men and women, which seems to worsen with time. This I found in stark contrast to Europe where men and women always seemed to genuinely like each other. I noticed any number of marriages and relationships in this country where couples simply don't seem to like each other. No wonder the divorce rate is so high here. (On the other hand, it has also become high in some European countries, such as nominally Catholic Austria.) I ascribe the difference in relationship to the fact that European women seem more feminine and the men more masculine than they seem in this country. I have been impressed that European women who have risen to high positions, of which there are quite a number, somehow manage to retain essentially feminine natures. I also have noticed a certain amount of insecurity in relationships here that lead to manifestations of jealousy that are much less common in Europe. (I am blessed, however, at having married a wonderful American woman who is surely one of the least jealous women in the world.)

The thing that I missed most coming home to the United States was the kind of broadly encompassing, prolonged serious conversation that one could experience in homes, bars, cafés, bistros, cantinas, or *Gasthaeuser* from Moscow to Madrid. With some exceptions, Americans seem inclined to avoid such conversations and nearly always shy from prolonged discussion of anything serious, be it social problems, literature, music, art, politics, history, or simply gossip. (Americans seem to prefer small talk, which I, alas, have never mastered.) I take it that, in general, they would rather spend their time on other, more useful, pursuits. Of course, it is true that these European conversations could at times well reflect a lack of knowledge on the part of some or all of the participants and could indeed turn out to be a waste of time. Still, I always found it an entertaining pastime and I miss it. I also have noticed that, unlike most Europeans, Americans seem to think it rude to look directly at people they don't know. This was most graphically illustrated one day as I was taking a bus in Georgetown. A young woman struggled on board carrying a huge toy panda that seemed almost as large as she was. I was absolutely fascinated by this scene but noticed that, incredibly, no one else was paying the slightest attention to her. Another difference is that when a European is leaving and saying goodbye, he will inevitably turn around one more time to wave. It was thus disturbing to Europeans to say goodbye to an American and then turn around to see that their host had already gone back into the house. Also when they saw someone off on a train, Europeans would wave until the train was out of sight.

As I noted in the Preface, when I first returned to the United States after nearly eighteen years of absence, I asked myself, "What are all these nice people doing in this nasty world?" More than forty-eight years later, I am still struck by how fundamentally decent, and yes, nice, most Americans seem to be. In Europe I could identify Americans at a considerable distance by their open and friendly facial expressions. Europeans and most others have closed, more serious expressions than we do, which reflect a more-reserved, less-sociable nature than we enjoy. One theory of mine as to why Europeans are less inclined to appear friendly is the relative permanence of most of their communities that discourages people from making friends with someone who might long live close by and have to be coped with for a long time. Our highly mobile society encourages more spontaneity in making friends since there is little danger of our being stuck for very long with such casually acquired friends. I also have noticed that while Europeans usually have one or more close friends in whom they can fully confide, we Americans often do not. This is especially true of men. In this country, there are two salient commandments: Thou shalt not be unhappy and Thou shalt not be unsuccessful. Thus, the occurrence of any setbacks is better not mentioned. Since most of us at one time or other are unhappy or unsuccessful, Americans are inclined only to confide in total strangers they meet on buses, trains, or airliners. Some, on the other hand, choose to confide in psychiatrists or other therapists. (A bit of counsel: psychiatric social workers are likely to be more empathetic [and much cheaper] listeners than psychiatrists. I know because I married one of the former.)

I believe that our more open facial expressions reflect a fundamental decency, fairmindedness, and charitableness that can be found in no other culture I know of. I am talking about the vast majority of Americans, but certainly not all Americans, many of whom, like people everywhere, obviously leave much to be desired. Most Europeans condescendingly tend to regard Americans as naïve, and I have frequently felt compelled to disabuse them of this mistaken notion. One British acquaintance of mine put it more diplomatically and somewhat more accurately when he observed that Americans tend to be "innocent," not naïve. This, I believe, is due to our generally having led more sheltered existences in the

United States that, next to Switzerland and perhaps Iceland, is the world's oldest democracy. That has provided us unparalleled political and social stability and security, the last with exceptions noted above. Therefore, we have been more inclined to think the best of people, even when not always justified. This tendency is changing with the times. Europeans, on the other hand, are inclined to be more cynical than are Americans. As I used to tell my students, cynicism and naïvete are but opposite sides of the same coin of unreality. This is why when I mention the naïve cynicism of Europeans it is not an oxymoron. A typical manifestation of this is an inclination to see base motives, conspiracies, and underhandedness where none actually exists.

I have talked to many Europeans who, while expressing gratitude for our postwar economic assistance to them, have insisted that we actually extended this aid only in our own national political interest. This view was usually expressed with regard to our Marshall Plan, proposed in 1947, for the economic recovery of Western Europe; this Plan was highly successful and effectively blocked the rise of Communism in Western Europe. In addressing this point, I would readily admit that this plan was most certainly greatly in our national interest, but also that essential popular, and, therefore, political, support of the plan was in large measure due to the innate generosity of the American people. As an example of this generosity, I always cited the millions of CARE packages unselfishly sent by individual Americans to hard-pressed Europeans. For instance, Eva's family in Austria received very welcome CARE packages from a simple Midwestern schoolteacher who certainly could not have had much money to spare.

One salient asset I brought home from Europe was the ability to enjoy simple pleasures in life that are generally common to Europeans. I sometimes think that we live to work whereas Europeans work to live. By this I mean Europeans have an ability to get the most out of leisure time, which they seem to treasure more than do we in that they demand, and get, much more of it than we usually have. For as long as I can remember, most people in the United States have not had more than two weeks of vacation a year, largely with the exception of government workers and educators, and many seldom take even two weeks at a time. Often when they take any time off, they're only partial vacations, since they remain in constant contact with their workplaces via cell phones and Blackberries. I remember my Austrian father-in-law who headed a small but eventually prosperous company producing metal fencing: he took two weeks or more off in winter and two or more in summer. During these vacations, he didn't even phone his company to see how things were going. People over there took real vacations and forgot about work, although perhaps this has now changed as Europeans pick up our bad habits. Of course, we often criticize Europeans for not having the limited vacations and longer working hours we have, since this decreases their economic efficiency.

How do Europeans spend their leisure time? Of course, they like to spend vacations in other places, preferably by the seashore. Other leisure time they spend by conversing with friends, as noted above, eating and drinking well, reading, listening to music, probably now watching TV, walking, hiking, and visiting museums and exhibits, all of which is easily affordable as well as pleasurable. I also discovered in Europe the pleasure of luxuriating in a hot tub bath (which also is more cleansing than a shower). After coming home, I realized that European men are far more interested in cultural pursuits than are American men, who often have to be dragged to cultural events by their wives. I believe that Europeans' enjoyment of leisure time still largely fits the above description, but things inevitably change with the times. For example, in the years after the war, Europeans were producing lovely and nationally individualistic popular music that made listening to the national variety of radio stations in Europe a pure delight. Now this charming and varied music has been largely replaced by little varied, unlovely, primitive assaults on aural nerves by rock music, a prime example of how Europeans and others manage to import the worst from our country along with fast food and sloppy attire. On the other hand, I also noticed when I lived in Europe a distinct adolescent streak in the way people tended to drive like unsupervised teenagers, far too fast for safety. Also Europe has lagged far behind the United States in instituting smoking bans in public places, like restaurants and bars. These are but two examples of where we seem to be more mature than Europeans, and there are others as well.

Class distinctions were far more pronounced in Europe than in the United States, and Europeans did not enjoy the considerable social mobility that characterizes Americans. Class distinctions manifested themselves most of all in speech, but there also were very minor differences that would not be noticed by most. For example, in Vienna addresses in districts used to be in Roman numerals. It was upper class to write them so that the horizontal bars on the top and bottom never touched the numbers in between. And there were a number of other such examples. I found the upper aristocracy (counts and above) to be the least obviously class-conscious and the upper-middle-class to be the most. Americans are loath to admit there is such a thing as an upper class in this country. We are all middle class—lower-, middle-, and upper-middle class. Classes here tend to be categorized according to income or wealth. I see many millionaires in this country I would place in the lower classes, which I do not define by material standards or even station in life. I do not, for example, equate lower class with working class (having a number of times been a worker myself and proud of it). Actually one of the most upper class of all my close friends, the late Peter Geyelin, had the least money of all my friends, but he had the most class. My parents, basically country people, moved easily among the rich and famous, but never considered themselves as belonging to any particular class (nor do I). My mother, for example, in later life included among her closest friends a widow living in an expensive home in an exclusive community and another widow living in a nice mobile home park.

I often have lamented that our greatest virtues seem to be little valued by Europeans and others. (Here I again largely exclude the British and Irish, who are more like us.) By this I mean our relative political maturity, our institutions of government, our legal and judicial system, and our sense of community, all of which, even considering their shortcomings, warrant emulating, but which, alas, are rarely forthcoming in Europe or in other countries. One reason why I could never again live in Europe or in any other country is that only in the United States is it possible for relatively unimportant citizens to make a difference. Anywhere else I would feel hopelessly frustrated and resigned when it comes to changing anything. One feature of our system that should be cherished and never taken for granted is the influence ordinary people can organize to influence members of Congress, especially in the House of Representatives whose members are constantly running for office and who are most dependent on continuous constituent support. Nowhere else on earth would it have been possible, with little money or political clout, to thwart a powerful institution like our Navy, which my able associates and I have been able to do on occasion, in respect to protecting the battleships, as I have described above.

There is one development that seriously threatens our national unity and well-being: the increased use of Spanish across the board, threatening to make this a bilingual country with all the problems this entails, as exemplified by the highly damaging disunity this has created in Belgium. I find it abhorrent that ballots are often now in Spanish. Should anybody who does not know enough English to vote have the right to vote in this country? As I see it, there are only two beneficiaries to this creeping bilingualism: employers who want to save money by keeping Latino immigrants in low-paying jobs and self-styled Latino "leaders" and Latino institutions that can thrive only as long as Spanish-speaking immigrants remain unassimilated and linguistically separate from the rest of the American population—unlike all our previous immigrants. By eliminating incentives for learning English these institutions render a grave disservice to Latinos who are arriving in increasing numbers—many, alas, illegally, which is another problem to be solved. The only Spanish that should be officially propagated in this country is the motto, *Sin inglés, siempre pobre* (Without English, [you will be] always poor). Any law eventually passed to resolve our huge illegal immigration problem should include a provision requiring learning English. I am very fond of Spanish as a language, however. I find it both powerful and beautiful. I believe many Americans should learn it, preferably at younger ages.

We have a stark warning example in Europe of the mischief bilingualism can cause a country. Belgium has long suffered from the rancor between the Dutch-speaking Flemings and the French-speaking Walloons. In line with the growing animosity between the two, several years ago it was decided to split off a new university from Belgium's leading University of Louvain, founded in 1426, creating two separate institutions along language lines. The decision on dividing the library especially dramatized the utter foolishness of this move. Shortly thereafter, I encountered the Belgian ambassador at a reception in Washington and said, "Mr. Ambassador, you won't believe what they're saying about your country, namely that the Louvain library was to be evenly divided with every other book going to the new university, leaving, for example, each library with only half of book sets, such as encyclopedias." The ambassador embarrassedly replied, "I'm sorry to say that this is true." A far more serious problem is that bilingualism constantly carries the threat of actually dividing this country along language lines. The Belgian example should give us pause as English–Spanish bilingualism constantly increases with its attendant expense and divisiveness.

One highly important and significant national characteristic that we enjoy is a genuine religiosity that is unique among the major Western powers, whereas in Europe Christianity is generally in a steady and disturbing decline (while Islam is clearly in the ascendancy). Unlike many Europeans, the vast majority of Americans believe in God and in an afterlife; to 65 percent of Americans religion is actually important (according to a 2009 Gallup poll). This is true despite the fact that the number of regular churchgoers has fallen off considerably in this country, at least among the leading denominations whose relaxing of standards and movement away from orthodoxy have driven people away, some to more-demanding denominations, such as Pentecostals and Mormons. Our religious beliefs provide us a moral compass and psychic stability that should not be minimized.

chapter 14

Vietnam

WHEN THE JETLINER I WAS IN REACHED THE SAIGON AREA, it began spiraling down onto the Tan Son Nhut airport and airbase to reduce the chances of being shot at by Communist forces surrounding the city—not a very encouraging introduction to my new post. When I got out of the plane and looked around, I was struck by the strong feeling that I was back in World War II southwest Pacific and that the twenty years since I left it had evaporated into thin air. The place had the look and smell of any number of wartime Pacific airbases. The canvas, Cosmoline, fuel, and other wartime smells; the lined-up old Douglas C-47s (DC-3) "Goony Bird" transport aircraft that had been our World War II workhorses; and the propeller-driven A-1 warplanes all served to transport me back in time. It was an eerie experience, to say the least.

When I was told that I was going to head the North Vietnamese Affairs Division of JUSPAO (Joint U.S. Public Affairs Office), I scurried around the State Department in search of expertise on North Vietnam. To my astonishment, we had no one working full-time on a country with which we had been de facto at war for nearly a year. There was one civil service officer who had this account, along with shared responsibilities for other countries. She was a good and competent officer, but had no experience with Communist countries. This typical gap in knowledge and experience among those in State and elsewhere who followed Indochina affairs accounts for many of the mistakes we made in that conflict, at least early on—of that I am convinced. I hated to admit it, but my being chosen to head the North Vietnam Division made perfect sense, given my years of dealing with Communist countries. Indeed, it turned out that I was the only officer in our Saigon mission with a Communist affairs background. It also helped that I was fluent in French, which enabled me to communicate with most educated Vietnamese. I left for Vietnam in early December 1965.

I soon found quarters in Saigon in a former French villa within walking distance of my office, which I had the great fortune to share with Tom Corcoran, deputy head of the political section; Corcoran had been living there for a while and had it well organized. Tom was an old Southeast Asia hand with an encyclopedic knowledge of the region. He was also a great raconteur from whom I learned a great deal. He had managed to hire the Vietnamese chef who had cooked for General Alessandrie, who had once commanded all the French forces in Indochina so we ate very well. JUSPAO, with which I was associated, unfortunately was largely staffed by officers from USIA with U.S. Army and Air Force officers also participating. The result was an organization that was predictably weak in substance and long on techniques. In all the JUSPAO meetings I attended, I rarely heard any discussion of *why* we were doing anything. It was almost always about *how* we were doing it. There were some exceptions, notably Don Rochlen, a maverick type with a real talent for bringing off public relations coups. I best remember his discovering that one of the leading Viet Cong (Vietnamese Communist, or VC) martyrs was actually still alive. He organized an Army operation to bring him back to his home village to demonstrate he hadn't died heroically after all. It certainly did help to discredit the VC.

It was obvious that my predecessor had known very little about North Vietnam or Communist doctrine and organization. He got most of his information about the North from Vietnamese who came south in 1954 to escape Communist rule in the North. More than ten years had elapsed since they left and much had changed in the interim. In other words, their knowledge about the North was hopelessly outdated. Our main vehicle for reaching the North Vietnamese civilians and soldiers were air-dropped leaflets. I went through all the leaflets then in the inventory and had a number of questions about them. I decided to show them to captured NVA soldiers to see their reaction. I was not surprised to note that they really didn't seem to understand the messages. For one thing there was a constant harping on the Chinese menace, which was consistent with the centuries-old Vietnamese anti-Chinese tradition, but which I doubted was then shared by most in the North. Chinese forces, especially artillery, were in large measure responsible for the decisive Communist defeat of French forces at Dien Bien Phu in 1954. China provided considerable military assistance to the North, and a lot of the consumer goods in the North, including most of the toys, seemed to come from China. In other words, I believed the people in the North had begun to look on the Chinese more as friends than as foes.

I set about to learn all I could about the North and its soldiers. One of the best sources of information was the Hanoi newspapers we received from the British

Consulate that, of course, reflected the Party's propaganda line, but also revealed some commonplace problems. These newspapers also turned out to be a prime source of intelligence. My very intelligent and diligent Vietnamese assistant and I set about to put out a new line of leaflets that I tested on NVA POWs. Some of them were incomprehensible to them, others seemed to have some meaning, although the case-hardened POWs were not about to recommend their use. The most successful leaflets were safe conduct passes in Vietnamese and English that looked official and could come in handy for any NVA soldier who had had enough and wanted to safely surrender. Others were designed to exploit problems in the North and demoralize the population.

The most popular leaflet we ever dropped over the North was a very good reproduction of a one dong (their currency) note with a message attached. We soon got reports that many were picking up these leaflets, cutting off the message and passing them off as legitimate currency. This prompted me to come up with the brilliant idea for throwing their economy into turmoil by dropping large numbers of much larger denominations with serial numbers and all the hallmarks of real money. Somehow the U.S. Treasury Department got wind of my scheme and killed it off decisively with the warning that, war or no war, the U.S. government never gets into the counterfeiting business. The leaflets we dropped were cut with certain exact dimensions that caused them to "auto rotate" around their longitudinal axis to give much longer range, making it possible for them to be released from aircraft at a much safer distance from the target than we would could get with just any old dimensions that simply fluttered down to the ground. The leaflets were loaded in bomb-like cases that opened up when dropped, scattering the leaflets all over the landscape. Leaflets were dropped over the North by fast fighter planes at high altitudes and several miles to windward from the target area.

The riskiest leaflet operations were those conducted over the Ho Chi Minh Trail, a network of paths and roads that began in Laos at the border of southern North Vietnam and continued south through Laos into Cambodia, with a number of branches into South Vietnam, Through it moved most of the NVA troops and supplies employed in attacking the South. I decided to meet with those brave lads who dropped leaflets over the Trail and paid a visit to their base somewhere up in II Corps. (I Corps was the northernmost region in the South and IV Corps was the southernmost.) After a briefing and pep talk that ended around 4 PM, I was prepared to get into my waiting chopper (helicopter) to return to Saigon when a group approached me. One of them asked, "You really believe in this operation don't you?" I replied. "Yes indeed. You are all doing a great job here." He then asked, "Well, sir, will you fly a mission with us tomorrow morning?" Prior to this I had been informed that the mission that took off that morning had not returned, which most likely meant it had been shot down. So far, the search aircraft had not found any sign of the plane or survivors. Clearly I had no choice, whether I liked it or not. These were my troops who risked their lives in implementing my plans and orders. Without hesitation I told them, "Tell my pilot that we're spending the night." I then spent the rest of the day until dinner being briefed on escape, evasion, and rescue techniques.

Early the next morning, I donned a flak jacket, an escape- and evasion-equipped jacket, a huge revolver, and a parachute. In getting into the old C-47 plane for the mission I felt like a fully armored medieval knight who had to be hoisted on to his horse: I practically had to be hoisted into the aircraft. I went forward to meet the pilot, a pleasant chap who had been in World War II and was still just a captain, not very encouraging. Also a bulkhead plate near the cockpit had U.S. Army Air Corps on it. I recalled that it changed into the Army Air Force in about 1943. In other words, we were flying in a very old plane. I expected to be flying over the numerous enemy troop concentrations on the Trail at about ten thousand feet. Instead the pilot wisely brought us in low in a long valley where we looked up at the mountain tops on each side. This way we came and went before anybody could get a really good shot at us. I knew we were being shot at because from a plane it looks like people rapidly turning flashlights on and off.

I assisted in shoveling leaflets into a chute from which they flew out of the plane. A couple of times I spotted leaflets I had ordered withdrawn because they were probably not very effective. I later made sure these were all destroyed. In combat situations, like many, I have to go more often. The plane's head was unfortunately located near the wide-open bay (the door had been removed to accommodate a machine gun that had just been removed) and the door to it had to be opened by standing next to the open bay, unbalanced by all the gear I was packing, and holding on to a longitudinal fuselage rib above with fingertips. Each trip to the head was scary, to say the least.

As soon as we mercifully finally landed at our base, the pilot jumped out of the plane and started to inspect the plane all over to see where we had been hit. Thanks to his skilled flying we didn't take a single hit. By then, I had dropped any concerns I had had about our pilot's ability. Still, I was glad to get in my chopper and head home. I can't say I really enjoyed adventures like this mission. I can't remember what happened to the ill-fated mission that had preceded ours. I expect they were all lost, which is why it has been blotted out of my memory like so many other unpleasant experiences. There were times when I really wondered if my whole operation was really worth risking lives. It was very difficult to assess how much good we were doing. True, enemy deserters were coming in waving our safe conduct passes, but not in large numbers. (By 1967, some seventy-five thousand VC and NVA soldiers had defected.) In the North we knew our leaflets upset the Communist authorities who ordered people not to pick them up. How much difference the whole program made in the overall scheme of things was certainly open to discussion. The pilots who flew our missions said we were bombing the enemy with b.s. Of course a lot of the ordnance we dropped on the enemy also made little difference in the overall scheme of things.

I frankly thought that my main contribution to our mission in Saigon was an improved knowledge of the enemy. We had built up quite a file of information on the enemy that at times came in handy. When the Army's MACV (Military Assistance Command Vietnam) acquired a state-of-the-art computer that filled a good-sized room, I was invited to check it out. I was to ask it any question I could think of, so I asked it for the number of times the enemy had called for special holiday truces. Wheels spun around. Lights went on and off and when everything came to a stop, nothing came out. I then invited the computer staff to come to my office and copy our files. (We had much information on truces.) They took us up on our offer and spent a couple days copying our files. I am sure that this huge computer had far less memory than any laptop today.

One of my JUSPAO colleagues, the late Douglas Pike, with the very best of intentions had done a great deal to mislead many on the nature of the enemy in his widely read book *Viet Cong* (1970). This book treated the National Front for the Liberation of Vietnam (NLF) as a real organization instead of the façade it really was. This was due to a woeful ignorance of Communist history. Communist fronts had their origin in a decision of the Moscow-dominated Comintern (Communist International) in July 1935, for Communist parties to enter into popular fronts (dominated by Communists) with other groups "against war and fascism." The first one was the French Popular Front (Front Populaire) formed in mid-1936 with Socialists and Radicals, which won the 1936 French elections and formed a government headed by a Socialist. From a Communist point of view it made eminently good sense to disarm the public by disguising its role in these fronts, since Communism was unacceptable to many. Ho Chi Minh, who, on orders from the Comintern, had founded the Indochinese Communist Party (ICP) in 1930, implemented the new Comintern line by forming the outwardly non-Communist Viet Minh Front in 1941.

In November 1945 the ICP went completely underground and officially (but not actually) ceased to exist, so anxious was Ho to "de-Communize" the Viet Minh Front. Despite all that, the Viet Minh Front became increasingly identified with Communism, which was costing it needed non-Communist support. Thus, in 1946, the Party also secretly created the Communist-dominated Lien Viet Front, which was created to attract those turned off by the Viet Minh Front. In 1955 the Party formed the Fatherland Front in order to appeal to more of the population than could the Lien Viet Front. In the meantime, in 1951 the Party had resurfaced as the Vietnamese Workers' Party (VWP), an anodyne title similar to those used by Eastern European Communist parties to disguise their true nature. As part of a major North Vietnamese effort to reestablish the Party in the South that had been decimated by Ngo Dinh Diem, the Party brought forth in January 1961 the National Front for the Liberation of South Vietnam popularly known as the NLF.

When the NLF's formation was announced from a number of places, Hanoi vehemently denied having anything to do with it. It was ostensibly an organization consisting of a number of non-Communist political organizations and groupings in the South designed to have a broad appeal to those who would be turned off by Communism. As Hanoi officially announced, on February 1961 the NLF was a grouping of "various political parties, peoples groups and religious and patriotic personalities." This deception worked remarkably well, and Doug Pike was one of those taken in by NLF propaganda. There was certainly enough material propagated in the South and elsewhere to fill a book, and that is what Pike did. There were also people in the embassy who believed that the NLF and its military wing popularly called by anti-Communists the VC could be enticed to split off from Hanoi, not realizing how completely the NLF and the VC were controlled by Hanoi. The enemy kept extensive records, which resulted in our capturing millions of pages of their documents. Those of the NLF were exclusively propaganda tracts and tactics with none ever directing any kind of operations. In other words, the NLF had no command authority. It was intrinsically a façade. Once the Communist side had won the war in 1975 and there was no longer a political need for deception, the NLF and its putative "leaders" were shelved and the Party again openly became the Communist Party.

Eventually Doug Pike realized that the NLF was a phony organization; when he retired from the Foreign Service, he established the Vietnam Center at the University of California at Berkeley, of all places. After some years, unwilling to cope with the increasingly hostile environment at Berkeley, Pike, his staff, and others loaded all the center's files and documents into a truck in the middle of the night and moved them to Texas Tech University in Lubbock where the center had a warm welcome and has flourished ever since. (After Doug's death it came under the able direction of Dr. Steve Maxner.) Thus did Doug, whom I always personally liked very much, make an outstanding, lasting contribution to our understanding of what actually transpired in Vietnam.

I had the great fortune to spend a fascinating evening with a former senior Communist officer, Colonel Chuyen, who headed the training unit of COSVN (Central Office for South Vietnam, Communist headquarters for the war in the South). By then he had been promoted to regimental commander and had hoped to get command of a division when he blotted his copy book by getting a local woman pregnant. I suspected there were probably additional reasons for Chuyen's setback. In any case, he came over to our side and was a goldmine of intelligence.

One evening in my quarters, while killing a bottle of good cognac, we had an intriguing conversation. (He spoke fairly good French.) He expressed surprise that our side never seemed to attack Communist installations or to lay ambushes along their lines of communications (LOCs). Thus the Communist side had pretty much a free ride throughout the country, and did not have to devote many assets for defense. On the other hand, we had to devote considerable resources to defend bridges, roads, and all our installations.

This conversation led me to come up with the idea of converting the thousands of trained enemy guerrilla and sapper troops who had deserted to our side to small teams for insertion into enemy territory to lay ambushes along their LOCs and attack their installations. This threat would surely tie down many troops and give us a substantial advantage. We would provide these teams with captured weapons and a week's supplies and then insert them by helicopter and retrieve them the same way after a week or so. The Marines had had excellent experience with their Kit Carson Scouts composed of defecting enemy troops, as were the Army-sponsored Armed Propaganda Teams that worked out very well when properly employed. So we knew we could depend, in large measure, on these defectors. When I tried to sell this simple, inexpensive concept to senior brass, American and Vietnamese, I ran into a brick wall. The Vietnamese generals insisted that these former VC could never be trusted. I explained that these teams would not be entrusted with guarding any of our installations and would be inserted into enemy territory where in the small chance they redefected back to VC units we would lose only some captured weapons, a radio, and a week's supplies. In point of fact, they invariably proved to be loyal and dependable, especially the Kit Carson Scouts, when put to the test.

I hate to say it, but I suspect senior U.S. officers were disinterested in a program that could be run by a colonel and would cost only peanuts at a time when we were spending more than a $1 billion a month (in 1966 dollars) on the war. In other words, it was a program too piddling to be bothered with. I still maintain that this scheme, plus the continuous presence of one or more battleships at relatively low cost, could have changed the course of the war decisively in our favor. I learned from the Vietnam experience that when one has too many resources, one is much less resourceful. I once, just half in jest, told the British ambassador in Saigon that if we gave the United Kingdom half a billion dollars a month to prosecute the war, the Brits would do as well as we were doing. He replied "Thanks, but no thanks."

On occasion and generally against my better judgment, I would go out on operations in order to be able to interrogate freshly captured enemy POWs before they had been worked over at the main interrogation center in Saigon. On one of these occasions I accompanied my old friend Rowland Evans of the well-known Evans and Novak column who wanted to see a bit of action. This was a fairly large operation in III Corps. We showed up at the line of helicopters that were ready to take troops into the landing zone (LZ). We were assigned a chopper, but soon became distracted by conversation, with the result that we missed our assigned chopper and took the next in line; Evans wound up in a seat by an open bay door with no seat belt. As the chopper jinked around to avoid enemy ground fire, poor Rowley had to wrap his arms around the seat back and hold on for dear life. We finally landed near a chopper that had just been shot down and which, we strongly suspected, was the one we should have been on. As we approached the downed chopper we saw a medic who was going through the dead pilot's pockets and who had just extracted his wallet from which photos of his wife and children tumbled out. For some reason, I always found something especially poignant about a dead soldier's boots, which the soldier had laced up and tied not long before he died.

One way to reach enemy troops in the southern delta areas was through boat-mounted loudspeakers. I decided to try this out on a Swift boat going down the Saigon River to the enemy-infested Rung Sat Special Zone. I had pretty well ascertained how this worked from a technical point of view and had no great incentive to go any farther. At this point, there came into view three PBRs (river patrol boats) returning to Saigon. These were the PT boats of the Vietnam War, and I was dying to drive one. (I had always wanted to drive a PT boat in World War II.) We hailed one that I, with great glee, drove back to Saigon. The next day I learned that a Swift boat had been attacked the day before in the Rung Sat Special Zone with 75-mm recoilless rifles, killing everyone on the bridge. I figured this had to be the Swift boat I had been on and that I would have been on the bridge when we hit the Zone. My Guardian Angel seems to have been working overtime. Actually it was a boyish whim that probably saved my life. I vowed to stay close to home more often in the future.

Saigon itself was anything but safe, and was infested with terrorists who liked most to attack the hotels where American troops were quartered. To protect them and other U.S. installations, barrels filled with concrete were positioned around the front to keep terrorist attacks at least some distance away. Favorite terrorist weapons, the IEDs (improvised explosive devices) of the Vietnam War, were bicycles with their frames filled with plastique charges that packed enough of a wallop to knock down the front of a fair-sized building. Cafés and bars had metal shutters and advertised themselves as providing "perfect safety." The one exception was the spacious wide-open verandas of the French-owned Hotel Caravelle that reportedly (probably accurately) was protected by paying off the VC. A favorite restaurant was the My Canh floating restaurant tied to a dock in the Saigon River. One evening it was hit with a Claymore mine, a circular mine that propelled numerous pellets horizontally, killing and wounding a number of people. When I was back in Washington at a reception at the Czech Embassy I encountered a correspondent friend who thought he was seeing a ghost, since he had heard I was killed in the My Canh attack. I never ate at the My Canh again without sitting on the river side ready to jump in it at the first sign of trouble.

One evening after work I went next door to the officers' club in the American-requisitioned Rex Hotel for dinner. Afterwards I came back to my office to discover a janitor trying to ream out my favorite pipe, given to me by my parents as a birthday present. I thought this was obviously a crude pretext for being in my office at that hour. I called security and had him held for questioning. It turned out that he was part of a terrorist squad that had lined our building with explosives due to be set off in a day or two. I lived in a residential area and in the some twenty months I spent in Vietnam I would guess that about three dozen people were killed by enemy action within three or four blocks of my quarters; most of these died in a rocket attack that hit a truck full of people. When I first arrived in country, one couldn't drive in any direction outside Saigon without risk of being shot at. This had improved somewhat by the time I left. One heard the constant sound of battle being waged around the city. At night there was a steady sound of explosions from H & I fire (harassment and interdiction) designed to discourage movement along known enemy routes and paths outside town. When I once went to Bangkok for R & R (rest and recreation), the absolute silence at night kept me awake.

There was much more terrorist activity in the countryside than in Saigon. Not long after I arrived, I learned that in a village not too far from Saigon two young women, a teacher and a nurse, were murdered by the VC because they were technically government employees. From 1964 to 1967 more than six thousand "government employees" such as hamlet chiefs, teachers, social workers, and nurses were assassinated by the VC. From 1957 to 1972, 36,775 civilians were assassinated and another 58,499 were abducted by the VC. Only about a quarter of them could be classified as government employees (*America in Vietnam* by Guenter Lewy, 1978). All this was designed to gain control through systematic intimidation and to discredit the Saigon government. This pervasive terrorism was hardly reported by the United States and other correspondents based in Saigon. I talked to many of them and they all told me that if they filed (or filmed) a story that was positive in respect to the U.S. and Vietnamese war effort, it was never used. Only negative stories (except those criticizing the enemy) wound up being used. The positive ones ended up in trash baskets or on the cutting room floor. (We have seen something similar in the Iraq War.) The result was that the American reading and TV-viewing public was badly misinformed about Vietnam, which contributed mightily to all the antiwar sentiment in the States. When I read what was being reported back to the United States I wondered if the correspondents who wrote them were really writing about the country I was in.

The most egregious atrocity of the war was hardly covered by our media. On January 30, 1968, during the Tet Offensive, Communist forces captured the old imperial capital of Hue in northern South Vietnam and held it for twenty-five days. Cadres with previously prepared lists of names on clipboards went from door to door arresting leading citizens of the community. In all, nearly six thousand people were led away, most likely to their deaths. Later a mass grave of some two thousand eight hundred bodies was discovered, with strong evidence that most had been buried alive. Moreover, on April 27, Hanoi took credit for this massacre, claiming that those executed were "hooligan lackeys who owed blood debts" to the people. In other words, this massacre was conducted as a matter of policy. The *New York Times*, which had the largest bureau in Vietnam, carried only a brief wire service piece on this atrocity. Its staff clearly didn't think it worthwhile to cover. In any case, this was largely a one- or two-day story in the U.S. media. I heard from an eyewitness about a television reporter who was present when a mass grave of Hue victims was discovered but refused to film it because he didn't want to disseminate what could become anti-Communist propaganda.

On March 16, 1968, members of an American Division company cold-bloodedly murdered nearly two hundred unarmed civilians, mostly women, children, and the elderly, in the hamlet of My Lai. First Lieutenant William Calley was held to be primarily responsible. The division kept this massacre a secret for a year. When it was finally exposed, there was a media coverage frenzy that went on and on. It was most certainly an outrage and unconscionable, but, unlike the Hue massacre, it was an aberration and completely against Army policy. In 1971 Calley was sentenced to life imprisonment. This sentence, due to an outcry on his behalf, was eventually reduced to parole. Back in the States when I would lecture on Vietnam at colleges and elsewhere, I would ask who had heard of My Lai and all hands would go up. When I asked who had heard of the Hue massacre, no hands went up. Such was the media impact back home.

There was always something negative to report about Vietnam. The Saigon regime was always pilloried for being corrupt and incompetent, which to some extent it surely was. And there were always accounts of military incompetence by both our troops and Vietnamese troops, the latter often being accused of avoiding combat, which they sometimes did. It is interesting how many Americans seemed to think there was something pristine about the discipline and determination of the Communist side compared with the corruption on our side. Little did they realize that corruption was far more widespread in the North than in the South because when everything, including the entire economy, is controlled by the regime, its cadres have countless opportunities to shake down peasants and others to enrich themselves. This corruption had gotten so bad that Ho Chi Minh himself had to go on the radio in 1967 to condemn this widespread practice. Of course, even if the American media knew about this, they never would have reported it.

One especially egregious example of our media's dereliction was their totally ignoring the Saigon regime's largely completing what was probably one of the most successful land reform programs in history, "Land to the Tiller," which by 1972 had made nearly every South Vietnamese peasant a landowner, greatly enriching the economy and strengthening support for President Thieu's regime. This incredible accomplishment was virtually ignored by the U.S. media. I was especially struck by how free everyone felt in Saigon, which was not only at war with a deadly enemy but which was virtually besieged. I was also struck by the fact that suspected VC terrorists often got a reasonably fair trial; some were actually acquitted. Of course none of this was ever reported. I am often wont to quote columnist George Will who wrote that to most of the media "*Good* news is an oxymoron." This certainly applied to Vietnam.

The coverage that was by far the most damaging to our cause in Vietnam occurred during the Tet Offensive. Tet, or the Chinese New Year as we called it, was to the Vietnamese our New Year, Christmas, and birthday all in one. Everyone received new clothes, gifts were exchanged, and special meals were prepared. During most Tets there was a kind of truce in the fighting and many troops would be on leave with their families. Tet in 1968 began on January 30. On this date the Communist side, in large measure the local VC, launched a major offensive to promote a general uprising of the population against the Saigon government, which it fully expected would succeed. These forces managed to penetrate or capture, or both, thirty-four provincial towns, sixty-four district towns, and all autonomous cites including Saigon—in short, nearly all of the cities and towns of South Vietnam. They penetrated Saigon itself and for a short time even occupied the grounds around the U.S. Embassy. The media incorrectly reported that they had occupied the embassy itself. This offensive obviously was an enormous media event, and the American public was bombarded with doom and gloom images of destruction and defeat. These images etched in peoples' minds played a key and continuing role in eroding American support for the war effort by seeming to indicate that the war was "unwinnable."

In reality the Communist side had shot its bolt, in effect. For example, many undercover VC cadre blew their covers by surfacing in support of the offensive and the expected "uprising" and suffered the consequences. Before long, the VC cum NVA troops were decisively defeated and driven out of all the towns and cities and of much of the territory they held. Instead of inspiring a popular uprising, the VC incurred the wrath of the people and greatly increased what had been weak popular support for the government. *The VC never recovered from this crushing defeat.* Thanks to U.S. media, however, this was scarcely reported, leaving a lasting impression that the offensive had succeeded. This attitude was typified by a leading TV star, the avuncular and very popular Walter Cronkite, who made a quick trip to Vietnam in late February 1968 after it was clear that the Tet offensive had been roundly defeated and the VC all but neutralized. Totally disregarding on-the-spot briefings he received to this effect, he returned to the United States and in a February 27 broadcast proclaimed that this offensive was an American defeat and that we should try to negotiate our way out of the war. President Johnson, after viewing this broadcast, reportedly declared, "If I've lost Cronkite, I've lost middle America."

Thus, thanks to our media, the Tet offensive, which was militarily a decisive defeat for the Communist side, was a significant psychological and political victory that contributed greatly to the ultimate success of the Communist cause in Vietnam. The significant demise of the VC led to a rapid acceleration of pacification of the countryside, which ensured the success of the land reform program described above. The great advance in security was dramatized in 1969 by a successful bicycle race from one end of the country to the other, something unthinkable a year or so before.

One of the correspondents I came especially to like and respect was Dwight Martin—I believe he worked for *Newsday*. I persuaded him to cover a positive story if I could find one. Not long thereafter, I got a call from one of our advisers to the Regional and Popular (militia) Forces (RF/PF, or "Ruff Puff," as we called them). He gave me an especially stirring account of how a Popular Force unit in a village in the Delta some distance southwest of Saigon had turned back a sizeable Communist attack the previous afternoon. Moreover, the village itself was something of a model of good program implementation. I called Dwight and we drove to the RF/PF headquarters to meet my U.S. Army contact there. He asked if I wanted to go down in his jeep or in my red Volkswagen. I was shocked, since I had assumed we would be going down to the village in a chopper. Evidently the poor cousins RF/PF didn't rate a helicopter. Dwight was still game to go, so I believed I had to go with him despite our having to drive through some fairly insecure areas, and the fact I had only two or three months left in my tour.

We took off in my car. I had a Colt .45 cal. automatic on my lap and the officer with us had an M-16 rifle. Dwight was unarmed. Before long the road we were on became disturbingly empty, always a bad sign. I picked up speed despite the potholes in the road to discourage being shot at. The village was indeed a good story. Not only had the PF unit fought bravely and well in repelling the recent attack, but the village itself had successfully implemented health and social programs that the Saigon regime kept trying to propagate in the countryside with varied success. All in all, it was a great success story and should have made good copy. (The photo of me on the cover of this book was taken at this time near the village.) As the afternoon lengthened, we decided we had better head back to Saigon before the VC began to close in, as they usually did just before dusk. On the way back I drove as fast as the road would permit, and we were shot at. Of course, I was enormously relieved to make it back to Saigon. That evening Dwight filed his story. Two days later, he told me it had been rejected. Obviously it was far too positive. So I could well understand why the media stuck to good old tried-and-true negative reporting.

I would like to describe an especially valued journalist good turn, now. For some reason I was out in the "boonies," in an area usually controlled by the VC after dusk, when we had a flat tire. My driver went to get the spare and discovered it had been stolen. We were in deep trouble. Come evening we were going to have to crawl into the underbrush and try to hide. Then along came CBS correspondent Dan Rather with a camera crew who rescued us and maybe even saved our lives. I have always wanted to thank Dan again for this, but never had the chance. Anyway, many, many thanks, Dan! This gives me a chance to say something nice about a famous correspondent.

The best description of the perverse role played by U.S. media can be found in what I consider to be the best of all books on the Vietnam War, *Vietnam at War, The History 1946–1975*, by Lt. Gen. Phillip B. Davidson USA (Ret.) (1988), from which I now quote:

> One correspondent with several years experience in Vietnam, Robert Elegant [whom I personally knew and greatly respected], who scathingly reproached his colleagues not only for their misleading reports, not only on the Tet offensive, but on the entire war. He wrote, "never before Vietnam had the collective policy of the media—no less stringent term will serve—sought by graphic and unremitting distortion—the victory of the enemies of the correspondents' own side. . . ." [T]here was the herd instinct. Most correspondents reported the war negatively because the other newsmen covered it that way. As Elegant points out, the reporter who refused to accept and report the negative views of his journalistic brethren risked professional and social ostracism. . . . But under these surface reasons for misleading the American people about the Tet offensive ran a deeper stream. Elegant in answering to his own question, "why was the press . . . so superficial and so biased?" writes, "Chief among many, I believe, the politicization of correspondents by the constantly intensifying clamor over Vietnam in Europe and America. The press was instinctively 'against the government'—at least reflectively, for Saigon's enemies." The television coverage of the Tet offensive revealed the awesome power of that medium to influence national events. On

18 July 1982 Tom Wicker, the columnist appeared on . . . [a] television program with . . . panelists [David] Brinkley, Sam Donaldson and George Will. This group, widely variant in ideological outlook, unanimously agreed that it has become impossible for a nation to fight a war if the blood and carnage of the battlefield appears nightly on the country's television screens. George Will cited the Battle of Antietam in the American Civil War as an example, saying, "if the North could have seen that battle in living color, it would have elected McClellan president, and we would be two nations today."

I harp on the perverse role of the press during the Vietnam War because it played a key role, if not the leading role, in ensuring a Communist victory and a tragic end to this conflict.

There was a pleasant side to living in Saigon, despite all. There were excellent restaurants, most of which were French or Chinese. There didn't seem to be many Vietnamese restaurants. Actually I found the Vietnamese cuisine to be more complex and interesting than Chinese food. Among its more exotic dishes, for example, was a soup made from the stomachs of baby ducks. The Vietnamese were very fond, as am I, of their national soup, *pho* (pronounced "fuh"), which they bought from soup pushcarts pushed from street to street with their owners clapping sticks together to signal their approach. A favorite way of getting around was in *cyclos*, a kind of rickshaw pulled by a bicycle. It was good to pop into one when it rained because they had folding roofs. It was always an interesting experience to go the movies at the Rex Theater. The subtitle captions (for U.S. films) were in French, Vietnamese, and Chinese, and covered half the screen. Also there were always large tame rats scurrying around, sometimes over ones' feet. More than once I observed rats sitting in the aisle actually watching the film (and I'm not making this up).

Horse races were always fun. Actually those running were more like ponies than horses and the races were fixed to a comical extent. I remember one horse being about four lengths ahead in approaching the finish line when the jockey suddenly reined his mount to a stop, coming in last. He wasn't supposed to win and apparently remembered only at the last moment. I also experienced, for the one and only time, a cockfight; this fight was attended by Vice President Nguyen Cao Ky, who had a cock in the fight.

I liked walking around Saigon. There was the unforgettable, ever-present sweet-sour smell of rotting garbage in the street gutters. The little houses on the streets were open and one could look inside to see the family altars dedicated to ancestors with a picture of one or two of them displayed. Then there were the graceful women and girls in their lovely *ao dais*, always a pleasure to watch. The numerous tall trees in Saigon were filled with cicadas that all in a chorus would loudly chirp then fall silent. South Vietnam was actually a quite beautiful country with great beaches at Vung Tau southeast of Saigon and farther north at Nha Trang and Danang. In the highlands there was lovely Dalat on a sizeable lake and with a great old French hotel that had clearly seen better days. It had been a great honeymoon spot. I was surprised to learn that malaria was largely confined to the highlands; we had to take antimalaria pills before going up there. Curiously malaria did not seem to be a problem in the lowlands. I found the Vietnamese I encountered to be intelligent and well-mannered having benefited from their Confucian tradition and French cultural influence both of which promoted education and learning and respect for those who were educated. We could train a Vietnamese who spoke adequate English to fly as quickly as we could train an American. These people definitely were anything but backward.

One day I got a call from the embassy's cultural attaché asking me if I would be willing to teach a course on international organizations at the local university's school of law two hours a week. In my ignorance I felt I could spare two hours and asked if the students understood English. I was assured they did, so I foolishly accepted, not realizing until later that an hour of college-level instruction requires at least three or four hours of preparation. At my first class I also discovered that most did not speak or understand English, but all were fluent in French. My French was rusty, and the course required a vocabulary I had hardly ever used. Also my French predecessor had spent half a semester on the UN Security Council alone, whereas I had planned to spend only one session on it. In other words there was no syllabus I could use, so I had to start from scratch. I decided to concentrate on international organizations that would actually be of use to Vietnamese, like the International Rice Institute at Los Baños in the Philippines. I still don't see how I got through this experience in French.

My European experience gave me this advantage: I knew to show up for class wearing a suit and tie, no matter how hot the weather, and I was neither surprised nor unprepared when I would enter the classroom and everyone would rise and remain standing until I told them to sit down. Then, when the class ended they would stand again until I left the room. I went along with all this assuming they were products of French secondary education. French education, which was very good, encouraged formality; it had remained in place after the French occupation ended. Mind you, these were all older graduate-level students in a law school.

We had some very well-qualified professional American professors in Saigon, most of whom, however, quickly lost students when they appeared before their classes in a sport shirt and told the students not to get up when they entered the room because that was not what American students did. They usually wound up teaching a handful of students in their apartments. This was a great pity because they had far more to offer than I did. The students simply didn't take them seriously for generally superficial reasons. Also, however, most of these professors knew only English, which posed a legitimate problem for a number of students. I wound up with so many students that some had to listen to my lectures through the large open windows on the side, although I really did not believe I was that good. I had civil servants and army officers among my students. I always wondered what happened to them when the Communists took over Saigon in April 1975. One of my army students was badly wounded before the class ended. I really did cherish this experience, in the end, and it made my later teaching at Georgetown University seem easy by comparison.

In September 1967, after more than twenty months in country, I returned to the United States. I stopped on the way home in Western Europe and Great Britain to brief some of our embassies on Vietnam. Among those I briefed in London was Adm. John S. McCain Jr. who commanded the NATO naval forces. We met not long before his son, Lt. John McCain, was shot down over North Vietnam; the younger McCain remained a POW in Hanoi until March 1973. He later became a U.S. senator and in 2008 ran for president of the United States. In 1968, Admiral McCain became Commander of all U.S. forces in the Pacific, which made him our most senior officer in the Vietnam War at that time. At other missions, I repeatedly discovered that the only officers who were trying to explain our war effort were political officers, since the USIS officers, with exceptions here and there, were liberals who didn't believe in the war and didn't want to explain it.

Chapter 15

Back in the State Department, White House Years Begin

I T WAS GOOD GETTING BACK TO THE STATES in one piece after more than twenty months in Vietnam. I was immediately faced with the problem of how I could avoid serving in USIA. Instead I was assigned to head the Indochina branch of the Voice of America, which was under USIA but was a separate entity. At least this kept me out of USIA and gave me a fair amount of freedom to work with State's Vietnam Working Group.

The main problem I encountered was a Voice of America policy to appear as objective as possible in choosing news items in order to preserve its credibility. The problem was that some of these news items were not only inaccurate, but actually harmful to our interests. I had a number of fights about this, but on the whole was not terribly interested in what went on in Voice of America. To me the real action was at State. After more than twenty months in this ambiguous bifurcated situation, an outstanding officer whom I had gotten to know in Vietnam, William Richard "Dick" Smyser, helped me get a job at State as head of the North Vietnam section in the Bureau of Intelligence and Research (INR), which made me a member of the "intelligence community," an eye-opening experience.

I had been in INR only about two months when I became involved in an incident that brought me my only, albeit brief and limited, moment of fame. A former acquaintance from my Soviet Desk days, a KGB agent with the Soviet Embassy by the name of Boris Davydov, invited me to have lunch with him at the Bird and Beef Restaurant on Thomas Circle on August 18, 1969. We were having a light conversation catching up on what we had been doing since we saw each other last, when I got a stiff jolt. I had a forkful of fish halfway to my mouth when Davydov casually asked me, "What would the U.S. do if we took out the Chinese nuclear installations at Lop Nor?" I put my fork down, thought for a moment then replied, "The U.S. would be gravely angered by such a clear threat to world peace, but would probably take no action." We then finished eating and parted company. I got back to State as quickly as possible and wrote the memcon (memorandum of conversation) of my life. It went immediately to the secretary of state and from there to the White House.

The reaction was akin to a low-yield nuke going off in one of the State Department's courtyards. The first thing I heard from the secretary's office was a scolding for having taken a position on such a serious issue without consulting anyone. I countered that no reply would have given the wrong impression. As it later turned out, State's policy guidance was taken verbatim from my memcon. In his memoir, *White House Years*, Henry Kissinger, then the president's national security adviser, described the reaction in the White House: "I took this sufficiently seriously to convene a meeting in San Clemente [the "Western White House" in California where the President then was] on August 25 of the Washington Special Actions Group (WSAG), the NSC subcommittee for contingency planning and crisis management. I asked them to prepare contingency plans for American policy in case of a Sino-Soviet war." This incident was taken especially seriously because the CIA a week or so earlier had predicted just such an attack, given the high degree of tension between China and the USSR as the result of Chinese border violations. As it turned out, the same threat was soon put out by the Soviets in New Delhi and elsewhere. Davydov's query was clearly the gambit in a war of nerves aimed at Peking (as Beijing was then called). Davydov sought me out because I would know how to handle his question, but posing it to someone on the Soviet desk would have been a kind of demarche that the Soviets wanted to avoid, since they weren't really being serious. Incidentally, my encounter with Davydov was described in two other books in addition to Kissinger's.

When I discovered that all in the chain of command above me in our section of INR were liberal "doves" who didn't believe we should ever have been in Vietnam, I knew I was in for trouble down the line—and I was right. I had a good group of junior officers under me who were not always "hawk" war supporters, but who did their jobs professionally. I did my best to get the good ones promoted, even if they disagreed with me on occasion. Incidentally, I always told all the officers who ever worked for me that to me the most insidious form of disloyalty was to agree with me when they actually thought I was wrong. I had difficulty getting my views passed up the line to the secretary, but I did get views out by sending my analyses to Dick Smyser in the White House and through correspondents who covered national security affairs in Washington. I would pass them unclassified information on "background"—that is, with no attribution to me.

At one point I predicted that the Communist side in Vietnam would offer to release the hundreds of POWs it held if we withdrew our troops. This was pooh-poohed by senior officers working on Vietnam as well as by my superiors in INR. So I shared this view with a few correspondents. When Hanoi indeed made this offer, a *Washington Post* correspondent, Chalmers Roberts, wrote an op-ed piece stating that not all State Department diplomats were "striped pants cookie push-ers." One of them, the op-ed piece went on, who didn't want any publicity but whose initials were "WLS," knew what he was doing and predicted the latest North Vietnamese negotiating ploy. This led to a guessing game in the department, with some guessing it was Dick Smyser (mentioned earlier), except that his initials are WRS. At that point, I believed I should set the record straight and did.

We were long troubled by the enemy's extensive use of Laos and Cambodia for military operations against South Vietnam. Laos was the main locus of the famed Ho Chi Minh Trail, the enemy's principal network of lines of communi-cations, whereas Cambodia was used as a base area with supply dumps, training facilities, and the main command structure, the Central Office for South Vietnam (COSVN). For domestic political reasons, U.S. operations against enemy forces in these countries had to be handled with care to avoid accusations of "broaden-ing the conflict." In 1969 it was decided to "Vietnamize" the war by withdrawing U.S. combat troops and turning over the actual fighting to Vietnamese troops. In preparation for this, U.S. Army leaders felt the need to deal a blow to key enemy sanctuaries in Cambodia. They were especially concerned about estimated large quantities of war materiel reaching enemy supply dumps from the Cambodian port of Sihanoukville (now Kompong Sam).

In late 1969 those of us in the "intelligence community" dealing with Vietnam met at CIA headquarters in Langley, Virginia, just outside Washington, DC, to draft a SNIE (Special National Intelligence Estimate) that was mainly cen-tered on the Cambodian Sihanoukville port problem. The representatives from the Army-dominated Defense Intelligence Agency (DIA) whose obvious objective was justifying an incursion of Cambodia, made a strong, and to me convincing, case that large amounts of war materiel were being received at this port and trans-ported to enemy supply dumps farther north in Cambodia. The senior CIA ana-lysts, reflecting the liberal bias of the analytical side of the CIA, clearly opposed a U.S. incursion and therefore downplayed the port's importance to the enemy, stating, in fact, that hardly any war materiel was entering the port. At this point a junior CIA analyst sitting against the wall (we principal players sat at a large table) stood up and had the temerity, or the exceedingly poor judgment, to point out that the CIA had received a substantial amount of intelligence showing that the port was indeed receiving large shipments of enemy supplies. The senior CIA par-ticipants all turned and glared at the poor young officer, clearly new at the game, and soundly if silently chastened this analyst, who slunk down in his chair and was never seen again at any interagency meeting. (I assumed he got the sack, but he may only have been put in his place.)

When our troops entered Cambodia on April 29, 1970, they discovered that a large percentage of the supplies captured had indeed come through Sihanoukville, and even the DIA estimates, which I thought might have been somewhat deliberately inflated, were low. We also captured about a million pages of very revealing intelligence. Unfortunately, on May 1 President Nixon indicated we hoped to capture COSVN headquarters. Those of us in the know were aware that this would be impossible since this installation was scattered over a large area and the principal generals and their staffs rotated around, making it impossible to capture them. I kept wondering what on earth prompted Nixon to make this statement, then one day my office received several large briefing-type photos of what were clearly former French rubber plantation buildings labeled "COSVN." When I stopped laughing, I wanted to cry. Somebody must have used these photos to convince Nixon that COSVN occupied a building complex that could be captured, instead of what it really was: a series of dugouts and huts scattered over more than forty square miles. The Cambodian incursions were well executed by both U.S. and Vietnamese troops and inflicted severe and lasting damage to the enemy's war effort in South Vietnam. Unfortunately, however, they resulted in widespread antiwar demonstrations in the United States especially on college campuses, most notably at Kent State University in Ohio where rioting students burned the ROTC building and later were fired on by ill-trained, ill-equipped, and ill-disciplined National Guard troops, killing four students and injuring nine. Most Americans, however, approved the Cambodian incursions.

I had entered the "Community" actually believing that there was something pristinely objective about intelligence analyses. After two years of inside intelligence exposure, I came to fully realize how politicized the whole process was. I left INR disillusioned. Subsequent dealings with the CIA and INR while in the White House only reinforced my disillusionment. I then resolved to find a better way to do intelligence if given the chance, and that chance came sooner than I could have hoped. Not surprisingly, in January 1971 my dovish superiors finally moved to get rid of me and to sink my career at the same time. I'll call my rating officer "Y" and his boss "X." X directed Y to give me an unsatisfactory efficiency rating, which, among other things, was against all precepts, since X was only the reviewing officer. In all my twenty plus years in the Foreign Service I had only received "very good" to "outstanding" ratings. This one was so bad and so completely unjust that it threatened to end my career. Good, reliable, and true Dick Smyser, thank God, came to the rescue and asked me to join the NSC staff, which I accepted instantly; I have been eternally grateful for his offer. He saved my career. After having thought they had permanently fixed my wagon, imagine X's and Y's chagrin when they learned I had gone over to the White House. Getting sacked from INR actually turned to be great for my career. Ten years later, (then-Ambassador) X finally got his comeuppance when, right after Ronald Reagan's election, he encountered in a State hallway a member of the Reagan State transition team, John Carbaugh, a former Senator Jesse Helms aide, who told him that he had heard all about him "from Bill Stearman." At that point X knew his career was finished, and it was. Justice finally, if belatedly, had been served. Or as they say in Washington, "What goes around eventually comes around."

Dick Smyser headed the Indochina staff of NSC and I, in effect, initially worked for him as the NSC's expert on the enemy in Vietnam. We all worked for famed Dr. Henry A. Kissinger, which was quite some experience. Dick dealt directly with Kissinger, whom we all called HAK, and had a far better rapport with him than I could ever establish. As soon as I was established in the White House, I wanted to file a grievance procedure against X for having violated Foreign Service precepts in dictating my unfair efficiency rating, but I was advised that this would be unseemly and was assured that HAK would take care of me, which he subsequently did. In any case, I was at last free to devise a better way to do intelligence. As a member of the "Community" I had gotten to know a number of working-level intelligence analysts and I chose four of the best from CIA, DIA, and the National Security Agency (NSA), plus Dr. Steve Hosmer of RAND, who had all the requisite clearances. We formed what was in effect a secret group that remained anonymous and autonomous and that met during the lunch hour on an ad hoc basis. Freed from the political and other predilections of our seniors, we combined to produce intelligence that was a whole order of magnitude better than that produced by the huge and expensive "Community."

The "shining hour" of our group was our incredibly accurate predictions related to the enemy's notorious 1972 "Easter Offensive." In the fall of 1971 we began to notice a number of articles appearing in Hanoi newspapers referring to the conscription of categories of men previously exempted from military service—for example, skilled technicians, Montagnards who didn't speak Vietnamese, Chinese, those previously declared physically unfit, and others. This meant only one thing to us: the enemy was scraping the bottom of the personnel barrel to mount a major offensive. We checked the seasonal weather patterns and concluded that it could come off in the spring of 1972. We were the first to predict a spring offensive in the coming year. We had a former Kansas farm boy from DIA who had an encyclopedic knowledge of the NVA order of battle. He eventually worked out the whole enemy order of battle for the offensive and was accurate to an amazing degree. Then, about ten days before the first attack began on March 30, our NSA member who was especially skilled in interpreting communications shifts accurately predicted the date of the initial attack. The whole "Community" didn't come close to our accuracy and detail. A week before the attack actually started, I passed our analysis to HAK's deputy, Gen. Alexander Haig. I never knew what he did with it, and kept forgetting to ask him when I later saw him socially.

Our use of Hanoi newspaper articles is a classic example of using open source material for intelligence analysis, a prime source badly neglected by intelligence analysts, especially in the CIA. The best example of the value of open sources was provided by the late William T. Lee, an independent analyst formerly with both the CIA and the DIA. Bill was the only American analyst who consistently accurately calculated Soviet defense expenditures, greatly surpassing CIA and DIA estimates. His figures later were confirmed by former Soviet sources after the fall of the USSR. Bill got most of his raw data from open Soviet sources, that long had been disdained by the CIA. Bill often said that the only way to get the CIA to take open source material seriously was to spread it out on a football field, take a satellite photo of it, and then give it a Top Secret TK classification. While in the first Bush White House NSC, I had a detached retina and had to cut my enormous reading load by half. I eliminated most of the classified material in favor of open source information provided by the indispensable Foreign Broadcast Information Service (FBIS), and the choice served me well. It was gratifying to read in 2007 that National Director for Intelligence John Negroponte had created a special open source capability.

By 1972 the Vietnamization process had been largely completed and there were no more U.S. ground forces in Vietnam except as advisers. However, we still provided air, naval, and logistics support. In 1972 the United States had only about two hundred killed in action, as opposed to an average of about seven thousand a year in previous years. Hanoi decided to test Vietnamization by launching its largest offensive of the war, the 1972 "Easter Offensive" with the equivalent of twenty-three divisions equipped with hundreds of Soviet-supplied tanks, long-range artillery, rockets, SAMs, and other modern weapons. In other words, this was the first mostly conventional enemy offensive of the war. South Vietnamese ground forces, Army of the Republic of Vietnam (ARVN) and Marines, with essential U.S. air, naval, and logistics support, stopped the offensive and launched counteroffensives. Shortly after the offensive began, however, President Nixon was concerned about the conflicting reports he was getting and directed General Haig to go to Vietnam and bring him back a report on what was actually going on. Haig took fellow NSC staffer Sven Kraemer and me along to check the field. Al Haig went to Saigon to consult with the top military and civilian brass, while Sven went up to eastern I Corps and I went to western II Corps.

When I landed at the Pleiku airport, it had already been taken under artillery attack. Indeed, I had wound up in the path of the major enemy thrust. Senior

U.S. official in II Corps, widely known and controversial John Paul Vann, took me in tow and organized a hair-raising tour for me. Vann constantly took incredible chances to the extent that I sometimes wondered if he didn't have a death wish. (He was killed in June 1972 when his helicopter hit a mountain south of Kontum at night.) He naturally expected me to take chances. He had me, accompanied by a U.S. Army colonel and an FSO, choppered into the ARVN 23rd Division headquarters at Tan Canh north of Kontum after it had already been taken under attack. The local fuel dump had been hit, sending up a straight very high column of black smoke, providing an ideal aiming point for the artillery targeted at the headquarters. We went into a bunker where we were briefed by some division officers. Before long, an enemy round exploded just outside the bunker. The U.S. colonel, an artillery officer, went out, picked up a shell fragment and pronounced it a 130-mm fragment. This was an excellent Soviet piece with a range of some thirty miles and a high velocity that could punch a round through the bunker we were in like a pin through tissue paper. I thought this was an excellent time to get the hell out of there since there was nothing more we could learn by staying any longer. I had our chopper called in and went out to the landing pad where I could see that our chopper was barely in sight. I lay down on the pad and shoveled recently dumped expended cartridge shells into my pocket. I would later use them as pipe tampers. It also gave me something to do at the time. Finally our chopper came in and hovered just above the pad as we quickly crawled on board; I expected a round to hit the pad any second. I believe one soon did. (Not long thereafter, the headquarters were overrun by tank-supported forces.) Next we were treated to a chopper run down "Rocket Ridge" where at another time enemy flak was so dense you could walk on it, as the saying goes. From there we went to Kontum where we got a very pessimistic briefing from a U.S. Army colonel adviser who didn't think the 23rd Division could hold the city. (He was wrong.)

At that point, I went to visit a friend and fellow FSO Chris Squire, who had been a P-40 fighter pilot in WWII and was a senior provincial representative. Squire was quartered just outside Pleiku in a cinderblock structure with a bunker out front. Just as we were having breakfast at about 6:30 AM we fell under attack by six-foot-long 122-mm Soviet rockets. We dived into the bunker hoping no rockets would hit it. The immense concussion of the rockets produced a tinnitus from which I still suffer. (The next time I saw Chris, he was our consul general in Leningrad and was living in a small palace.) When we finally left Vietnam, I was not very optimistic about our side's chances, since it seemed that I had been under fire for most of my stay. When you have to keep spending time in bunkers and slit trenches, things are not exactly looking up. Actually my firsthand observations led me to wrong conclusions about how things were really going. Two developments had greatly changed the scene in Vietnam since I had left in 1967. The quality of

U.S. troops, by then all support troops, had deteriorated considerably. General Haig was shocked at the change. Also the enemy had acquired Soviet handheld SA-7 Strella antiaircraft missiles that greatly affected air operations. Helicopters would have to go straight up to ten thousand feet, fly at that altitude, and then drop straight down on landing. The highly effective Vietnamese-manned A-1 attack aircraft were rendered excessively vulnerable due to their slow speed.

There was considerable discussion in the White House about how we should respond to this massive attack. Initially, HAK and others feared that Nixon's desire to bomb Hanoi and the central port of Haiphong might well derail the upcoming U.S.–Soviet summit meeting in Moscow. HAK later concluded that the bombing with the addition of blockading Haiphong by mining its harbor would not result in Moscow's canceling the summit that I believed, at the time, was more far more important to the Soviets than to us because it was a key element in the latest Soviet détente campaign. Henry, who for some time had been fruitlessly negotiating with the North Vietnamese outside Paris, had hoped that maybe the Soviets and even the Chinese might persuade Hanoi to make concessions leading to a negotiated settlement. I could never see what either Moscow or Peking had to gain from taking this monkey off our back.

What finally led Hanoi to make concessions was the effective defeat of by far the largest offensive, which ended with their losing some one hundred thousand troops killed in action, about twice the number we had suffered in the entire war. Bear in mind that the enemy, as noted above, had to scrape the bottom of the personnel barrel to launch this offensive. I'm afraid I was so influenced by my recent negative experience on the ground in Vietnam I later could not realize the seriousness of the enemy's ultimate postoffensive weakness. The intelligence I was getting from the CIA did not reflect this, since its analysts had long since concluded that the war was for us unwinnable and tended to emphasize the negative, not unlike the U.S. media. The key evidence of the extent of the enemy's defeat was the expulsion by South Vietnamese marines, on September 15, 1972, of all Communist forces from the northernmost provincial capital of Quang Tri, the only provincial capital taken in the offensive. Quang Tri was the strongest position held by the enemy in all South Vietnam. There, they had their best troops and equipment as well as the very shortest supply lines of communication to North Vietnam less than twenty miles away. Clearly, if they couldn't hold Quang Tri they couldn't hold anything else and were on the way to being totally expelled from the South. Unfortunately, I had finally taken a few days leave at a Delaware beach and was out of touch on September 15. When I returned to the White House, I learned nothing of this key turn of events in reading the latest CIA reports, which, as noted above, were not inclined to stress or even convey positive developments.

Sometime after Hanoi had won the war in 1975, a former top commander in the South, Gen. Tran Van Tra, stated in the Party organ *Nhan Dan* that his troops, by late 1972, were on the ropes and seemed on the verge of defeat. As former CIA Director William Colby wrote in his 1983 book *Lost Victory*, "[By the fall of 1972] on the ground in South Vietnam the war had been won." I still believe that, as HAK's expert on the enemy, had I been able to convince him that the other side was on the verge of defeat he might have been emboldened to take a tougher position in negotiating with Hanoi's representatives or, better still, might have postponed negotiations pending a more favorable position on the ground. Maybe I'm just dreaming, though. On September 26 Kissinger entered into talks in Paris with his longtime North Vietnamese negotiating partner, Le Duc Tho (whom we all called "Ducky"), who indicated his side was willing to make concessions sought for years by our side. This intrigued Kissinger, who had been dedicated to negotiation. Formal negotiations began on October 8, 1972, outside Paris in the former studio-home of famed French Communist artist Ferdinand Leger. Thus Henry Kissinger, with the best of intentions, began the process that finally snatched defeat from the jaws of victory, as President Lincoln famously said about General Burnside. Kissinger pocketed Tho's concessions, but conceded an earlier agreement to *a cease-fire in-place that would leave North Vietnamese forces in South Vietnam.*

John Negroponte, a mid-level FSO who usually accompanied Kissinger at these negotiations, courageously put his career on the line by unsuccessfully going mano a mano with Kissinger in opposing this fatal concession. Kissinger, wrongly in my opinion, believed that the Watergate scandal (later to become public), congressional opposition, and even the upcoming presidential election would impede extending the conflict long enough to expel all North Vietnamese troops from the South. This is the profound miscalculation that lost Vietnam. Thanks, I believe, to our intelligence gap, Kissinger did not fully realize how close to victory Thieu's forces were; as noted, I wasn't much help to him in this regard.

The North Vietnamese side craftily leaked that a negotiated peace was near. This was later confirmed by Kissinger (much to his regret). Once Congress heard this, interest in continuing the war rapidly waned. However, since South Vietnamese forces were on a roll, Thieu understandably wanted to continue fighting until the North Vietnamese troops were expelled. Accomplishing such a victory would no doubt have produced a change of attitude on the war in the United States. Thieu had to be brought into line with threats, often issued in the (usually not consulted) president's name. Hanoi's delegation, believing it had the better of us, began to renege and broke off talks. It took the "Christmas" bombing campaign (which produced remarkably little collateral civilian damage) to bring them back to the table. Kissinger described that, in contrast to Le Duc Tho's prebombing hostility, upon returning to the negotiating table Tho embraced Henry with such ardor that, for a brief moment, as he later joked, he thought he was the object of a homosexual attack. The "Paris Peace Accords," signed on January 27, 1973, were immediately and massively violated by Hanoi's forces. Initially these were mostly violations of the cease-fire and some were committed by our side. The most serious and prolonged violations were the massive infiltration of men and equipment. The primitive old Ho Chi Minh trail was in effect converted to a kind of superhighway. All these violations were later described in detail by the North Vietnamese Chief of Staff General Van Tien Dung in an April–May 1976 series of articles in *Nhan Dan.*

A plan to meet this serious threat called for new negotiations to be preceded by U.S. air attacks on Communist forces. The Communist side agreed to the talks. Alas, Nixon, preoccupied with Watergate, cancelled these air strikes, but unfortunately we were stuck with going ahead with these, to me farcical, if not humiliating, talks at Leger's old place outside Paris in May and June 1973. In the June meeting, Kissinger threatened to resume air strikes if the violations continued, whereupon the Hanoi delegation derisively laughed as Tho observed that Kissinger apparently was unaware of what the U.S. Congress had done. He was referring to the June 4, 1973, Case-Church Amendment that would cut off all funding for U.S. military operations in Indochina. I had never seen Henry quite so nonplussed. He could simply grumble that this was a domestic matter and none of Tho's business. At that point, I knew that all was lost, because, without the threat of U.S. retaliation, Hanoi had zero interest in adhering to the Accords. As General Van Tien Dung later put it in his articles, "The [Paris] agreement represented a big victory for our people and a big defeat for the U.S. imperialists and their lackeys."

In addition, a Democratic-led Congress, with significant Republican support, reduced military aid to South Vietnam from $2,270 billion in fiscal 1973 to $700 million for fiscal 1975. This had a devastating effect on the morale and combat effectiveness of South Vietnamese forces, which greatly contributed to their defeat, in April 1975, by North Vietnamese forces well supported by their *loyal* allies, China and the Soviet Union. Van Tien Dung stated in his articles, "The decrease in American aid made it impossible for Saigon troops to carry out their combat and force development plans." As Dung put it in his book *Great Spring Victory* (cited in Davidson, *Vietnam at War*), "Nguyen Van Thieu was forced to fight a poor man's war. Enemy firepower had decreased by nearly 60 percent . . . its mobility was also reduced by half." Once our troops and POWs had returned to the United States, Congress simply lost interest in Vietnam.

In January 1973 I had taken over as head of the NSC's Indochina Staff, probably making me our government's most senior official who dealt only with Indochina (Vietnam, Laos, and Cambodia). This meant I had the thankless task of trying to garner support for South Vietnam from the Pentagon and other government agencies. After our troops had left Vietnam and all our POWs had returned, there was, alas, precious little interest in Washington in supporting our Vietnamese allies. If it weren't for Col. P. X. Kelley, Joint Chiefs of Staff liaison with the White House (who later became the 28th Commandant of the Marine Corps, which I had predicted), I doubt I would have gotten any help at all from the Pentagon. What help I got from the CIA was largely thanks to Ted Shackley, one of the operational field types, the good guys of the CIA.

In March 1975 the Communist side launched a full-scale assault against a South Vietnam weakened and demoralized by our disgraceful near abandonment. President Thieu made the fatal mistake of withdrawing his forces from the northern half of the country to form a consolidated defense of the more populous South. The South Vietnamese forces had proven themselves formidable in the defense, but in the retreat, especially from Kontum and Pleiku in the western highlands, troops intermingled with civilian refugees crowding the retreat route and lost unit integrity, making them fair game for the enemy. This was very similar to what happened to French troops retreating from the Germans in 1940. As enemy forces closed on Saigon, our ambassador, Graham Martin, and Saigon leaders, incredibly detached from reality, actually hoped that the last-minute replacing of Thieu with the legendary Gen. Duong Van Minh ("Big Minh") could somehow lead to a negotiated cease-fire, inter alia, enabling an orderly evacuation of Vietnamese who were in danger, especially those who worked for us.

Martin would not order or approve evacuations for fear of causing a panic in Saigon, which was likely to some extent—but better to have a panic before the enemy was near. Kissinger deferred to Martin. Thus Martin wouldn't use two large ships, at one point docked at Saigon, which could easily have evacuated most of the endangered Vietnamese. When the end came, the evacuations outside Saigon were largely independently organized by FSO provincial representatives. The result was the disheartening spectacle of the helicopter evacuation from the roof of a building in Saigon. On April 30, 1975, North Vietnamese forces entered Saigon, and tragedy and death subsequently befell hundreds of thousands of South Vietnamese. North Vietnam's victory had cost it an estimated 1 million troops killed in action (as a percent of the population, equivalent to about 17 million in the United States).

On October 25, 2004, the History Channel presented a documentary on the Vietnam War that included fascinating interviews with knowledgeable North Vietnamese who made the following points, among others: About 2 million North Vietnamese lost their lives in the war, mostly through hostilities and disease. The VC forces in the South Vietnam were almost completely wiped out as the result of the 1968 Tet Offensive. The VC, in any case, were always under the complete control of Hanoi. U.S. and South Vietnamese troops could have effectively blocked the Ho Chi Minh Trail, which was the principal enemy supply route through Laos and

Cambodia. Had the North feared an attack on North Vietnam, or had a ground attack been actually launched, it would have tied down most of North Vietnamese forces in the North, which would have ensured victory for our side.

After the fall of Vietnam we were faced with a crisis in Cambodia, which had just been taken over by indigenous Communist forces who captured an American container ship, the *Mayaguez*, on May 15. President Ford ordered a carrier in the area to bomb Cambodian air bases and ordered an attack on the island where the ship along with its crew was being held. Marines transported in Air Force helicopters soon landed on the island but met with unexpectedly heavy resistance. Our forces did their best despite some foul-ups due to the Marines' never having operated with Air Force assets. When the island was taken, it was discovered that the forty-man crew had been removed from the island. When the crisis began, a high-level group, including Secretary of State Kissinger and Donald Rumsfeld, a top White House staffer, forgathered in the White House West Wing, having just come from a black tie dinner. There they stood around in their tuxedos trying to determine what to do next.

I suggested that we contact the Communist capturers by coming up on their internal communications network. Kissinger thought it was a good idea, but the National Security Agency, which would have to implement this suggestion, shot it down on the grounds of not wanting the Cambodian Communists to know that we could listen in on their communications. In the end, the Cambodians let the crew go, after we had lost fifteen Marines killed and a number wounded. Kissinger insisted that the air base bombing continue, but I opposed this as being unnecessary and risking the lives of American flyers. Kissinger, as it turned out, wanted to use the bombing as a sort of show of force to discourage the North Koreans from taking advantage of our defeat in Vietnam to launch an attack on South Korea. Some ten years later, a graduate student at Berkeley called me, having somehow learned that I was the "crisis manager" in this case about which he was writing and wanted to know what crisis management model we used. I said we didn't use any model, which is always the case in real life. He insisted that his professor required a model, so I pieced together one based on various models he described.

The question always arises, "Was the Vietnam War worth it all?" I say yes, explained as follows. In April 1954 President Eisenhower opined that a Communist victory in Indochina could topple Southeast Asian countries like "dominos." While pooh-poohed by many liberals in the United States, subsequently the leaders of Australia, New Zealand, Cambodia, Malaysia, Singapore, Thailand, and India essentially agreed with Eisenhower's "domino theory," as did leaders in Hanoi, Peking, and Moscow. For example, China's famed Marshal Lin Piao stated in September 1965 that revolutionary warfare could encircle developed capitalist countries and that the defeat of "U.S. imperialism" in Vietnam would show the people of the world "that what the Vietnamese people can do, they can do too." In July 1964 Vietnam's Defense Minister General Vo Nyuyen Giap declared that "South Vietnam [the VC] is the vanguard fighter of the national liberation movement in the present era . . . and the failure of the special war unleashed by the U.S. imperialists in South Vietnam would mean that this war can be defeated anywhere in the world" (Lewy, *America in Vietnam*). The war bought time for strengthening the Southeast Asian regimes, the potential "dominos," while wearing down North Vietnam and effectively eliminating its threat to Southeast Asia. In the 1970s Indonesian leaders Suharto and Malik confirmed to columnist Robert Novak that they had earlier told U.S. officials that our introduction of combat troops in Vietnam in March 1965 substantially encouraged their resistance to a nearly successful October 1965 Chinese-backed Communist coup that would have toppled a number of dominos, had it succeeded and that in turn would have no doubt triggered our treaty obligation to come to the aid of the Philippines in the face of a massive Communist threat that would have dwarfed the threat we faced in Indochina. Norman Friedman pointed out that our troop commitment to Vietnam also encouraged the successful British defense of Malaysia against a Communist invasion launched from Indonesia. As noted in Chapter 8, we got into World War II as a result of our opposition to the Japanese takeover of what later became Vietnam, so this area was of interest to our national security even at a time when it was far more remote in travel time than in the 1960s. On the whole, George Kennan's ultimately successful "containment policy" largely worked in regard to our Vietnam policy. The outcome of the Vietnam War should thus be regarded as a tactical defeat, but a *strategic victory*.

Here I would like to include the cost of the war to South Vietnam as described in an April 30, 2002, lecture by Dr. Lewis Sorley, a West Point graduate who saw much combat in Vietnam and who served in key Pentagon offices and on the faculties of the Army War College and West Point. Most notably he wrote one of the very best of the countless books on Vietnam, *A Better War* (1999). He cited a Seth Mydans piece in the April 24, 2000, *New York Times*: "More than a million southerners fled the country after the war ended. . . . Some 400,000 were interned in camps for 're-education'—many only briefly, but some for as long as seventeen years. Another 1.5 million were forcibly resettled in 'new economic zones' in barren areas of southern Vietnam that were ravaged by hunger and extreme poverty." To this Dr. Sorley added,

> The price paid by the South Vietnamese in their long struggle to remain free proved grievous indeed. The armed forces lost 275,000 killed in action [U.S. KIAs were 47,424]. Another 465,000 civilians lost their lives, many of them assassinated by Viet Cong terrorists or felled by the enemy's indiscriminate shelling and rocketing of

cities, and 935,000 more were wounded. Of the million [escapees] who became boat people, feared to be many, lost their lives at sea. [The International Red Cross estimated 300,000.] In Vietnam perhaps 65,000 others were executed by their self-proclaimed liberators. As many as 250,000 more perished in the brutal "re-education" camps. Two million, driven from their homeland, formed a new Vietnamese diaspora."

Dr. Sorley ended his talk with this eloquent thought, with which I heartily concur:

> By way of conclusion, I will just state my conviction that the war in Vietnam was a just war fought by the South Vietnamese and their allies for admirable purposes, that those who fought it did so with their mightiest hearts, and that in the process they came very close to succeeding in their purpose of enabling South Vietnam to sustain itself as a free and independent nation. A reporter once remarked that General Abrams [who commanded U.S. forces in Vietnam 1968 to1972] was a man who deserved a better war. I quoted that observation to his eldest son, who immediately responded: "He didn't see it that way. He thought the Vietnamese were worth it." As do I. Thank you.

What we did wrong in Vietnam and what we should have done:

- We should have supported Ngo Dinh Diem, difficult autocrat that he was, instead of encouraging his ouster which destabilized South Vietnam for years. We also should have realized that Buddhist anti-Diem rioting was political, not religious in nature. (They later also rioted against his successors, which helped the VC no end.) Diem, a Catholic, certainly did not persecute Buddhists and indeed had a number of Buddhist pagodas built.

- Vietnamization should have begun in 1966 when things were somewhat stabilized in Vietnam. We should have concentrated on training ARVN and marine officers and noncoms. Instead, our general attitude was, "Stand aside, you little guys, and let us do it better." I personally plead guilty to not having made any effort to help train my Vietnamese counterparts.

- Service tours should have been between twenty and twenty-four months. Twelve months was simply too short. With one-year tours, by the time a soldier learned his job, he was on his way home. Units should have been deployed intact. The steady infusion of casual replacements was not good for unit integrity.

- Only volunteers should have been sent to Vietnam, with draftees sent to Germany, South Korea, and other places where we had troops stationed. (As it was, two-thirds of those who served in Vietnam *were* volunteers.) If there weren't enough volunteers, National Guard and reserve units should have been activated. Also, we were far too generous in granting student deferments. Many students have told me that they strongly opposed the war because they felt guilty about staying in school, while the less fortunate were drafted and sent to Vietnam. Most of the vocal opposition to the war came from students—largely, I would guess, for this reason.

- We should have organized the tens of thousands of trained guerrillas and sappers who defected to our side into teams based on the Armed Propaganda Teams and especially on the highly effective Marines' Kit Carson Scouts. These teams should have been inserted in enemy areas to attack enemy installations and lay ambushes along their lines of communications, including the Ho Chi Minh Trail. This would have tied up many enemy troops in static defense roles.

- We should have had a credible amphibious capability, located just below the DMZ, which would have conducted regular amphibious exercises, as well as launched feints and forays along the North Vietnamese coast to tie down troops in defense of the North.

- The Marines should not have been used in static defense in places such as Khe Sanh, but should have been redeployed from the north, where they first landed, to the delta area, from Saigon to all the area to the southwest, with its large rivers and tributaries, where the Navy primarily operated. Being in the naval service, this was a natural environment for Marines.

- Our use of firepower was often profligate, which was costly in dollars and in loss of popular support. This was especially true of continuous random H & I fires, which were eventually mostly terminated as not being all that effective. In general, I concluded from our experience in Vietnam that when one has near limitless resources, as we had, one is no longer resourceful.

- Our "tooth to tail" ratio was all out of whack. When we had more than five hundred thousand troops in Vietnam, only about eighty thousand were in maneuver battalions—that is, actual combat troops. Also, our troops, including officers even at the general level, should have been living in Quonset huts or under canvas, instead of in residences and hotels, which, among other things, were less secure. I found it somehow obscene to see our top commanding Army general living in a relatively large house with its own tennis court where the general could be seen decked out in whites playing tennis within the sound of firefights just out of town.

- We should have taken out missile sites in North Vietnam as soon as they were being built and not worried about killing Soviets involved in building these sites.

- We should have mined Haiphong (and possibly also Sihanoukville) harbor early on to block shipments of war materiel. We should also early on have bombed or shelled Haiphong's docks.

- Bombing of military targets should have been done on a continuous basis without "bombing pauses" to encourage negotiations. Actually such halts logically removed incentives to negotiate and enabled the enemy to recuperate from our air attacks. This should have been obvious.

- The war should not have been micromanaged (or mismanaged) from Washington as it was by LBJ and Secretary of Defense McNamara. The best commanders should have been sent to Vietnam and then trusted to make the right decisions.

- Two battleships and two to four heavy cruisers should have been dedicated to Vietnam service, as recommended by a Navy panel in November 1964. The development of extended-range sixteen-inch rounds should have been encouraged. Instead, very promising and inexpensive tests of such rounds were cancelled by the Navy in 1968. The numerous targets in both North and South Vietnam within range of 16-inch guns generally should have been attacked by battleships, not aircraft, whenever possible.

- The U.S. government should have done a much better job explaining the war to the American public. The only really good and persuasive official publication on the war that I ever read was put out by the Australians. This is a sad commentary, indeed.

- We should have postponed negotiations with the enemy until we had an absolutely dominant position on the ground (This would have required effective explaining to the U.S. public and to Congress.)

- We should not have seriously entered into negotiations with the enemy when we did. By continuing the fighting for some additional months into 1973, our negotiating position would have far stronger. If it were shown by this that we were winning, it would probably have been supported by public opinion and even Congress. (I believe this could have had much the same effect as the "surge" later had in the Iraq War.)

- The North Vietnamese and the United States concluded a solemn accord, the 1973 Peace Accords, which cost us some fifty-eight thousand lives and countless billions of dollars to achieve. The North Vietnamese massively violated this agreement and imposed a Communist regime on our Vietnamese allies. We should have insisted, at a minimum, on substantial reparations as the price of our diplomatic recognition of Communist Vietnam.

Most the above observations will be of negligible use in future conflicts, but they do help explain why we did not have greater success in Vietnam.

I can't end this section on Vietnam without a word about the famous Vietnam Memorial Wall in Washington, DC. I found it very impressive, deeply moving, and wrong—not only wrong, but profoundly wrong. This long gash in the earth is completely negative, to give the impression that the some fifty-eight thousand Americans whose names are inscribed on the Wall died for nothing. This was undoubtedly the objective of its designer, then–Yale student Maya Lin, who must have been strongly influenced by the pervasive anti-Vietnam, anti-military culture of a university that would ban the ROTC from its campus.

Were it not for Frederick Hart's moving sculpture of the three soldiers and the American flag flying from a small pole, this could easily just as well be a monument to fifty thousand Americans who were killed in traffic accidents during one year of the Vietnam War. Both of these additions, incidentally, were strongly opposed by Maya Lin and the Vietnam Memorial board who wanted the Wall to remain pristinely negative. Most of the combat veterans of the war I know strongly object to what the Wall stands for. The most vociferous critic of the Wall is the son of one of my best friends who, as a Marine in Vietnam, was so badly wounded he will never fully recover. He feels deeply affronted by a war memorial that more than implies that all who fought in Vietnam did so for nothing, and I totally agree with him. (He also noted its stark contrast with the more recent positive World War II monument in Washington.) The *New York Times* (March 6, 1997) quoted one veteran as labeling it a "black gash of shame and sorrow." I was not surprised when someone who knew told me that no Vietnam veterans were on the panel that approved the Wall design.

While I was engaged in coping with the trials and tribulations associated with Vietnam, Laos, and Cambodia, the Watergate scandal was developing with the whole scandalous cover-up occurring within about fifty feet of my office in President Nixon's office in the OEOB (Old Executive Office Building; most of the White House offices, including those of the vice president, are located in that building). The Watergate scandal resulted from the June 17, 1972, break-in at the Democratic National Headquarters in the Watergate apartment complex, in the Foggy Bottom section of Washington, by five men who were arrested on the spot by DC police. In time it became known that these men had connections with the White House, with suspicion falling on President Nixon himself. I have always doubted that Nixon ordered the break-in or even approved it. He was far too intelligent to initiate any scheme so insane and so unnecessary. The break-in seems to have been intended to find something of use for the upcoming presidential election, which Nixon was certain to win, in any case. His opponent was the hapless George McGovern who didn't have a chance of winning. (In fact, he carried only Massachusetts.) All this rendered this criminal act not only terribly wrong, but incredibly stupid.

The Watergate mess largely simmered beneath the surface until the notorious "Saturday Night Massacre" on October 20, 1973. As it turned out, Nixon taped everything that went on in his offices. When that got out, these tapes moved to center stage in the ever-more-apparent cover-up of White House involvement in the break-in. Archibald Cox had been appointed special prosecutor in this and insisted on having direct access to the tapes. Nixon refused and sacked Cox, precipitating the resignation of Attorney General Elliot Richardson and his deputy, William Ruckelshaus. Kissinger who was much closer to what was going on, though in no way involved in the cover-up, was deeply disturbed by the implications of Watergate almost from the very beginning. This, I believe, to some extent sapped his confidence in getting the support he needed in coping with the problems confronting him and surely affected his policy on Vietnam, which I at times found wanting, as I have explained earlier. As I noted above, I was physically located about fifty feet from Nixon's working office in the OEOB on the floor beneath mine, but still, throughout most of the developing scandal, all I knew was what I got from the media. I believed that Nixon engaged in this notorious cover-up due to a misplaced sense of loyalty to those involved. Others believed, as I did, that he should have fired the lot of them and expressed outrage at the break-in. Of course, if he had actually approved the break-in, as I have always doubted, this course of action would not have worked. In any case, it was always assumed by many that Nixon was in on it from the beginning.

Kissinger almost completely monopolized NSC contact with the president. I later could understand why, since he had a tenuous relationship with the very complex and often unfathomable Nixon, who at times was clearly jealous of all the attention Henry got, especially in the media. The only direct contact I ever had with Nixon was in April 1973, in the informal surroundings of the well-guarded Western White House at San Clemente, on the Pacific coast about halfway between

Los Angeles and San Diego. He and Pat Nixon occupied a nice Spanish-style residence nearby. I was there because this was where President Thieu was to spend most of his long-awaited four-day visit to the United States to avoid the apparent threat of hostile demonstrations against him. I found this threat disgraceful in light of Thieu's being a staunch ally and friend of ours whose country was a remarkably free democracy, considering all it had gone through. Ironically, tyrannical and hostile leaders of Communist or other leftist countries hardly had to worry about hostile demonstrations when they visited the United States. I ran into Nixon a few times and we chatted about things that were unrelated to politics and foreign policy. He struck me as a bit strange and uptight and I wondered how he ever could have succeeded in politics.

I liked it out there because the food was very good and I had a chance to meet some of the famous White House big shots like John Ehrlichman and Bob Haldeman whom I had only read about in newspapers. I liked fellow fisherman Ehrlichman, but Haldeman left me cold.

Kissinger managed to become secretary of state on September 22, 1973, which gave him a complete monopoly of foreign policy. When soon thereafter the UN General Assembly had its annual fall gathering primarily of the foreign ministers of UN countries, I went to New York to accompany Kissinger in his meetings with my Southeast Asian clients. We all stayed at the famed Waldorf-Astoria Hotel, which was quite a treat, since this was a luxury I could never afford on my own. When I awoke late on the Saturday morning of October 6, 1973, I heard on the radio that Egypt and Syria had attacked Israel on Yom Kipper. This created great turmoil and involved Henry in frenzied activity, beginning early in the day because the threat of war seemed imminent. Interestingly, the day before, Friday October 5, Henry had had lunch with the Arab delegates, including the Egyptian and Syrian ones, and everything had seemed normal with them.

Kissinger's main preoccupation initially seemed to be to dissuade Israel from launching preemptive attacks to counter this threat. He need not have worried, since Israel had not seemed to expect them before they began. Unfortunately, the day before, the head of the NSC Middle East staff, highly capable and very knowledgeable Harold "Hal" Saunders, learned his wife had been killed by a fall at home and he had to rush home. This deprived Henry of a right-hand man at a very critical time. We immediately began providing beleaguered Israel with war materiel, which made my efforts to get military aid for the Vietnamese even more difficult. Soviet involvement, especially on behalf of the Syrians, made this crisis especially menacing.

By 1974 Nixon was so absorbed by his Watergate travails that his chief of staff, Gen. Alexander Haig, had largely taken charge of running the country. At a birthday party for Henry in 2008, I at long last finally got round to asking Haig what he thought of my often-expressed view that for nearly a year he was the de facto president of the United States. He looked me in the eye and replied, "Bill, I never made a decision without first clearing it with the president." This statement really did not change my mind. The nation owes Al Haig an enormous debt of gratitude for holding things together in those terribly troubled times. On February 21, 2010, the day after Al Haig died, the *Washington Post* aptly referred to him as the "37 1/2th president" (Nixon being the thirty-seventh). Henry Kissinger writing in *Time* magazine of March 8, 2010, noted that Haig held "our government together as its presidency disintegrated in the worst constitutional crisis since the Civil War."

After the House Judiciary Committee voted for articles of impeachment on July 27 and 29, we knew Nixon's days were numbered. We felt the power of the White House quickly ebbing away and fully expected our requests to the government bureaucracy would be met with scorn and derision. Interestingly, the opposite seemed true. Everybody seemed to believe we were doing our best to hold things together and that we needed their help, which we usually got.

On August 8, 1974, Nixon announced his resignation, and the following morning his cabinet and the White House staff gathered in the East Room for a farewell. At 9:15 AM the president and Mrs. Nixon entered the room to the strains of "Hail to the Chief." As he began his final speech, he put on glasses for the first time in public. He had a folded sheet of yellow legal pad paper in his inside coat pocket that kept sliding in front of his tie and that he kept pushing back. His rambling, sometimes incoherent, very personal speech was so pathetic and heartbreaking that there was scarcely a dry eye in the room. His wife Pat and their two daughters with their husbands stood stoically beside him, bravely controlling the emotion they had to be feeling. Then they left the room, and we all went out on the South Lawn to wave goodbye to the two. We watched them walk along a red carpet that seemed somehow out of place to their waiting helicopter. At the top of the stairs, Nixon turned and gave us his typical over-the-head wave, then got in and was whisked away to the clattering sound of the helicopter. (My future wife, Joan Crotty, was also present. She was on Pat Nixon's and later Betty Ford's staff. My daughter Betsy recognized me from behind on TV from my bald spot.)

A short time after the Nixons took off, Vice President Gerald Ford was sworn in as president in the East Room. Most of us on the White House staff were not invited to this event, but my deputy, FSO Kenneth Quinn, and I decided to try somehow to crash it. We got on the elevator that stopped at the second floor and there were two Secret Service men and Ford, waiting to get in. We told the vice president that we would get out to make room for them, but Ford told us to stay put. We all got out of the elevator together and, as a group, crossed West Executive Avenue, went into the West Wing, and strode past the guards unhindered—it being assumed that Ken and I were with Ford. Not long before on the same day, the walls of the West Wing corridors had been covered with photos of Nixon with family and notables. They had all been quickly replaced by Ford-related photos. It was weird. When we entered the East Room, there were the same cabinet members sitting where they had been not long before, plus others from the judicial and legislative branches. The atmosphere in the room had been completely transformed into a jovial, happy, festive occasion, however. Apart from combat, this was the most surreal event in my life.

With Ford as president, Kissinger in November 1975 finally relinquished his role as national security adviser and was replaced by his deputy, former Air Force general, Brent Scowcroft. From then on Henry was only secretary of state, although he continued to dominate the foreign policy field. All the ultimate disaster in Indochina happened on Ford's watch. Nothing remained to do but pick up the pieces left by the disastrous Communist takeovers in Indochina. Since there remained little left for me to do in the White House, in January 1976 I left it for a new job back in the State Department building.

chapter 16

Arms Control Agency, Georgetown University, and a Return to the White House

I N JANUARY 1976, I WAS HAPPY TO ACCEPT AN INVITATION from my old friend and NSC colleague John Lehman to go over to the State Department building and join the Arms Control and Disarmament Agency (ACDA), then an independent agency located in the old east wing of the State Department. Lehman, at that time, was deputy director of ACDA. My new title was deputy assistant director for multilateral affairs, the equivalent of a deputy assistant secretary of state. The assistant director was Leon Sloss, who was very knowledgeable in the field and a great guy to work for. The Multilateral Bureau of ACDA was responsible for all of our arms control agreements and negotiations with more than one other country. Our most important negotiations were the bilateral ones with the Soviets and our principal agreements with them were those reached during the Strategic Arms Limitations Talks (SALT). Among our most important multilateral agreements was Multilateral Balanced Force Reductions in Europe (MBFR). Our bureau also was responsible for our negotiations in Geneva in the Committee on Disarmament, which handled a host of arms control issues.

Eventually I became the federal member of the president's General Advisory Committee on Arms Control and Disarmament (GAC). There were very interesting people on the GAC, most especially Dr. John Wheeler, one of the world's leading astrophysicists and the one who first described the "black hole" phenomenon. John was a polymath ne plus ultra (a "renaissance man") with whom one could discuss virtually anything. Having always had broad, if often shallow, interests, I loved to have lunch with him. I found him to be one of the most interesting persons I had ever known. I have long held that most people at the very top of their fields, like John, often have broad interests.

In November 1976 Jimmy Carter was elected president. When he took office ACDA Director Fred Iklé and his deputy John Lehman resigned and Leon Sloss took charge of ACDA until the new director, Paul Warnke, was confirmed. Paul was a confirmed and somewhat controversial liberal, and it took until March 1977 until he was confirmed by the Senate. I had replaced Leon as head of our bureau. Early on, Carter decided to withdraw the U.S. Army 2nd Infantry Division from South Korea, which would have seriously tempted North Korea to attack its southern neighbor. The North attacked the South in 1950, primarily, I believe, as the result of our having withdrawn our troops from South Korea in 1949, not, as commonly believed, because Dean Acheson on January 12, 1950 (and Douglas McArthur in March 1949) drew a U.S. Asian defense perimeter that left out Korea. Stalin gave North Korean leader Kim Il Sung the go-ahead for the attack on South Korea on January 17, 1950 (according to Friedman); so he must clearly have made up his mind before Acheson spoke, although he was no doubt reassured by Acheson's statement. Thus Carter's decision was a prime example of why he will go down in history as one of the worst presidents in the twentieth century. Leon and I were part of a government cabal to thwart this insane move. As I recall, it even included newly named National Security Advisor Zbigniew Brezezinski, as well as many in the Pentagon. Leon Schloss and I convinced Warnke that a strong arms control case could be made against Carter's move.

In January 1977 I was asked to become an adjunct professor of international affairs at Georgetown University. This came about through my having gotten to know Dr. Peter Krogh, dean of the School of Foreign Service. I was asked to take over a course that had been taught up to then by a rather liberal individual who had been involved with the leaking of the classified Pentagon Papers on Vietnam, a move made in order to discredit our war effort. He had received a position with the new Carter Administration and didn't have time to teach anymore. He had focused in the course almost entirely on Vietnam decision making, whereas I transformed the course into one on the general process, entitled "National Security Decision Making."

When Warnke finally was confirmed in March 1977 he set about purging all the nonliberals on the staff. I was a career FSO who, like military officers, had loyally served under both Democratic and Republican presidents, but I suppose I had served too long in a Republican White House; moreover, although I had long been a registered Democrat, I had no real liberal credentials. I was replaced by a certified liberal who had had a senior position in ACDA under the Republicans. I have observed that while Republican administrations will tolerate liberals, liberal Democratic administrations try to get rid of all nonliberals. So I was out of a job and knew I would get nothing in that administration. I then went into a kind of exile at the National Defense University (NDU) in some kind of statistical research project the point of which I never quite fathomed. NDU was located at Ft. McNair on the other side of town. It was connected to Georgetown with a bike path all the way, so I could bike to work in good weather. Ft. McNair was named after Lt. Gen. Lesley J. McNair, commander of Army ground forces during World War II, who was accidentally killed in Normandy by one of our B-17 strikes not long after the 1944 landings. It is the oldest Army post and was the scene of the hanging of the Lincoln assassination conspirators in 1865.

In October 1978 the State Department offered retirement to those eligible, with an annuity based on the highest one-year salary as opposed to the usual average of the last three highest years. Sixty-four of us jumped at this chance. Then the State Department reneged. This led to our organizing and hiring a lawyer, who fortunately had been a State Department lawyer. Our group was led by Phil Manhard who had been captured during the Tet Offensive in Vietnam and had been a POW for more than five years. I was his deputy. We won hands down. I was out of the Foreign Service after twenty-eight years of service, having retired as a senior officer with a rank equivalent to rear admiral and with more than thirty-two years of federal service, including my Navy time. I really didn't need to earn much more and I certainly didn't earn much teaching part-time at Georgetown, but I loved teaching. In fact I had earned a PhD in the first place so that someday I could teach at the college level. Georgetown is one of the best universities in the country, and for the study of foreign affairs it is the very best.

I got the best of Georgetown's excellent students because I was very demanding, giving my students in the beginning class two pages of requirements. The weaker ones immediately dropped out, leaving me the crème de la crème. Even these students had serious deficiencies resulting from having gone to high schools at a time when learning facts was denigrated as mere memorization, always preceded by the pejorative "rote." I gave each class a blind (no names) geography test at the beginning of each course and never ceased to be amazed by some of the answers I got. For example, the Korean peninsula was a thousand miles from Japan, and the United Kingdom had a contiguous *land* border with the Federal Republic of Germany. (I'm not making this up.) When it came to history, things were even worse. I used to tell my students that if you don't know history and don't know geography, you will never fully understand what's going on in the world.

I cited two examples to illustrate this. In 1968 the Soviets invaded Czechoslovakia to prevent it from straying from the Soviet flock. History told Moscow that the Czechoslovakians did not have a record of being stalwart soldiers, as exemplified in the World War I story of the pacifist "Good Soldier Schweik." Moreover, geography made intervention important to Moscow, since the country formed a bridge from NATO member West Germany to the always politically sensitive Ukraine, which broke away when it had the chance in December 1991. As I will note later in this chapter in discussing the 1980–81 crisis in Poland, I was alone in predicting that the Soviets would not "invade" Poland. History informed Moscow that the Poles were fighters. In 1920 the new Polish army defeated Moscow's Red Army, and when the Soviets put pressure on the Poles in 1956 (as described in Chapter 12) the Poles were clearly ready to fight any Soviet troops that invaded and any already in the country that tried to move on Warsaw. That was the history. Poland's geography reduced any threat to the Soviets, since it was entirely surrounded by loyal Communist states and Soviet troops and had nowhere to go.

My course required that each student prepare the kind of action memoranda for the president that the NSC staff prepared to help the president make national security decisions. This consisted of a description of the problem, its background information, and a critique of various possible solutions with a recommended choice. The solutions were listed at the end with each followed by two check-off boxes labeled "approved" and "disapproved." I required that each student interview at least one expert in the field covered for background and advice. Students always protested that this would be difficult because "who of any importance or knowledge would want to talk to a mere student." I assured them that people in government and elsewhere loved to talk to students because, unlike others, they wanted nothing but time and wouldn't embarrass them by revealing normally not-revealed facts. I often steered them to people at State or in the White House whom I knew. The students were always amazed by the ease with which they got appointments with officials and others, some of rather high rank. For example, the top NSC Middle East expert gave a student an hour of his time in the midst of a Middle East crisis. The smart ones interviewed several such people. I encouraged this by telling them that these interviewees might someday be useful contacts. Indeed, some of these interviews did lead to jobs for these students.

My lectures consisted of a number of case studies of actual decision making in coping with various actual challenges and crises, such as Israel's various wars with its neighbors. As I noted above, I was one of the most demanding professors at Georgetown. At the beginning of each course, I would tell the students they, their parents, or both were paying about $1,600 for this course and I was going to see that they got their money's worth. Although I taught only upperclassmen and graduate students I took attendance; I was perhaps alone in the university in doing this. Papers that did not meet deadlines suffered rapid grade deterioration with each day they were late. I would point out that in the work world late papers could be worthless and that there an "F" could mean "fired." Each was also required to give an oral presentation on the subject of a given day's lecture. After my lectures I would query the students, but I don't remember ever giving final examinations, except in geography, which I insisted they master, and which most of them did. I also marked papers down for English mistakes over the protests that mine was not an English course. I simply pointed out the downside of making English grammar mistakes in the job world. My standards were put to the test when one of my students, a Chinese student from a wealthy Hong Kong family, failed to return from vacation in time to give his oral presentation. Given his not-great performance in general, I gave him an F in the course. Neither his family nor the university complained, despite the family's previous donation of a substantial sum to the university. No doubt in their culture the son had brought disgrace on the family

By the time I began teaching, professors at most universities and colleges were rated by their students. I first thought this was a terrible idea, but as it turned out, even though I initially believed I would be considered an unreasonably demanding SOB, I wound up with an average 4.86 out of 5 rating—with, over the years, a number of students anonymously noting that, "Professor Stearman really cares for his students." They were mature enough to appreciate that it's much harder to be a demanding professor than a lax one and that I was demanding for their own good. They also appreciated that, unlike most professors, I had had a great deal of real-world experience in my field. Many of my students turned out to be quite successful, often earning far more than I had ever earned. One student I taught wound up for a while as the de facto director of the CIA.

I remain friends with some of my students to this day. One whose friendship I especially cherish is that of Jeffrey Cimbalo, who went on to earn a masters degree from Harvard and a law degree from the University of Virginia (after having also been admitted to the Harvard Law School). He now has his own law firm in Richmond, and we count Jeff and his lovely wife Susan among our closest friends. Not long ago we attended the christening of their baby daughter in the Virginia country church where George and Martha Washington were married.

Another student with whom I remained friends was a very personable Jordanian by the name of Hassan. In 1980 he invited me to visit him in Jordan and I took him up on it. I first flew into Beirut in an Arab airliner. Coming in to land I could see the terrible destruction that the mostly religious civil war, which began in 1975, had been wreaking in this once lovely city. Before that war, one could swim in the surf and ski in the mountains on the same day. Before we landed most of the passengers were unfastening their seatbelts and walking around, which was ignored by the flight attendants. The small, crowded waiting room in which we waited for connecting flights was full of armed guards. I finally landed in Amman, Jordan, and was met by Hassan, who took me to the new Intercontinental Hotel. When I was checking in I noticed that everyone seemed to know him. When I remarked on this, he replied, "That is because I own the hotel." Hassan's father was president of the parliament and as such was driven in a limousine with the license plate "1."

We made a tour in this chauffeur-driven car, first to the extensive Roman ruins north of Amman and then down to the Dead Sea along a road with one hairpin turn after the other, which did not inhibit our driver from passing in one blind curve after the other. It was a white-knuckled ride all the way, and I thanked Heaven that we made it down alive. The Dead Sea is a kind of beach resort with cabanas scattered here and there, but I could see that it had been receding for some time because its source of water was mostly being siphoned off before it could reach the Sea. This diversion of water also caused the famed River Jordan to look like a muddy little creek full of reeds, an enormous disappointment after all I heard about it over the years. From the east bank of the Jordan I could see the ancient city of Jericho off in the distance on a hill under Israeli control. The area east of the Jordan seemed unusually devoid of people, and there was a palpable tension in the air, even though it had been thirteen years since Jordan and Israel were at war. While in Jordan I learned that the best way to avoid an upset stomach and other related maladies in the Middle East is to eat plenty of yogurt and garlic.

In 1980 I was asked to become director of Georgetown's Russian Area Studies (graduate) Program (RASP). I readily accepted and soon was introduced to academic politics. As Henry Kissinger was reported to have said, "Academic politics can be so vicious because the stakes are so small." And I came to realize how right he was. To begin, some professors who taught Russian or Russian studies thought they were better qualified than I who had only a skimpy knowledge of Russian. What I had that they didn't have was years of real-world experience in actually dealing with matters related to the Soviet Union and its satellites, including four and a half years of negotiating with the Soviets. These professors thought RASP should drop its doctoral program since it was too thinly supported. I disagreed. They also strongly opposed my efforts to introduce a major in Soviet military studies, probably the only such program in the nation and one that would have considerable appeal in the local defense community and elsewhere. I was defeated on this point, and after two years I was out, the probable victim of the liberal cabal that had opposed me from the beginning.

By now, some readers might begin to wonder if I am not suffering from some sort of persecution complex resulting in a seemingly special aversion to liberals. I am not, in fact, one of those rock-ribbed conservatives who dislikes all liberals as a matter of principle. I share some of my liberal friends' views. I have simply learned from experience that, where liberals hold sway, only liberal views are tolerated. This is evident on most campuses throughout the United States where clearly only liberal views are tolerated and the basic First Amendment freedoms of speech, expression, assembly, and even religion are generally denied those not sharing liberal views. This statement can be easily documented a hundredfold and is not some figment of a conservative imagination.

For some reason I became a career counselor at Georgetown. Most such counselors there and at other colleges and universities had received special training and, in theory, should have been far more professional than I, and in some respects they were. Nearly all, however, had no experience beyond the ivy-covered walls of academe, whereas I had had a wealth of real-life experience, a fact that was appreciated by a number of students. I eventually had students coming some distances from other universities to talk with me. I even met with some who were taking courses in their thirties, forties, and even older. When I would jocularly ask these older ones, "What do you want to be when you grow up?" they took the question seriously. (I could never pose this question to younger students, of course.) They usually were generally unhappy with their current line of work and, for the most part, lacked job satisfaction, a widespread complaint. I usually would ask my "clients" what they liked to do best and what they would be best at doing. More often than not, they had the same answer to both questions. I would throw out a few suggestions, but on the whole they mostly found their own solutions, while I just listened sympathetically. They basically simply needed someone with whom they could kick around their ideas. In teaching I had long been taken by Henry Adams's observation in his classic *Education of Henry Adams*: "A teacher affects eternity; he can never tell where his influence stops."

When Ronald Reagan was elected president in November 1980, former ACDA Director Fred Iklé asked me if I would be willing to join Reagan's NSC transition team. Each department and agency of the executive branch had a transition team to prepare for the new administration. I noted that I was registered Democrat, albeit of the [Senator] "Scoop" Jackson variety—that is, hardline on national security issues but somewhat liberal on domestic issues. Fred said other Democrats were joining the Reagan administration, which indeed welcomed them. (Most of us subsequently became Reagan Republicans.) The NSC team was lodged in an office building in downtown DC. We sat together at a long table and talked about policy, personnel, and other related items. I sat next to Richard Armitage, who would later wind up as the number two officer at State. When the team was disbanded just before the inauguration, I rode down in the elevator with National Security Advisor–delegate Dick Allen who asked me to join his NSC staff. I told him I would be happy to do so, but needed flexibility in order to continue at Georgetown. He assured me that this was no problem. To be on the safe side, I opted to forgo any salary and keep my ample annuity that I would have had to give up if I were on a government payroll. On the payroll I was bound to lose some flexibility. This arrangement came in handy before very long.

It was great being back in the OEOB; it has French Second Empire design and spacious, nearly twenty-foot-high ceiling offices that often have balconies and fireplaces, although the latter no longer work. The corridors all have floors of black and white checkerboard patterned marble in which one could often spot the outlines of ancient mollusks. The walls of the building were of massive granite. It is replete with elaborate design features down to the doorknobs. It is, in essence, a late Victorian structure. It was built from 1871 to 1888 to house the War, Navy, and State Departments, which it continued to do until 1918 when the Navy left. In 1938 the War Department left, leaving the building to the State Department. This gives an idea of how enormously the federal bureaucracy has grown since World War II began. Imagine a time when all the organization housed in the massive Pentagon and in numerous other buildings would fit into a little more than two-thirds of the OEOB. President Eisenhower in 1957 agreed to a board recommendation to demolish this great structure to build a larger more modern one with many more and smaller offices to house his burgeoning staff. (Wags said he wanted to turn it into a parking lot.) There then ensued an uproar of protest from preservationists, architects, and many others. Moreover, tearing down a structure this massive would have been enormously expensive. Ike ultimately gave up the idea. It is, therefore, beyond ironical that a few years ago the OEOB was renamed the Dwight D. Eisenhower Executive Office Building.

One of the great perks one had in the White House was the use of the president's nicely appointed suite, including a restroom and small fridge stocked with little bottles of champagne, at the Kennedy Center for the Performing Arts, which we could occupy when the president or his friends were not using it. It could accommodate eight guests, making it ideal for entertaining friends or professional contacts, since everybody understandably regarded being invited to this as a signal privilege on the Washington scene. One evening, for example, we had in the box renowned economist Arthur Burns.

My favorite people in the White House were the Southern, middle-aged, cleaning ladies. They were dear. I often surprised visitors by stopping to give one a big hug. Believe me: I was not putting on an act. I really very much liked those dear ladies. In the Kissinger era I used to work late and would often wind up, close to midnight, dragging myself home on my two-mile walk to Georgetown. The cleaning ladies used to visit me and exchange Southern recipes late at night. One morning, one of them came in, closed the door, and told me that I had left my safe open, a safe that contained a great deal of highly classified material. I could see a major security violation staring me in the face. She told me that she had closed and locked the safe. She should have reported it to security instead, and what she did could well have cost her job. When I finally left the White House in 1993 my cleaning lady friends came in to wish me farewell. Most were crying. I was, of course, deeply touched. I also had a good relationship with the White House police. When the Queen of England came to the White House I went over to where the ceremony was being held only to be told I needed a special pass, of which I was unaware. One of my police friends simply escorted me to the VIP section. I always believed that one should treat everyone with courtesy and respect. It's the right thing to do, but sometimes it can also pay off.

In 1981 I was hired to partner with famed Soviet affairs scholar Professor Richard Pipes of Harvard to handle Soviet and Eastern European affairs. He was the senior partner charged with big picture policy formulation. Actually he would have much preferred to retreat to Harvard's great library to fulfill his perceived mission of producing overarching policy papers. I was to be the detail person. The small "actions" I handled were in themselves seldom of earthshaking interest, but it has been my experience over the years that actual policy often results from an accumulation of such actions, usually carried out at the mid-level of the bureaucracy. When Reagan entered the White House in January 1981, Poland was in the midst of a crisis. In August 1980, the newly formed workers' movement, Solidarity, organized a strike in a Gdansk (former Danzig) shipyard. The success of this strike unnerved the country's ruling Communist party and created an ongoing crisis that greatly disturbed the Soviet leadership.

Not long after I came on board at the White House, I attended an interagency meeting of several dozen of the government's top Soviet and Eastern European experts who had been called to discuss the situation in Poland. I was the only one present who insisted that the Soviets would not "invade" Poland by introducing more troops than were already in the country. The reasons I gave were along the lines I described above to my students. I only recently obtained some inside information confirming that the Soviets expected stiff resistance from the Polish Army as well as from guerrilla forces if they invaded. In addition, I believed that the Soviets would not want to give the West any justification to strengthen its defenses. I long have been convinced that some of the military present at the meeting secretly hoped the Soviets would invade so that U.S. defense expenditures would increase, and the Europeans would be discouraged from having any thoughts of détente with the USSR and would be more supportive of U.S. defense efforts in Europe. The Soviets had largely succeeded in creating a spirit of détente in the 1970s, which generally evaporated with the Soviet invasion of Afghanistan in December 1979.

President Carter's reaction to the invasion of Afghanistan was to negate all the détente-promoting agreements that had been worked out between the USSR and the United States. We know now that Soviet leader Leonid Brezhnev opposed invading Poland in the hope that the badly battered détente still might be resuscitated. Eventually Polish premier and Party leader General Wojiech Jaruzelski declared martial law on December 31, 1981, gaining control of the unruly situation, at least for the time being. At this point most had backed off from the belief the Soviets would invade. As with my Berlin Wall prediction, nobody in government ever mentioned to me that I had been right when all the others had been wrong. In fact, the only person ever to mention this to me was a former NSC colleague and Soviet expert, the late Bill Hyland, then head of the Council on Foreign

Relations, whom I just happened to run into while walking up Connecticut Avenue near the White House.

Early in his administration, on March 30, 1981, Reagan was shot just after addressing a CIO-AFL meeting at the Hilton Hotel on Connecticut Avenue and was rushed to The George Washington University Hospital. As the doctors prepared to operate on him, he reportedly quipped, "I hope you're all Republicans." According to press accounts, when the top brass immediately gathered in the White House, Secretary of State Alexander Haig stated that he was the "vicar" there and was in charge. (In point of fact, he was fourth in the line of succession should the president actually be incapacitated. The vice president was obviously first.) I believed at the time that this was a kind of reflex action on Al's part, since he had in effect been the de facto president for nearly a year at the height of the Watergate crisis, as I earlier pointed out. I never had the nerve (or the indiscretion) to ask Al what had prompted his declaration. Some attributed it to the postcardiac operation medication he was on.

In November 1981 my boss, National Security Advisor Dick Allen, hit a bad patch when $1,000 and a seemingly incriminating note were found in an envelope in the safe of an office he had recently occupied. At first blush, this seemed to smack of hanky-panky, but it turned out, according to *The Reagan Diaries* (Ronald Reagan, 2007), that apparently the $1,000 had been sent to Nancy Reagan by a Japanese magazine as a well-intentioned, routine token of appreciation for an interview she had granted. To save embarrassment all around, Dick intercepted the envelope with the money and note and gave it to his secretary who put in the safe, after which everybody forgot about it. Eventually, an FBI investigation rightly absolved Dick of any wrong doing, but this result had to be reviewed by Justice where, after months, someone leaked it. Reagan wrote that he "suspected bureaucratic sabotage" aimed to embarrass his administration, not just Allen. As Reagan noted, it was highly unlikely that Allen would have moved and left $1,000 in his old safe, if he had taken the money for himself, which in itself was highly unlikely. The president realized, however, that the press, as well as Democrats in Congress, were not going to let up on this case as long as Allen remained in his position. On January 4, 1982, Dick was asked to resign, and he did. Welcome to Washington and its pathetic but often vicious little intrigues. Dick went back into private business and has been doing quite well ever since.

Dick Allen was replaced with one of Reagan's old friends from California, William "Bill" P. Clark, often referred to as "Judge" Clark for having been an associate justice of the California Supreme Court. He had begun in this administration as the deputy to Secretary of State Alexander Haig. Apart from this, he had had little or no experience in national security affairs. In fact, of all the eight national security advisers I served under, he had the least such experience; however, of all eight

I liked and respected him most. Because of his paucity of expertise, he relied more on his staff, at least certainly more on me, than did any of the others. He was the only one who took me along when he briefed the president on subjects I covered. Also he sent nearly all of the analytical pieces I wrote to the president. I thought this was just great. He was a very unassuming, down-to-earth, decent person. He loved living on his ranch and wore cowboy boots to the office, which on him did not seem affected. On the wall of his modest office he had hanging a glass case displaying his former sheriff father's iconic Old West Colt single action six-shooter. I loved this little decorating touch. As a former cowboy I found it easy to relate to him.

A few months into Judge Clark's tenure, I became the object of a curious and unfathomable plot to oust me. When I took this to the good Judge, he quashed it. It was difficult to fire me since I was not on the NSC payroll, so no one could justify doing so. (I preferred to keep getting my annuity rather than be on the White House payroll.) To this day, I wonder what prompted all this. I believe I know the identity of at least two of these backstabbers, both of whom later went on to top jobs in the government. Actually I never felt important enough to be plotted against. That's what puzzled me. Speechwriter Peggy Noonan, in her masterful book about her time in the Reagan Administration, *What I Saw at the Revolution* (1990) noted that this administration was noted for the amount of backstabbing that went on, and I can believe it. In any case, I somehow survived both Reagan administrations, which included several national security advisers. My survival may well have been due to my not being on the payroll, meaning I couldn't be fired as an "economy measure."

Unlike his predecessors, Reagan entered office convinced that the Cold War could be won if the United States and the West in general went on the offensive. This new U.S. approach was soon manifest, to the special alarm of KGB chief Yuri Andropov, who insisted that the United States was preparing a surprise attack on the Soviet Union, a threat he instructed his overseas agents, especially those in the United States, carefully to monitor. (When Leonid Brezhnev died, on November 10, 1982, he was replaced as Soviet leader by paranoid Andropov.) Before long, Reagan had begun a substantial military buildup, which was to contribute considerably to the decline and fall of the Soviet empire. The new "Reagan Doctrine" called for supporting resistance groups fighting the Soviets or their proxies—for example, the Cubans in Angola and Mozambique and, later, those Afghans fighting the Soviets in Afghanistan. This also came to apply to "Contras" fighting the Communist-dominated regime in Nicaragua, a position that was to cause Reagan's administration serious problems.

The July 19, 1979, deposal of Nicaragua's corrupt and somewhat oppressive ruler, Anastasio Somoza, was widely popular among all levels of the population and had the support of the United States that, in the following months, provided the new successor regime with substantial economic and humanitarian assistance.

Unfortunately, this new regime was soon dominated by the Sandinista National Liberation Front (shades of the Viet Cong's National Liberation Front), which was led by case-hardened Cuban-trained Marxist–Leninists, who later openly admitted to being Communists. The new Sandinista regime became increasingly oppressive, especially as manifested in religious persecution. Moreover, the regime began to greatly expand its armed forces with ample aid from the Soviet Union. The avowed objective of this military buildup was to spread Communism throughout Central America. Eventually, the Soviets promoted the construction of a twelve-thousand-foot runway at Punta Huete in western Nicaragua that could accommodate Cuban-based Soviet Tu-95 "Bear" long-range bomber or reconnaissance aircraft. These aircraft, rebased or refueled at this airstrip, could cover the entire western coasts of the United States and South America and fly west as far as Honolulu.

Clearly, the Soviet-backed Sandinistas were beginning to pose a serious military threat. By 1981 a resistance movement had been formed. It was popularly known as the "Contras," and most of the members at first were poor peasants; eventually about a quarter of the members had been in Somoza's discredited National Guard, which Contra foes used against them. In March 1981 Reagan approved covert action against the Sandinista regime. This in time produced a negative reaction in Congress resulting, on December 8, 1981, in Congress's unanimously passing the notorious Boland Amendment to the Defense Authorization Act that would block, in effect, any military aid to those seeking to overthrow the then-Communist-dominated Nicaraguan regime. The Boland Amendment was aimed at blocking U.S. aid for the Contras on the specious, if not absurd, grounds that Nicaragua, of all places, could become another Vietnam for us.

There also were a number of members of Congress who had been misled into taking a benign view of the Sandinistas. It was the imaginative ways of getting around this ill-advised amendment that was to lead to the major scandal of the Reagan administration. In any case, this amendment was all too reminiscent of the congressional obstructionism that lost us the war in Vietnam, especially the June 4, 1973, Case-Church amendment (see Chapter 15). I pointed out to the NSC's congressional liaison officer, Dr. Christopher M. Lehman (John's brother) that by citing the 1936 *U.S. v. Curtiss-Wright* Supreme Court decision that established executive branch primacy in foreign affairs we could get the Boland Amendment declared unconstitutional. I was clearly preaching to the choir. Chris's position, as he later described it, was,

> I was totally and unalterably opposed to the Boland Amendment
> in its several forms and when I came to the NSC in early 1983, I
> agreed fully that it was an unconstitutional provision and should
> be vigorously resisted/defeated in the next legislative cycle. At

> some point later in 1983, I wrote a memo to [then Reagan's Chief of Staff] Jim Baker through the National Security Advisor expressing a strong recommendation to veto the Appropriations bill containing the second Boland amendment because [it] was clearly intended as a "poison pill" which would allow the Democrats to attack the administration at a later date because of the ambiguity of the Boland language.

Nothing came of Chris's recommendation.

Chris was heavily involved in supporting the insurgency headed by Jonas Savimbi that sought to overthrow the Soviet- and Cuban-backed Marxist regime installed in the capital of Angola. He also played a key role in the repeal of the 1976 Clark Amendment banning military aid to Savimbi. In addition, he did much to convince Congress to support Reagan's strategic modernization program.

The year 1983 was notable for those of us engaged in Soviet and East European affairs. March 1983 was especially eventful, to say the least. On March 8 President Reagan gave a talk in which he accused the Soviet Union of being "an evil empire." I believe that my friend and NSC colleague Sven Kraemer had inserted this language. At that time, I would have preferred criticizing the USSR by citing specific faults and derelictions instead of using this kind of broad rhetoric. I was wrong. Reagan's label apparently had considerable impact in the USSR. More important, this was a facet of Reagan's generally offensive stance against the Soviet empire. The crowning blow to the Soviets came soon thereafter when, on March 23, Reagan announced plans to launch a Strategic Defense Initiative (SDI) that would render all nuclear weapons "impotent and obsolete." SDI was soon nicknamed "Star Wars."

The SDI initiative had a tremendous impact on Soviet leadership because it was widely believed among Soviet military experts that we could make it work. I remember, several months later, sitting next to a Soviet general at a dinner and asking him if he thought SDI could work. It was as if I had asked him if the sun would rise tomorrow. Of course you can make it work, he replied. At about this time I had read an authoritatively sourced report that top Soviet military brass believed that, given our technical and engineering competence and resources, SDI could be at least 55 percent effective, which would radically alter the strategic balance in our favor. Actually the Soviets had been working for some thirty years to achieve a defense against ballistic missiles with little success. As a key element of our military strength emphasis at that time, I am convinced SDI played a crucial role in shaping events that led to the collapse of the Soviet empire. Vladislav M. Zubok, in his revealing and very informative book *A Failed Empire* (2007) noted, "CIA's Robert Gates [now secretary of defense] assumes that 'SDI did have a significant impact on the Soviet political and military leadership' by presenting it with the prospect of an 'incredibly expensive new arms race in an area in which the USSR could hardly hope to compete effectively.'" This sums it up well and cogently.

The part of this year that I actually enjoyed was my obligatory "familiarization trip" to the Soviet Union and Eastern Europe, which I had taken twenty years before while at State. This time, coming from the White House, I was given VIP treatment. The highlights of this trip included a stay at Ambassador Jack Matlock's residence, a palatial mansion in Prague that had its own park and an indoor swimming pool. It had been built by a rich industrialist before World War II. My then-fiancée Joan got word to Jack that I would be celebrating my sixty-first birthday as his guest. After dinner on that day, the butler brought in a huge birthday cake with sixty-one candles burning. It took a while to blow them out. As I noted earlier, I have long regarded Prague as one of the most beautiful cities in the world and it was great to be back there again. The next really enjoyable part, indeed the most enjoyable part, was visiting my old friend Chris Squire, then our consul general in Leningrad (now St. Petersburg) and with whom I had been on the receiving end of a number of six-foot Soviet rockets in Pleiku Province during the 1972 "Easter Offensive," as described in Chapter 15.

What a contrast between his Leningrad residence, the former relatively modest town palace of a prince in czarist times, and Chris's cinderblock quarters in Vietnam! That's the Foreign Service for you. Chris took it upon himself to show me the city, then somewhat on the drab, neglected side, the most impressive part of which was the huge cemetery with a series of mass graves in which were buried a large number of the some 1.2 million people of Leningrad who died, most of starvation, during the German siege of the city from September 1941 to January 1944. The graves were a number of large elongated grassy mounds with a memorial column and statue in the center. Night and day there came over the loudspeaker system the haunting strains of Chopin's funeral march. It was an incredibly moving experience.

On a much lighter note was the great Leningrad circus to which Chris and his dear wife Patricia took me one evening. Many cities in the Soviet Union had permanent circuses that generally feature animal acts, which was especially true of this one. The bear acts are always great. The bears ride bicycles and motorcycles, toss a ball around, dance, and do other routines. Because bears are relatively easy to train, these performances, while quite entertaining, were not very impressive acts. What followed, however, was something I had always thought impossible: trained cats. There were four or five of them doing little dance routines and other maneuvers in unison. It was not until later, when I finally had a cat, that I fully realized what a prodigious effort must have been required to get these cats to perform anything, let alone as a group. There also were a number of performing dogs, like the bears a not-too-impressive act. The finale of the dog act was the lot them, about ten small ones, running madly around the foot-high and foot-wide ring that enclosed the animals. One dog stopped to poop and all the other dogs collided with it, with dogs scattering all over the place.

Leningrad was clearly the highlight of my trip; although I must say I also much enjoyed staying at Spaso House, the ambassador's imposing residence in Moscow, another carryover from pre-Revolution times. Spaso House was run by a beautiful young Russian woman who could well have been used by the KGB to seduce important visitors staying there. I never heard that this was ever a problem, however.

In October 1983 I was saddened to learn that Judge Clark was being eased out of the White House to become secretary of the interior. Rumor had it that Chief of Staff Mike Deaver had persuaded First Lady Nancy Reagan that Clark was too hardline vis-à-vis the Soviets and had to go, which Clark did with typical good grace. This must have been a very painful decision for Reagan, who regarded Clark practically as a son. His going to Interior was announced on October 13, and on October 17 it was decided that Bud McFarlane would replace him. Bud, then the Judge's deputy, was the one who had earlier told me I was fired. What followed was a mixed bag of national security advisers. Some of them, including McFarlane, would later fall prey to the burgeoning Iran-Contra scandal. Of those who followed, I had the most respect for Gen. Collin Powell, whom I considered to be the most capable and compassionate person I had ever worked for. I was shocked and disappointed, therefore, when he turned against the Republican Party that had consistently promoted his career in October 2008. When Richard Pipes had to return to Harvard, I agitated for bringing in Jack Matlock to replace him. As noted before, Jack had been our ambassador to Czechoslovakia and then was our chargé d'affaires in Moscow. I did the necessary spadework to bring him on board as the first active-duty FSO in Reagan's NSC staff. State was reluctant to let him go, but relented in the face of a White House request.

Nancy Reagan unwittingly played the key role in blocking my one chance to become an ambassador, the goal of all FSOs. The White House Presidential Personnel Office recommended that I become our next ambassador to Austria, a dream assignment for which I clearly had all the requisite qualifications and then some. I even spoke German with a Viennese accent. Unfortunately, Nancy's good friend, cosmetic queen Estée Lauder, wanted her son Ronald to have that post, and of course he got it. Ronald Lauder seemed to have had a chip on his shoulder vis-à-vis the Austrians. Many Jewish Americans believed that Austria unjustifiably escaped much of the blame for its Nazism—which to some extent was true. In any case, Lauder did not help U.S.–Austrian relations. Fortunately, he was eventually succeeded by former *Time* magazine chief editor, Henry Grunwald, the son of Alfred Gruenwald, the well-known librettist for Emmerich Kalman's beloved Viennese operettas and for favorite Viennese songs. A former Austrian himself who, being Jewish, had to leave Austria when the Nazis took over, Grunwald was enormously popular with the Austrians and did much to get U.S.–Austrian relations back on track.

The president himself, as history will note, kept his eye on the "big picture," notably undermining the Soviet empire, and tended to scant issues he believed were of lesser importance. This used to exasperate those who tried to sell their ideas and projects to the president in NSC and other meetings. Sometimes during a presentation his eyes would glaze over or he would almost doze off. More than once, I had one incensed colleague come back from a meeting chaired by the president exclaiming, "There is no president!" after Reagan had almost dozed off when my friend's pet project was aired. Peggy Noonan, in the book cited above, quoted TV star Leslie Stahl asking Peggy, "I'd give a lot to reconcile these two things: that Reagan is, so the rumors have it, disengaged and uninvolved and lazy—and yet on certain issues he is totally unmovable, wouldn't give in no matter what the pressure. How could he be so uninvolved and yet cling, with determination, on taxes and SDI?"

I had relatively little direct contact with Reagan, especially after Clark's departure, but I know enough about him to strongly recommend reading Peggy Noonan's book in order to understand Reagan and his administration. From 1984 to 1989 Peggy had frequent and continuous contact with the president and knew him as well as anyone could. Here are excerpts describing Reagan from Peggy's book (*What I Saw at the Revolution*):

> He [Reagan] didn't have to be the man pulling the switch, he wasn't in it for the ego, he was actually in it to do good. He was probably the sweetest, most innocent man to serve in the Oval Office. He was a modest man with an intellect slightly superior to average. His whole career, in fact, was proof of the superior power of goodness to gifts. "No great men are good men," Said Lord Acton, who was right, until Reagan. Toward mankind in general he had the American attitude direct and unillusioned: He figured everybody is doing as much bad as he has to and as much good as he can. He wasn't artless, or an angel; he didn't expect a great deal. . . . James Baker said, He is the kindest and most impersonal man I ever knew. An aide said, "Beneath the lava flow of warmth there is something impervious as a glacier. . . . Imagine a president with no personal enemies. This has never happened before. Imagine a man nobody hates, or no one who knows him."

The year 1984 was, next to my birth date, the most important year of my life in that I took the wisest step in my life. On May 5, I married my longtime, dearest friend, Joan Frances Crotty in the old Georgetown University chapel. The officiating priest was Father Zrinyi, a wonderful Jesuit (of the old school) professor of economics who had been born a Hungarian count. My best man was my friend and NSC colleague Marine Lt. Col. Oliver North who was, in a few short years, to become nationally famous, if notorious, for his part in the ill-fated Iran-Contra scheme. I had first met Joan one morning in March 1972 on the corner of Thirty-fourth and M Streets in Georgetown when we were both going to work. It turned out that we were close neighbors and that both of us worked at the White House. Joan worked for Pat Nixon and then Betty Ford and I, of course, worked for Henry Kissinger. There were subsequent gaps in our contacts, but eventually we became closer and closer friends. While I had been dating some fine young women, it increasingly occurred to me that none could come close to Joan. She was one of nine children in a Catholic family with the heritage of an Irish father and French (Alsatian)–Anglo Saxon mother. She had a strong moral character uncommon in those (and present) times and was caring, kind, giving, gracious, intelligent, and last, but certainly not least, she was beautiful and more than once was taken for actress Candice Bergen who was not much older. My mother adored her and used to insist that I wasn't really good enough for her.

Next to her late mother (an ideal mother-in-law), she was the least jealous woman I have ever known. In fact she really liked the last pre-engagement woman I dated. Joan has long been director of admissions of the Medical School of the Uniformed Services University of the Health Sciences (USUHS), which trains doctors for the armed services and the Public Health Service. She has been with USUHS ever since it began accepting students in 1976. She has a masters of social work from Catholic University and for some time was a licensed, but nonpracticing, therapist. Joan was among the first of the Boomer Generation and I, of course, am a member of the "Greatest Generation." Americans seem to have a hard time understanding how a marriage between two people of different generations could possibly work. As to the age difference, Joan's main complaint had long been that she didn't have my energy level. Things finally evened up a bit in this regard when I had a heart attack in 2007. Actually she had long believed she had more in common with my generation than with her own. Our marriage, from the very beginning, has been a happy one and has gotten better with each year. We have over the years simply become increasingly devoted to each other.

My wife Joan and I enjoyed an especially pleasurable interlude when the Austrian government invited us to come to Vienna in May 1985, to celebrate the thirtieth anniversary of the Austrian State Treaty. I was mainly invited because of my dissertation-turned-book, *The Soviet Union and the Occupation of Austria*, which explains why the Soviets finally agreed to sign the Treaty and leave Austria (an explanation, incidentally, that still holds water). I suppose I was also given a bit of credit for having battled the Soviets for four and half years when they tried to suppress "First Amendment" freedoms in Austria. We were put up at my favorite Viennese hotel, the historic five-star Hotel Sacher, which was long monopolized by the Austrian aristocracy, and which has long been known for its great cuisine, especially that delectable cake, the Sacher torte. The highlight of our stay was a wonderful performance of my very favorite opera, *Der Rosenkavalier* by Richard Strauss.

In May 1988 we enjoyed another invitation to Europe when West Germany's leading bank, the Deutsche Bank, invited me to be the principal speaker at a symposium in Duesseldorf. We were put up in a flower-bedecked suite in Duesseldorf's fine five-star Hotel Breitenbacher Hof and were well wined and dined. I addressed the convention extemporaneously in German for about fifteen minutes on U.S.–Soviet relations and then answered questions. I have long found this format is the best, because the questions would tell me what my audience was really interested in. (There was no conflict of interest here because I didn't accept any money, and I never had any professional contact with banks.)

In November 1986 the Iran-Contra affair that had been simmering beneath the surface broke out into the open. Here is how it began: On June 15, 1986, a TWA jetliner with more than a hundred Americans on board was hijacked and flown to Beirut, Lebanon, where the passengers were held hostage. Most were released in a prisoner swap involving the Israelis, but five remained held. Those in the White House charged with this problem, principally National Security Advisor Bud McFarlane, sought a solution. Bud came up with a plan described by Reagan in his diary in a December entry as follows: "It calls for Israel selling some weapons to Iran. As they are delivered in installments by air our hostages will be released. . . . We then sell Israel replacements for the delivered weapons." This assumed that Iran had considerable influence over those holding the hostages, which it indeed had. Also involved in this operation were Deputy National Security Advisor (later to replace Bud as National Security Advisor) Vice Adm. John Poindexter and NSC staffer Marine Lt. Col. Oliver North, whose account included conflicts in Central America. The Israelis made a profit on the weapons sales to Iran, which they deposited in a secret Contra Swiss bank account. North had come up with this idea of funneling profits to the Contras fighting in Nicaragua. This was a violation of the Boland Amendment, of course, but as I have already stated, Chris Lehman and I regarded that amendment as unconstitutional.

On November 6 it became known that a press story in Beirut reported that we had bought the freedom of hostage David Jacobsen with arms deliveries to Iran. This created a flurry of reaction in the media and in Congress. The president subsequently was more than vexed that North had not told him about the Contra arrangement and "worst of all John Poindexter [who had replaced McFarlane who retired late in 1985] didn't tell me." Poindexter resigned shortly thereafter and was replaced by Frank Carlucci who had been deputy CIA director. The NSC was in turmoil, to say the least. I don't believe there had ever been an NSC turnover at the top this frequently. When Poindexter resigned, the focus shifted to North, but by 1987 everybody connected with Iran-Contra was getting in trouble. In February 1987 Bud McFarlane attempted suicide in despair. The star of the Hill hearings was clearly Ollie North, who had had to resign from the NSC. He had been summoned to appear on July 7 to testify in a joint Senate–House investigating committee that convened in the Senate Caucus Room in the Russell Senate Office Building. He appeared in uniform with a (well-deserved) chest full of medal ribbons. He had seen a great deal of action in Vietnam where he had been severely wounded. He made a spirited, stirring, and convincing televised defense of what had been done to aid the Contras and why it had to be kept secret, which gained him a great deal of public support, to the chagrin of those interrogating him.

In the end, North and Poindexter were convicted of withholding information from Congress and of obstructing justice. Both charges were vacated on appeal. McFarlane pleaded guilty to withholding information from Congress, but was pardoned by Reagan's successor, George H. W. Bush. The charges against these men were outrageous. In the first place, the Boland Amendment that was the root cause of all those accusations was a clear example of unconstitutional overstepping by the Congress. Aiding the Contras was clearly in our national interest. Without the Contras there would have been no armed opposition to the oppressive Sandinista regime, which ultimately led to a 1989 peace agreement calling for free elections. Even the Soviets were confident that the Sandinistas would win a fair election. To everyone's surprise the 1990 election resulted in a decisive victory for the United Nicaraguan Opposition, headed by democratic-oriented Violeta Chamorro, widow of and successor to the editor of La Prensa, whose assassination triggered the upheaval that deposed Somoza in 1979, as mentioned above.

Since the Soviets were involved with Nicaragua, I had a special interest in aiding the Contras and volunteered to help my friend Ollie with this problem. Fortunately, he declined my offer with thanks. Ollie at that point was stretched very thin. His accounts included not only Communist insurgencies in Central America but also counterterrorism and continuity of government in case of a major attack on the United States. Any one of these was a full-time job. Ollie simply didn't want to give any of them up. Before the whole Iran-Contra imbroglio emerged, Ollie had been ordered by the Marine Corps to proceed to Camp LeJeune to take command of a battalion. Ollie clearly preferred to remain in the far-more-prestigious White House to finish what he had started, and the president agreed he should stay. I have long believed that if Ollie had taken over the battalion, not only would he have escaped his subsequent Congress-instigated trials and travails but eventually he could well have become commandant of the Marine Corps. (I correctly predicted that P. X. Kelley would become commandant when he was only a colonel.)

Ollie North wasn't the only friend of mine who was given a bad time in 1987. In February 1987 my good friend John O. Koehler, former director of Associated Press's Worldwide Service, was chosen by the president to be White House Director of Communications, replacing departing well-known former news commentator Pat Buchanan. What happened next is described in Reagan's *Diaries*:

> Learned that our W. H. press corps has learned that Jack Koehler who I have picked to replace Pat B. at 10 years of age joined the Hitler Youth movement in Germany. They are raising a fire storm over this. They ignore that he came to this country served in our military & went from Corp. to Capt. with 14 years of active and reserve duty—including service in our mil. Intelligence. He's been top man at A. P. and had a lifetime career there heading the International Bureau among other things. Well I'm not going to back down in the face of a lynch mob.

Not long thereafter, realizing that his situation had been made untenable, Jack stepped down and left the White House.

In the first place Jack had "joined" not the Hitler Youth but, being only ten, the Jungvolk (Young People) organization. After only six months of membership, he was spotted by his mother as he stood in formation with other kids, She ran up to him, pulled him out of the line and shouted, "*Weg von hier*" (Get away from this). Jack remembers, "My mother was irate. My father had been fired from his professorship at the Dresden Technical University in 1934, because he was a Social Democratic Party member, even months before a Jewish friend lost his job. Fortunately, he got a job at a tea packing company where he built the first tea bag machines, the first few of which were sold to the Lipton tea company in the U.S." When Jack turned fourteen, he was pressured to join the Hitler Youth. Instead, he volunteered to become a messenger for the air raid police where he served during the disastrous 1945 firebombing of Dresden. Generally, in this totalitarian dictatorship, young people had little choice but to join the two Nazi youth groups. Jack has always declared all of the above in getting up to top-secret security clearances. His being pilloried by the press was beyond outrageous.

In November 1988 Vice President George H. W. Bush was elected president, defeating Massachusetts Governor Michael Dukakis. The last time I saw President Reagan was in January 1989 just before he left office. I was having my picture taken with him and began to chat. At that point the old film star in him came out when he directed me "to look at the camera." Reagan's remarkable contribution to the country and to the world, particularly his key and decisive role in helping to bring about the fall of the Soviet empire, is increasingly recognized.

The NSC, indeed the whole White House under Bush, was substantially different and more stable than it had been under Reagan. What I found puzzling was that we Reaganauts—that is those of us who had served under Reagan—were treated as if we were all members of another and hostile political party and were shunned. In other words, none of us was to continue serving in the White House. The new (and only) Bush national security adviser was retired Air Force general Brent Scowcroft, who of all the eight in this role under whom I had served was intellectually best prepared for the job, even exceeding Kissinger in this regard. I had served under Brent in the Ford administration and he had learned to fly in a Stearman, so I decided to take my chances by simply staying on; I was not one who had to be hired, in any case, since I was willing to continue serving *pro bono publico*. When I showed up at the first NSC general staff meeting, Brent looked at me and said, "Are you still here?" That was the last time I attended a staff meeting. (I eventually learned from Bob Woodward's book *The Commanders* [Simon and Shuster, 1991] that Scowcroft was very critical of Reagan's Soviet policy and thought he was ill-served by his "national security team," of which I was a member, hence his bias against us all.) I hunkered down and was taken care of by the administrative people who had taken care of me in the previous administration. In time, Scowcroft got used to my being there when he started getting analytical memos from me on subjects in which he was interested.

On the one hand—and this is important—I believe I was blessed to be in the White House working on Soviet bloc affairs at one of the most critical and far-reaching junctures in modern history: the dissolution of the Soviet empire. On the other hand, I feel remiss in not having had a better feel for what was transpiring in the Soviet bloc, since prior to this I had a fairly good batting average in figuring out what Moscow would do next. For example, in December 1994 I had sent National Security Advisor Bud McFarlane a memo predicting that the Soviets were about to launch another détente campaign designed to thwart our development of SDI. As I describe above, the Soviets were deeply concerned about SDI because they believed we could make it work eventually. It had long been my theory that when the Soviets believed they were falling behind us militarily they would launch a détente campaign to convince us that we had nothing to fear and could safely throttle back our defense capabilities. This theory is more fully developed below.

I also believe that most American policy makers did not adequately appreciate the extent to which military power was the key—indeed the decisive—element of Soviet political and diplomatic power. Thus when we were ahead militarily, Moscow viewed us as harder to cope with on the world scene. As I mentioned in Chapter 12, the impact of our belief in the "missile gap" on our negotiating position in the 1959 Foreign Ministers Conference in Geneva revealed to me for the first time the real purpose of strategic arms: they were the blue chips in diplomatic poker with the Soviet Union. I still fervently believe in maintaining a highly credible strategic strike capability, even should the Pentagon conclude there is no perceived need for this capability. One never knows when one is going to need these diplomatic poker chips in dealing with threatening or unruly nations in an uncertain future.

Many will disagree with me, but I do not believe that the Soviet Union really *planned* to attack either the United States or Western Europe. (They hoped to achieve their objectives in Europe through subversion and pressure.) To be sure, the Soviets with their European satrapies had *plans* to do both. We have even seen some of them and they were quite detailed, realistic, and convincing. The United States most certainly had *plans* for attacks on the Soviet empire, but we never expected to use those plans except in retaliation or to counter an imminent threat. I was quite intrigued by a Soviet–U.S. attack scenario worked out by our top analyst of the Soviet military, William T. Lee mentioned in Chapter 15. Based on masses of intelligence he had gathered, Lee believed that if it came to a nuclear war the Soviets would try to minimize the total yield it laid down on the United States for two reasons. First, in such a case, the Soviets had hoped to occupy a defeated United States and didn't want to inherit mostly destroyed and smoking cities and economic infrastructure, especially since the Soviet Union itself could be largely in ruins. Second, given the prevailing westerly winds in the Northern Hemisphere, the fallout from such an attack would plague and poison Western Europe, which they would hope to have occupied, as well as the Soviet empire itself.

This, Bill concluded, would mean that the Soviets would stick to relatively low-yield ICBM weapons targeted at our defense infrastructure to avoid collateral damage. Bill believed that Washington, DC, as a command and control center, would probably be the only major U.S. city, qua city, targeted. In addition to fear of fallout, despite extensive Soviet efforts to defend against retaliatory U.S. strikes, such strikes would certainly have wreaked havoc in the Soviet Union itself. This raised a fundamental controversy within the defense and arms control community. The prevailing view supported the concept of mutual assured destruction (with the apt acronym MAD). In this scenario both sides are deterred by the inevitable destruction each power would incur from retaliatory nuclear strikes should one launch a first-strike attack. This view was most commonly, but not exclusively, held among liberals.

Conservatives (including me) generally believed that the Soviets had not bought the MAD concept, but instead were wedded to the much different damage limitation concept. The elements of this concept were these: an extensive deep shelter complex that would protect their key players; a budding but still far-from-successful antimissile defense capability that employed at least one large-phased array radar, among others, which violated the 1972 ABM (Antiballistic Missile) Treaty; and the deployment of SAMs that could possibly double as ABM weapons. Also there was their ace in the hole: ballistic missile submarines to be deployed in waters controlled and well protected by the Soviet Navy (for example, the northeast reaches of the Sea of Okhotsk) ready to retaliate. In other words, while we generally scanted defensive systems, the Soviets were devoting considerable assets to building a capability to survive a U.S. strike and to retaliate effectively. Interestingly, Defense Secretary Harold Brown, under President Carter, in his fiscal year 1981 Defense Posture Statement described the Soviet measures listed above as "a concerted effort to take away the effectiveness of our second-strike forces." In other words, the Soviet Union had adopted a *damage limitation strategy*. I would love to see some contemporary scholar check out all these above-mentioned theories using newly declassified Soviet documents.

Picking up on the reference to Soviet détente policy above, here is a brief history of the Soviet policy of switching to détente tactics to retard military advantages over the Soviet Union we accrued from time to time. When NATO was first formed in 1949, Stalin called off the failing Berlin blockade and tried to placate us otherwise. Stalin, however, was temperamentally singularly unsuited to effectively promote détente that, in any case, would have disintegrated in June 1950 when North Korea attacked South Korea with Stalin's blessings, if not his encouragement. The second and most effective détente campaign of all began soon after the death of Stalin on March 5, 1953. Its primary goal must have been to dampen and reverse the enormous U.S. defense buildup resulting from the Korean War. As I mention earlier, we had unilaterally almost completely disarmed after World War II, whereas the Soviet Union had not. Stalin's death before long resulted in an end to the Korean War with an armistice agreement signed at Panmunjom on July 27, 1953. Stalin's death also encouraged unrest in Eastern Europe, especially in East Germany (see Chapter 11). This post-Stalin détente reached its zenith in 1955 under Party First Secretary Nikita Khrushchev, who made a number of dramatic and unexpected moves that included a conciliatory visit to Stalin's former archenemy, Yugoslav President Josip Broz Tito; handing back to Finland the Soviet naval base at Porkkala; and establishing diplomatic ties with West Germany. But most dramatic and far-reaching of all, an agreement was made to conclude a State Treaty, signed on May 15, 1955, which was to end the quadripartite occupation of Austria after ten long years. (On May 14 an illusory Soviet bloc NATO counterpart, the Warsaw Pact, was created to provide a legal basis for maintaining Soviet troops in Hungary and Rumania that had previously been justified as "lines of communication" troops supporting Soviet forces in Austria.)

Khrushchev was keen on crowning his détente campaign with a Big Four (U.S., British, French, and Soviet) summit conference. One of the conditions President Eisenhower had set for his participation in such a meeting was Soviet agreement to an Austrian State Treaty. This treaty resulted in the July 1955 Geneva Summit that generated a spirit of goodwill soon exploited by the Soviets as the Spirit of Geneva. This was the crowning achievement of this détente and was soon paying dividends. For example, the Icelandic Parliament on March 28, 1956, resolved that "in view of the changed situation" the United States should withdraw the troops it had operating a vital air base. Testifying in a Senate committee in April 1956, former U.S. Chief of Staff General Omar Bradley stated, "I am concerned . . . because Russian propaganda is having an effect on the integrity of NATO" (*New York Times*, April 17, 1956). This Soviet détente, which was clearly succeeding, however, went down in flames when Soviet troops suppressed the Hungarian Revolution in November 1956 (see Chapter 12). The Icelandic Parliament subsequently changed its mind and asked that U.S. troops remain. One thing that no doubt encouraged both Polish resistance and the Hungarian Revolution was Khrushchev's denunciations of Stalin's crimes in a secret speech before the XX Party Congress in February 1956. It didn't remain secret long and its leaking out created a bombshell of reaction. In the Soviet Union Khrushchev promoted and encouraged significant domestic liberalization, exemplified in the cultural "thaw."

The following détente campaign resulted from Khrushchev's reaction to his badly failed 1962 Cuban missile adventure and also no doubt to the knowledge that, at the time of the crisis, the United States had something like a ten-to-one superiority in strategic weapon delivery systems. In April 1963 the United States and the USSR agreed to establish a telephonic "hot line" to facilitate rapid, leadership-level, direct communications in crisis situations. In June the two nations signed a nuclear test ban treaty banning aboveground tests. About this time Moscow also stopped jamming Voice of America broadcasts to the Soviet Union. A main contribution to this détente's demise was the active military assistance, especially SAM installations, Moscow provided to the North Vietnamese beginning in 1965.

The next Soviet détente campaign began in the early 1970s and was no doubt designed, through restricting arms control agreements, inter alia, to counter the U.S. development of MIRV (multiple, independently targeted reentry vehicle), an ICBM with multiple warheads that have different targets. This system, which could overwhelm Soviet missile defenses, was considered a major threat by Moscow. In 1972 the ABM (antiballistic missile) Treaty was signed, which Moscow knew would limit U.S. development of this system while they (unsuccessfully) sought to perfect one of their own, as we now know. Also agreed on was a provisional SALT agreement, which I thought at the time was to the Soviet Union's advantage, as were subsequent similar agreements. This fairly successful (at one point) détente began to wane as relations between President Carter and Brezhnev worsened, mostly due to differences over strategic arms control issues. Détente came to a quick end when the Soviet Union invaded Afghanistan in December 1979.

We now come to the final, and for the Soviet Union fatal, détente campaign, but first a bit of background. As noted above in this chapter, in December 1994 I wrote Bud McFarlane a memo in which I predicted another détente campaign aimed at countering our very considerable military buildup and especially at derailing SDI. It actually took another six months or so for this to develop. In November 1984 Ronald Reagan, age seventy-three, was elected to a second term, burying Democratic candidate Walter Mondale in a landslide. This was great news to all of us, of course. Not long into President Reagan's second term came a development in the Soviet Union that would later prove to be of transcendent importance. Andropov had died on February 9, 1984, and had been succeeded by Konstantin U. Chernenko, who subsequently died on March 10, 1985, followed by Mikhail Gorbachev, the youngest member of the Communist Party's Politburo. Gorbachev would unwittingly bring about the end of the Soviet empire within five years.

Gorbachev remained to the end a dedicated Communist who firmly believed in the validity of Marxist–Leninist doctrine. But he also was dedicated to innovating and improving the existing system. The two watchwords of Gorbachev's reign were perestroika (restructuring) and glasnost (openness); these two words signaled a sincere intention to better the lot of Soviet citizens. On the other hand, Gorbachev soon revealed an earnest interest in arms control and in blocking the development of SDI. This was made especially clear in his first interview of note published in the United States in early September 1985 in *Time* magazine. Gorbachev made it crystal clear that the SDI program must be strangled in its crib. I found this interview of special interest, although at the time it was generally overlooked. In fact, I couldn't believe that virtually nobody else seemed to have picked up on this quite revealing piece. I wrote a memo flagging this interview for high-level attention, which went to the president. Gorbachev was far and away the most successful Soviet leader when it came to promoting the fifth and final Soviet détente, because he genuinely desired better relations with Western leaders and, far more than other Soviet leaders, actually felt comfortable in their company. He indeed became quite popular in the West and even acquired the nickname "Gorby." Can you imagine any other Soviet leader being given a nickname? In any case, however, he remained concerned about his nation's military posture and was stubbornly determined to seek the elimination of what he viewed as the major potential threat to his country's defense, SDI.

SDI remained a major bone of contention between Gorbachev and Reagan. This issue came to a head when the two met, October 11 and 12, 1986, in Reykjavik, Iceland, to discuss arms control. Reagan laid out his remarkable and incredibly far-reaching proposal to eliminate all nuclear weapons by 1996, but Gorbachev adamantly insisted that any arms control agreement between the two nations was contingent on Reagan's total renunciation of SDI, including laboratory testing. This is how Reagan described this exchange in his *Diaries*: "He [Gorbachev] wanted language that would have killed SDI. The price was high but I wouldn't sell & that's how the day ended. . . . I pledged I wouldn't give away SDI & I didn't but that meant no deal on any of the arms reductions. I was mad—he tried to act jovial but I acted mad & it showed."

In 1987 Gorbachev revealed that the quite genuine reforms he was introducing in the USSR also should be introduced in the European countries in the Soviet bloc. Subsequently he began to speak of applying a Sinatra Doctrine in his dealings with Eastern Europe. By this he was referring to Frank Sinatra's signature song "My Way," implying that Eastern Europeans would be free to apply "their way," as opposed to the Soviet way, in their internal affairs. The clear implication was a total rejection of the interventionist "Brezhnev Doctrine," which justified the Soviet-led invasion of Czechoslovakia in 1968; in any case, that doctrine had lapsed. I was convinced that the Sinatra Doctrine was only a détente gimmick and not for real. I believed that Gorbachev had to realize that the Soviet empire was held together by force or at least by the real threat of force. I was very wrong, as it turned out. Sincerely convinced of the validity, merit, and durability of Communism, Gorbachev actually believed that Communist rule in Eastern Europe was genuinely popular, not realizing how fragile it was and to what extent it had been based on force and terror. The Sinatra Doctrine was officially confirmed by Gorbachev at a critical Warsaw Pact meeting in Bucharest in July 1989 that turned out to have been a critical turning point.

Still quite wrongly, I refused to believe Gorbachev's Bucharest pronouncement was for real. It was opposed by the leaders of Bulgaria, Czechoslovakia, East Germany, and Rumania, who realized how much this would undermine their positions. The more independent and confident Polish and Hungarian leaders welcomed Gorbachev's pronouncement. I later felt considerably better about my profound misreading of the developing situation in the Soviet bloc in 1988–89 when I read a piece by *Washington Post* staffer Robert G. Kaiser (November 7, 1999) observing the tenth anniversary of breaching the Berlin Wall: "A computer-assisted search of the archives—extensive but not exhaustive—discovered no analyst or statesman, no commentator or professor who understood then the hole in the Wall would be quickly followed by the utter collapse of European Communism and the Soviet Union, soon producing a weak and bumbling Russia half the size of the U.S.S.R., with a fraction of its importance."

In any case, with benefit of hindsight and subsequent revelations, this fateful 1989 Warsaw Pact meeting marked the beginning of the end of the Soviet empire. Once Gorbachev's position became public, Communist Eastern Europe began unraveling. Succumbing to popular pressure, the East German regime in November 1989 finally permitted free travel to the West. This immediately resulted in the highly symbolic tearing down of the infamous Berlin Wall. Communist regimes throughout Eastern Europe were crumbling under the popular opposition unwittingly encouraged by Gorbachev. This infection spread to the most recently acquired part of the Soviet Union, the Baltic states of Estonia, Latvia, and Lithuania, which were forcibly and brutally seized in 1940 as the result of the August 1939 agreement between Hitler and Stalin, a move that set the stage for World War II. After an unsuccessful attempt to use force to bring Lithuania in line in January 1990, Gorbachev seemed not to have had the heart to subdue the Baltic States by force, and so lost them. Prior to the Soviet empire's unraveling, President George H. W. Bush had taken office in January 1989 and had made very knowledgeable Soviet scholar, Condoleezza Rice, his principal adviser on Soviet bloc issues. I had little contact with her, since I worked directly for Brent Scowcroft as his full-time, in-house special consultant. I spent most of my time poring over large amounts of intelligence, classified and open source (mostly from FBIS), wrote only information memos, and took no actions. Condy Rice and her team handled all the Soviet bloc–related actions.

I represented the NSC at the regular interagency Soviet Warning Meetings held at CIA headquarters in Langley, Virginia. At one meeting about this time, I suggested that the Baltic States breaking away would most certainly encourage the Ukraine and perhaps other Soviet regions to follow suit. This view was generally pooh-poohed. I later learned that there was strong sentiment in the White House against a breakup of the Soviet Union for fear of the chaos that could result from a nuclear-armed world power like the USSR coming apart at the seams. (A breakup of Yugoslavia was apparently also opposed—as it turned out for good reason, given the bloody chaos that eventually resulted from this event.) Since at that time I was removed from the White House inner circle, I was not privy to this kind of thinking. Incidentally, I was spectacularly wrong when it came to Gorbachev's position on German reunification.

West German chancellor Helmut Kohl met with Gorbachev in July 1990 in the resort town of Arkhyz in the North Caucasus to negotiate the details of a German reunification; in September 1990, and not being completely privy to Allied negotiations elsewhere on Germany, I was unaware of that fact when I sent Brent Scowcroft a memo making a closely reasoned case for the Soviet Union's never agreeing to a peaceful reunification of Germany. Sometime later I got the memo back with Brent's writing on the first page, "Well argued, but wrong." German reunification had been announced on October 3, 1990. Seemingly incredible, Gorbachev had even agreed that a reunified Germany could be a member of

NATO, though it later came out that he preferred a reunified Germany locked into NATO than being on its own. Soon thereafter Gorbachev was awarded the Nobel Peace Prize, a basically justified recognition of Gorbachev's role. In large measure thanks to Gorbachev's persistent well-intentioned fecklessness and incredible naïvete, the Soviet Union itself finally and mercifully came to an end on December 25, 1991, thus ending the Cold War. (For details on how the Soviet empire came to an end I recommend two books mentioned above: *The Fifty-Year War* by Norman Friedman and *A Failed Empire* by Vladislav M. Zubok.)

In 1992 my mother passed away. We assumed she was well into her nineties, but never knew how old she really was because when her birth certificate had been lost in a courthouse fire, she took a number of years off her age. She pulled it off by remaining relatively young through daily exercise, including golf and tennis. In fact, she was playing tournament golf into her eighties. She was an ace bridge player and played in bridge tournaments into her nineties. She also always associated with women much younger than she. She was a character and kept coming up with quips like, "Before long bottled water will be labeled cholesterol-free." When peanut farmer Jimmy Carter became president, the subject of my mother's father also being a peanut farmer came up at a family dinner. She kept getting questions about raising peanuts, which did not particularly interest my mother. When told that peanuts had to be roasted, someone asked, "How did you know when they were done?" Tired of this conversation, my mother replied, "We knew when they were done when someone would yell, 'Omygawd, the peanuts are burning.'"

I consider one of my crowning achievements in the Bush administration to be a revealing report I wrote on Nelson Mandela before he made his June 1990 trip to the United States. He was lionized everywhere he went and was scheduled to appear before a joint session of Congress and the United Nations General Assembly, and to visit the White House. I felt compelled to provide Brent Scowcroft, and through him the president, with the facts about Mandela's disturbing Communist connections. There is no doubt that Mandela symbolized and encouraged the increasing resistance to the apartheid regime in South Africa. He has been indeed a giant on the world scene at a time when most public figures have been relative pygmies. One must give the man his due. However, I knew that he was not the free agent he pretended to be. In point of fact, he was in thrall to the South African Communist Party (SACP), a fact that State and the CIA chose to ignore or cover up, or both. CIA had plenty of information on this which I used, but which the CIA generally neglected. Given that one of my main specialties at the time was Soviet machinations in the developing world, I couldn't in good conscience look the other way. In any case, I believed I had ensured that the president knew all about Mandela before he came to the White House. I believe this had something to do with the reserved reception Mandela received there.

Mandela had long been a key member of the African National Congress (ANC), which by the 1950s had been completely taken over by the SACP; he was a cofounder in 1961 of its militant branch Umkhonto we Sizwe (Spear of the Nation, or MK), which carried out the ANC's terrorist attacks, earning it a place on State's list of terrorist organizations. (Clueless State, for diplomatic reasons, delisted it in 1988, the year in which the MK's attacks peaked. Shopping malls were its principal targets.) In 1964 Mandela and other ANC members had been sentenced to life in prison on well-documented charges that they were planning to take over South Africa by armed force through instigating a widespread revolt in the planned Operation Mayibuye (Zulu for "return"). In 1973 Mandela was offered a release to free black Transkei, but he refused. In 1985 he was offered a release on the condition that he renounce the use of force. He refused and remained in his relatively comfortable confinement, becoming a globally famous symbol of resistance to apartheid in South Africa. He was finally released, on February 10, 1990, by President F. W. de Klerk who was seeking some kind of modus vivendi with the ANC by ending the ban on the ANC and by ending apartheid, thus eventually ending the international sanctions that were harming the country's economy.

Mandela's first postrelease speech, on February 11, 1990, began, "Comrades and fellow South Africans" and continued, "I salute the South African Communist Party for its sterling contribution for democracy. . . . The memory of great Communists like Bram Fischer and Moses Mabhida will be cherished for generations to come. I salute [SACP] General Secretary Joe Slovo, one of our finest patriots. We are heartened by the fact that the alliance between ourselves [the ANC] and the Party remains as strong as it ever was." Mandela was clearly currying favor with the SACP, which would decide his future, since it held the levers of power in the ANC. On February 13 the usually liberal *Washington Post* in an editorial found Mandela's praise of the SACP "passing uncomfortable" and asked, "But how can a [Communist] party that now stands revealed almost everywhere else in the world as repressive, corrupt and bankrupt win top billing at one of the century's great celebrations of freedom." The *Post* then speculated that, "caught in . . . a time warp," Mandela might have been paying old debts for past Soviet and Communist support, adding,

> But that does not entirely explain why Communist Party members still dominate the executive council [*sic*] of the African National Congress and why they also have a strong position in the ANC-oriented Mass Democratic Movement [an ANC front]. Nor does it explain why the ANC's lumpily Marxist formulation of 1955 known as the Freedom Charter [drafted by an SACP member], remains the organization's ideological beacon . . . their people

and friends elsewhere still want to know that the destiny of South African freedom movement . . . is not to create another of the cruel, undemocratic and inefficient state-centered regime that are collapsing in other parts of the world."

Sad to say, the exceptionally well-informed staffer who wrote this editorial seems never to have been heard from again. Neither the *Post* nor any other leading publication or media figure ever again associated the virtually canonized Mandela and the ANC with the SACP, both of which have continued to have a largely free ride in the media outside South Africa.

The degree of Mandela's subservience to the SACP was clearly demonstrated when, in his May 2–4, 1990, initial meeting with President de Klerk at Groote Schuur (the official residence of the leaders of South Africa), he was accompanied by SACP General Secretary Joe Slovo (a white Lithuanian rumored to have been a KGB colonel) and three other SACP members who were on the ANC's executive committee. Clearly, Party leaders were not sure they could rely on Mandela. He was a global celebrity, whereas they were relative nobodies. Could he then be trusted to take direction from the Party? (Although an avowed Marxist, he was not an SACP member.) That had to be the reason they took the obvious political risks of accompanying him and monitoring his performance in the meeting. Not only did this embarrassingly reveal ANC and Mandela's dependence on the SACP, it outraged many South African whites. De Klerk's predecessor, ex-President P. W. Botha, resigned in protest from the National Party, to which he had belonged since 1936, because de Klerk had met with Slovo (a cofounder and the head of the MK) who had masterminded from London much of the ANC terrorist activity in South Africa. Fortunately for Mandela and the ANC, all this received little or no media attention outside South Africa. Mandela could simply do no wrong in world opinion. (In 1993, he and de Klerk together received the Nobel Peace Prize.)

At the time of Mandela's release, then–ANC president (and SACP member) Oliver Tambo was terminally ill and generally out of it. It seemed perfectly logical under these circumstances that someone of Mandela's international stature and reputation should soon have replaced him as president. Instead, the Communist Party made him the ANC vice president. It was not until June 1991, sixteen months after his release, that the Party finally trusted Mandela to become president. In the interim, reliable Party member Alfred Nzo (later to become South Africa's foreign minister) actually filled in for Tambo, leaving Mandela with few real responsibilities. On November 16, 1991, enormously popular and charismatic senior ANC official Cris Hani, who, before he was assassinated in 1993, was Mandela's probable successor and was soon to become SACP general secretary, made a remarkably candid public statement on the role of the SACP in the ANC. "We in the Communist

Party have participated in and built the ANC. We have made the ANC what it is today and *the ANC is our organization*" (emphasis added). In 1992, as the ANC was entering into power-sharing negotiations with de Klerk, the Party deemed it politic to lower the SACP profile in the ANC. Hani, therefore, advised some senior Party officials in the ANC to "resign" from the Party for cosmetic reasons. Two of those who did, Thabo Mbeki and Mac Maharaj, later became senior members of the new ANC-dominated South African government, at which time they referred to themselves as "former Marxists." It defies logic to imagine that case-hardened old Communists like these two would actually resign from the Party on the brink of its coming to power.

When the new South African government was announced on May 11, 1994, just after the ANC's landslide in victory in an unusually well-run and fair general election, for Africa, the offices assigned to known SACP members provided a textbook example of the posts Communist parties consider key to controlling a country. It also reads like a veritable "Who's Who in the SACP." First was Nelson Mandela's designated replacement, First Deputy President Thabo Mbeki (who later replaced Mandela as planned). Key ministries assigned to SACP members were these: Defense, Joe Modise and his deputy Ronnie Kasrils; Safety and Security (which controls the police), Sidney Mufamadi; Foreign Affairs, Alfred Nzo and his deputy Aziz Pahad; Post, Telecommunications, and Broadcasting (which includes national radio and TV), Pallo Jordan; Trade, Industry, and Tourism, Trevor Manuel; and Transport, Mc Maharaj. Three other ministries also went to SACP members. (On April 29, 1998, SACP member Sphiwe Nyanda took command of the South African armed forces as chief of staff.) When this list was published, only one, Sydney Mufamadi, was identified in the media (*New York Times*) as a Communist and the media regularly refer to Mbeki as a "former Marxist." Clearly his 1992 "resignation" ruse has worked.

Most of the black population (which is about 79 percent of the total population of South Africa) that brought the ANC to power would not have been particularly bothered by the SACP role in the ANC. The Party's main concern was presenting a non-Communist face to world opinion that played a key role in pressuring the South African government, through sanctions and denunciations, to abolish apartheid, lift the ban on the ANC, and allow the free elections that were bound to bring the ANC to power. In order not to discourage foreign investments or encourage "white flight," the Party has soft-pedaled its avowed ultimate goal to establish a "socialist South Africa" and has moved the government only cautiously left. Nevertheless, *The Economist* (London), which had been largely supportive of the new regime, felt compelled to report, on July 25, 1998, "The ANC government is slowly undermining most of the institutions that could serve as a check on its powers. Provincial governors can do little without approval from the capital. The independence of the judiciary could be compromised by the decision to appoint an ANC hack to the new post of national director of prosecutions. Now with Mr. Mdoweni's appointment [as governor] to the [Reserve] bank, South African businesses will find themselves even more in thrall to the government: the central bank has the power to veto large investments abroad."

The reader must be wondering why I have devoted so much space to South Africa. While most of the events on the world scene I have previously described have generally been extensively covered in many books and other writings, this is most decidedly not the case with South Africa. Indeed the reader would be hard pressed to find anything in print that covers what I have described above. For example, I know of only one authoritative book on the ANC/SACP, *Inside the ANC*, by Morgan Norval (Selous Foundation Press, Washington DC, 1990); that book provides an exceptionally well-documented history of the ANC and SACP. I mention a number of facts not covered by Norval or anyone else here, however. I believe that in order to understand Africa's most important country today, knowledge of its recent history is essential. For example, many seem puzzled and perplexed that Thabo Mbeki, who has offered to broker a political settlement in chaotic Zimbabwe that has been driven into the ground by its ruthless and mindless dictator, Robert Mugabe, insisted on siding with Mugabe. This would become more understandable when one realizes that Mbeki regards Mugabe as an old Marxist revolutionary comrade-in-arms. The machinations described by *The Economist* above make more sense when one realizes the extent to which South Africa is controlled, albeit covertly, by members of the SACP. Conversely, the ANC-ruled government promises to be the most stable in Africa. Despite burgeoning crime, corruption, unemployment, AIDS cases, and its internal fissures, the ANC will no doubt continue to have the support of the majority of South Africans for the foreseeable future. In 2009 SACP member Jacob Zuma was elected to replace Mbeki as president.

In any case, the demise of Communism in the disintegrating Soviet Union and in its European satellites, which had, in large measure, provided essential support to the ANC/SACP, rendered indigenous Communist influence in South Africa far less important than would have been the case were it able to provide the Soviet Union with a strategically valuable toehold in southern Africa in grateful repayment. This had been my principal concern all along when I became involved with South Africa, not realizing that my concerns would be overtaken by events before long. Moreover, it should be emphasized that even with the SACP in a controlling position, South Africa has by no means become anything like a Communist country. Apart from state-run enterprises that existed before 1994, few more have been created. By and large the country enjoys a substantial degree of freedom. The new SACP/ANC ruling class has benefited very substantially in the new regime and is also keenly aware of the importance of not alienating world opinion. Hosting the summer 2010 World Cup soccer matches certainly improved its international cachet and has given South Africa a national shot in the arm.

South Africa today was well described in a fourteen-page special report in *The Economist* (London) of June 5–11, 2010. Here are some salient points it made:

> "Everyone loved Mr. Mandela, whites as well as blacks, for his calm dignity and generous spirit of reconciliation. But he was more of an idealized figurehead than a leader . . . " The ANC's leader, secretary general Gwede Mantashe, is a Communist [clearly indicating that the SACP remains in political control]. "Freedom House [in Washington] . . . gives South Africa a respectable rating of 2 in its 'freedom of the world index' . . . 1 is completely free and 7 totally unfree." Living conditions for a large part of the population have significantly improved and a substantial black middle class has emerged. Exports have doubled, public debt has halved and double digit inflation of the 1980s has now shrunk to 5.1%. "Today South Africa is a lot happier, wiser and more prosperous." On the other hand, unemployment is 30% for blacks and 6% for whites. South Africa has one of the world's highest crime rates. For example its murder rate is nearly seven times that of the U.S. Corruption is rampant as is government incompetency. The general quality of education at all levels is low, and there is a serious nationwide AIDS/HIV epidemic. At least, however, the Communists (or soi-disant "former Communists") now running the country are far more realistic, intelligent, humane and freedom-loving that those who created so much misery and mischief in running countries in the former Soviet bloc. No doubt they will remain in control for a long time, because there is little incentive (or possibility) to throw them out.

With the disintegration of the Soviet empire, my main specialty had all but evaporated except in providing retrospective analyses that had only an academic or historic application, such as those that I have used in this book. President Bush's term in office expired in January 1993, and with it my last tour in the White House. I always regretted that I had had so little time with the president; when we did talk it was mostly about his adventures as a naval aviation cadet during World War II learning to fly Stearmans in the wintertime. When I left office, I had served on the NSC staff for seventeen years, longer than any other professional in the history of the NSC, beginning with its creation in 1947. Sometimes I wonder if I might not actually have served in the White House longer than any other professional in our history, but confirming this would require years of research. When I left in 1993, I had served in the U.S. government under about a quarter of all U.S. presidents, beginning with Franklin D. Roosevelt. While I admired Roosevelt's wartime leadership, of all these presidents Harry Truman was my favorite because he saved Western Europe and brought an end to World War II through his courageous use of the atomic bomb. Also his quick and decisive action saved South Korea. When he left office his popularity rating was very low because of the Korean War (nearly as low as George W. Bush's at the end of his administration). Truman is followed on my list by Ronald Reagan, who played a key, if not decisive, role in ending the Cold War. My least favorites were Lyndon B. Johnson who, I believe, did this country untold and lasting harm, followed by the feckless Jimmy Carter. Actually, I was not very fond of Dwight D. Eisenhower, either. John F. Kennedy was the most fun and interesting to serve under, although he screwed up badly in the first part of his administration, as I have described in Chapter 12. I believe that both Jerry Ford and George H. W. Bush continue to be underrated.

About the same time that I left the White House, Georgetown University instigated a rule requiring the retirement or resignation of all faculty members seventy or older. (This later proved to have been illegal.) Since I was then nearly seventy-one, I was out. My students all thought this was preposterous, since none regarded me as too old to teach, but what could I do? In any case, this freed me to pursue my new career of writing and becoming a naval fire support advocate. The days were over when I would ever again work in an office of any kind, which I later found to be of great advantage.

One of my most interesting and gratifying experiences at this time was being knighted in 1997 in the ancient Equestrian Order of the Holy Sepulchre of Jerusalem (KHS), a papal order, that according to tradition was founded in 1099 by the leader of the First Crusade, Geoffrey de Boullion, to guard the Holy Sepulchre. Its present mission is to support the much-put-upon and rapidly dwindling Christian population in the Holy Land. The ceremony took place in the spacious old church at the Franciscan Monastery in Washington, DC. Carrying our white robes, we initiates knelt in turn in front of Washington-area Archbishop Cardinal Hickey who, acting for the Pope, dubbed us on each shoulder with a sword after which we arose as "sir knights." It was a scene right out of the Middle Ages. I owe being knighted to the late Dr. Bernard Ficarra who founded the Middle Atlantic regional lieutenancy (chapter) of the Order. He was also a Knight of Malta, and was a leading New York surgeon and physician to the Metropolitan Opera, a fine gentleman indeed. Prior to World War II, knights of this order were mostly European aristocrats, still true to some extent in Belgium and Italy. (When I told my old friend Prince Karl Schwarzenberg [now the Czech Republic foreign minister] that I had been knighted in the Order he noted that his father had also been a KHS.) Now most knights are plain old commoners, including many non-Europeans, like me.

Thanks to Dr. Fecarra, I was honored to be named an academician in the Catholic Academy of Sciences of the United States. Sciences here are used in the broadest sense to mean simply fields of knowledge, which included my field of international relations. Later, the George W. Bush administration appointed me a member of the Army War College Board of Visitors and subsequently a member of the Secretary of the Navy's Advisory Subcommittee on Naval History. I found both to be very rewarding and interesting experiences. I very much enjoyed and appreciated the days I spent at Carlisle Barracks in Pennsylvania and at the Navy Yard in Washington.

I would now like to end with two favorite poems:

Here is a favorite snippet from what many scholars regard as the greatest poem in the English language, Thomas Gray's *Elegy Written in a Country Church-Yard*.

> *The boast of heraldry, the pomp of power,*
> *And all that beauty, all that wealth e'er gave*
> *Awaits alike the inevitable hour:*
> *The paths of glory lead but to the grave.*

(I used to tell my students to look to these words for perspective when clawing their way up bureaucratic or institutional ladders.)

The other poem is Henry Wadsworth Longfellow's *Psalm of Life* (What The Heart of the Young Man Said to the Psalmist):

> *Tell me not, in mournful numbers,*
> *Life is but an empty dream!*
> *For the soul is dead that slumbers,*
> *And things are not what they seem.*
>
> *Life is real! Life is earnest!*
> *And the grave is not its goal;*
> *Dust thou art, to dust returnest,*
> *Was not spoken of the soul.*
>
> *Not enjoyment, and not sorrow,*
> *Is our destined end or way;*
> *But to act, that each to-morrow*
> *Find us farther than to-day.*

Art is long, and Time is fleeting,
And our hearts, though stout and brave,
Still, like muffled drums, are beating
Funeral marches to the grave.

In the world's broad field of battle,
In the bivouac of Life,
Be not like dumb, driven cattle!
Be a hero in the strife!

Trust no Future, howe'er pleasant!
Let the dead Past bury its dead!
Act,—act in the living Present!
Heart within, and God o'erhead!

Lives of great men all remind us
We can make our lives sublime,
And, departing, leave behind us
Footprints on the sands of time;

Footprints, that perhaps another,
Sailing o'er life's solemn main,
A forlorn and shipwrecked brother,
Seeing, shall take heart again.

Let us, then, be up and doing,
With a heart for any fate;
Still achieving, still pursuing,
Learn to labor and to wait.

Epilogue

IT WAS NOT LONG AFTER I LEFT both government service and academe that I took up the Sisyphean task of promoting the reactivation of our reserve *Iowa*-class battleships in order to provide our Marines and soldiers essential, lifesaving naval surface fire support (NSFS).

I became acquainted with battleships in World War II when they were providing highly effective fire support for our amphibious operations in the Pacific. I first took up the cause of their reactivation when the Communist side began massively violating the Vietnam Peace Accords signed in January 1973 soon thereafter. I realized that the one weapon system we had that absolutely terrorized the enemy was the *Iowa*-class battleship *New Jersey*, which operated for six months off Vietnam September 29, 1968, to April 1969. I asked the last captain of *New Jersey* when it was off Vietnam, Capt. Ed Snyder, to come to the White House to brief me. He told me he had strict orders not to promote battleships, but agreed to brief me when I promised not to tell anyone at that time of his visit to me. What he told me about his ship's performance in combat confirmed my view of the efficacy of having this ship stationed off the demilitarized zone (DMZ) ready to retaliate for any further violations. Unfortunately, I failed to sell my idea to Henry Kissinger, but I did make a battleship believer out of my NSC colleague and friend John F. Lehman Jr. When he became Reagan's secretary of the Navy, John had all four *Iowa*s returned to active service as part of his large Navy buildup program.

After we lost two aircraft during the August 1964 Tonkin Gulf incident by attacking targets that could easily and safely been taken out with naval guns, some in the Navy took note, apparently. In November 1964 a commission headed by one of the Navy's top gunnery experts, Vice Adm. Edwin B. Hooper, recommended activating two *Iowa*-class battleships and two heavy cruisers for future Vietnam contingencies. The admiral commanding the Pacific Fleet and the chief of naval operations (CNO, who heads the Navy), both aviators, strongly opposed returning the battleships to active service. Groundless hostility to battleships by aviators (and some others), which exists to this day, dates at least to the Pearl Harbor attack when two of eight battleships in the Harbor were lost and six were damaged but later raised, repaired, and returned to combat. We never again lost a battleship in combat, but some eleven carriers of all sizes were sunk in the course of the war in the Pacific (and I believe one in the Atlantic).) One could even go further back in time, to July 21, 1921, when Brig. Gen. "Billy" Mitchell led a fifteen-hundred–plane bomber attack that sank the helpless, unmanned, and defenseless former German battle cruiser *Ostfriesland* as it was anchored off the U.S. East Coast, thereby "proving" that aircraft could sink battleships. By 1967 top-level Navy opposition to battleships was contributing to the loss of a plane a day in Vietnam. In fact, we lost 1,067 aircraft attacking targets in North Vietnam, 80 percent of which could have been taken out with a battleship's 16-inch guns. For example, between 1965 and 1968 we lost fifty aircraft in seven hundred unsuccessful sorties to take out the strategically important Tanh Hoa Bridge that could have been permanently destroyed with one 16-inch nine-gun salvo dropping the span and destroying the bridge's abutments.

Finally, pressure from Chair of the Senate Armed Services Committee Richard Russell and Marine Commandant Gen. Wallace M. Greene Jr., in addition to the retirement of the incumbent CNO, resulted in the decision to reactivate *New Jersey*, which reached the gun line off Vietnam on September 29, 1968, and performed magnificently before eventually departing on rotation to the United States in April 1969; it was scheduled to return to Vietnam in September. Then unexplainably it was decided to retire her instead, no doubt delighting many battleship foes in the Navy. Later it was reported that she did not return to Vietnam because the North Vietnamese had complained that her presence off Vietnam was "impeding peace talks." (They didn't mention the four carriers usually present off Vietnam.) Anecdotes and reports of *New Jersey*'s stellar performance off Vietnam are legion. For example, Gen. James L. Jones, once commandant of the Marine Corps, later NATO supreme commander who, in December 2008, was named by President-elect Obama to be his national security adviser, had these comments: "*New Jersey* once saved my life." "Within the arc of fire of a battleship's guns war evaporates." "When *New Jersey* would just show up during an enemy attack everything would go quiet."

It could take out deep, well-protected targets that were immune to air attacks, even by B-52 heavy bombers. It absolutely terrorized the enemy because there was no protection against its 16-inch guns that left a crater more than twenty feet deep and forty or fifty feet across. On one occasion these guns reportedly destroyed an enemy complex seven stories deep, which repeated air strikes only dented. After *New Jersey* was retired, Marine Corps Commandant Gen. Leonard Chapman had this to say about her performance: "*Thousands of American lives were saved* by the speed, accuracy and enormous penetration power of the battleship's heavy guns. Unlike B-52 bombers, tactical aircraft and Marine artillery, *New Jersey* was always there day and night, in good weather and bad, and her guns were always ready for any target, whether a troop concentration or a fortified bunker. Just knowing that *New Jersey* was there bolstered the morale of our fighting Marines" (*USS* New Jersey, by Robert F. Dorr, Motorbooks International, Osceola, WI, 1988; emphasis added). If *New Jersey* "saved thousands of American lives" in only six months, think how many could have been saved by having had a battleship off Vietnam for the whole seven years we fought there. In other words, one could say that, in effect, a groundless prejudice against battleships in the Navy needlessly cost thousands of American lives during the Vietnam War. Battleships' continued absence from the fleet could well needlessly cost us numerous American lives in evitable future conflicts in littoral regions, for want of effective naval surface fire support (NSFS).

Soon after Ronald Reagan became president, he sought to significantly expand our armed forces as part of a more aggressive anti-Soviet stance. This included a very substantial Navy buildup under the guidance of Secretary of the Navy John F. Lehman Jr., who succeeded in getting all the *Iowa*s reactivated: USS *Iowa*, USS *Wisconsin*, USS *New Jersey*, and USS *Missouri*. In a speech honoring the recommissioning of *New Jersey* on December 28, 1982, Lehman gave me credit for having gotten him interested in bringing back the battleships. He also recognized the key role of Charles E. "Chuck" Myers Jr., who had been both an Air Force pilot and a naval aviator, and who deserves a lion's share of the credit in getting essential congressional and other support for battleship reactivation.

Contrary to media reports, the *New Jersey* performed exceptionally well off Lebanon in 1983–84. On December 3, 1983, the NSC, with President Reagan presiding, met to discuss retaliation for a Syrian attack on a U.S. reconnaissance plane over Lebanon's Bekaa Valley. The president recommended using *New Jersey*'s 16-inch guns. An admiral representing the Navy, either out of pure ignorance or sheer duplicity, misinformed the president that 16-inch guns had neither the range nor the accuracy for this mission; he added that this mission should use airstrikes. The airstrike launched on Bekaa Valley targets from a carrier the next day cost us one pilot killed, one captured (a Lieutenant Goodman), one A-6 (aircraft) and one A-7 lost, and another A-7 damaged. Ten days later, when we encountered the same problem, 16-inch guns were used, and with eleven rounds silenced six Syrian anti-aircraft missile sites in the Bekaa Valley with no losses whatsoever.

On February 8, 1984, after Syrian artillery had bombarded Christian-held areas in West Beirut with more than five thousand rounds, *New Jersey* fired 270

16-inch rounds that completely silenced all the Syrian batteries. (At the time, I happened to be on the phone with NSC colleague Navy captain Phil Dur who was there, and I could hear the sound of the gunfire.) Based on an interview with a Syrian spokesperson, CBS News reported that *New Jersey*'s barrage had killed only innocent civilians and goats; this grossly misleading report gained currency and produced a widespread misconception of 16-inch accuracy. Actually there were some accuracy problems resulting from map deficiencies and firing at ridgeline targets where missing by only a few feet could send a round miles off target, but, as we have seen, on balance these big guns were extremely effective.

When Lehman left office in 1987, there was a move in the Navy to retire battleships. This move was heightened by the tragic and still not definitively explained April 1989 Turret Two explosion on the *Iowa* that killed forty-seven sailors. This was the first such accident on any battleship commissioned after World War I. Carriers have had far worse accidents without their resulting in a call to end carrier use. Incidentally, some weeks later the *Iowa* resumed firing its 16-inch guns. By the outbreak of the Gulf War in August 1990, only *Missouri* and *Wisconsin* were still in commission. When we began engaging in hostilities in that conflict these ships were used to launch the first Tomahawk missile attacks against Iraqi targets. Otherwise they were simply being utilized as logistic support ships. The Navy did not want the ships to use their 16-inch guns because this could be used to justify their continued active service, and the Navy wanted to retire them. Other ships could launch Tomahawks, but only battleships had the big guns.

Reportedly, U.S. Commander Gen. Norman Schwarzkopf ordered the reluctant Navy to use the battleships' guns to provide NSFS for our ground forces, especially in supporting them during our successful Desert Storm offensive, which kicked off on February 24, 1991. None of the other eighty or so naval combatants present could perform this vital task. The two battleships were extremely effective, as testified to in the Defense Department's April 1992 *Report to Congress: Conduct of the Persian Gulf War.* They were also essential to the credibility of the Marine Corps' amphibious landing feint, which faked Iraqi troops out of position, substantially facilitating the success of our final flanking attack. The battleships' massive fires so terrified the enemy that Iraqi marines holding Faylaka Island off Kuwait City surrendered to one of *Wisconsin*'s UAVs (unmanned aerial vehicle), fearing it was the harbinger of a 16-inch gun attack that could blow away the island. The Navy did nothing to publicize the battleships' feats, and thus they were all but ignored by the media after they launched their initial Tomahawk strikes. One of the few exceptions was the Soviet newspaper *Sovetskaya Rossiya* of February 19, 1991, which reported, "Their [the two battleships'] salvos . . . are producing a 'strong impression' on the Iraqis; they are abandoning their [reinforced concrete] coastal positions and pulling back northwards tens of kilometers."

Regardless of the two battleships' stellar performance during the Gulf War, they were retired and mothballed by the Navy in 1992, thus eliminating the only source of NSFS available to our Marines and soldiers. This ill-considered move was initially protested in vain by Adm. Stanley Arthur, who had commanded our naval forces during the war. Admiral Arthur had high praise for the 16-inch guns' performance and believed the battleships should remain in the active fleet. It was striking testimony to the battleships' psychological impact in the Gulf War that, in late 1991, the Sultan of Oman offered then–Secretary of Defense Richard B. Cheney to pay the operating and maintenance costs of two *Iowa*-class battleships as long as one was kept in the Persian Gulf area for nine months of the year. He never received a reply. (I understand the request was initially routed through the State Department. Maybe it never reached Cheney.)

In December 1994 I was informed by my former student and friend, Jeff Cimbalo (mentioned in Chapter 16), who was the "token conservative" on President Clinton's Defense Roles and Missions Committee, that the Navy was quietly plotting to sell the four *Iowa*s to South Korea as scrap. I subsequently learned that the Navy had quietly, if not surreptitiously, stricken the four ships from the Naval Vessel Register (NVR) on January 24, 1995, without informing anyone that it was doing so. Even higher-ranking Navy Department officials and officers were unaware of this move. For example, in April 3, 1995, congressional hearings, Assistant Secretary of the Navy (and former student of mine) Nora Slatkin and Deputy CNO for Resources, Warfare Requirements and Assessments Adm. Thomas J. Lopez both stated that they were unaware of the Navy's decision to strike these ships from the NVR. In fact, Lopez indicated that the Navy was upgrading their main guns.

Perhaps even CNO Admiral Boorda never saw the actual striking order that was signed "by direction" by a Navy civilian. Boorda wrote Sen. John Warner of the Senate Armed Services Committee (SASC) on May 31 "that these ships can be returned to mobilization status in a reasonable period of time." Did he know that the striking order called for these ships to be so demilitarized that they could never be reactivated? They were designated eligible for donation as museums. (If it had initially planned to sell them to South Korea for scrap, the Navy no doubt had realized that this would impolitic.) In February 1995 I informed the SASC of the Navy's decision to strike the battleships. The Committee was more than put out by having been ignored by the Navy in making this decision. Members of the SASC, including senators Strom Thurmond, John Warner, Sam Nunn, John Glenn, Edward Kennedy, and John McCain, made clear to the Navy their displeasure at its antibattleship move, and, on June 29, 1995, the SASC, dissatisfied with the Navy's responses to their queries, voted seventeen to three in favor of keeping at least two battleships on the NVR.

An SASC report stated, "The conferees believe that the Department of the Navy's future years defense program, presented with the fiscal year 1996 budget, could not produce a replacement fire support capability comparable to the battleships until well into the next century. The conferees consider retention of the battleships in the fleet's strategic reserve a prudent measure." Preceding action on the Fiscal Year 1996 Defense Authorization Act, the SASC, on July 8, 1995, described the *Iowa*-class battleships as the Navy's "*only remaining potential source of around-the-clock accurate, high volume, heavy fire support*" (emphasis added). The following legislation resulted from SASC deliberations:

> Excerpts from Public Law 104–106, Section 1011 of the Fiscal Year 1996 National Defense Authorization Act: "The Secretary of the Navy shall list on the Naval Vessel Register [NVR], and maintain on such register, at least two of the *Iowa* class battleships that were stricken from the register in February 1995 ... [selecting] the *Iowa* class battleships that are in the best material condition. . . . The Secretary shall retain the existing logistical support necessary for support of at least two operational *Iowa* class battleships in active service, including technical manuals, repair and replacement parts, and ordnance. . . . The requirements of this section shall cease to be effective 60 days after the Secretary certifies in writing [to congressional armed services committees] . . . that the Navy has within the fleet an operational surface fire support capability that equals or exceeds the fire support capability that the *Iowa* class battleships listed on the Naval Vessel Register would, . . . in active service, be able to provide for Marine Corps amphibious assaults and operations ashore.

This law protected at least two battleships for the next ten years. In early 1998 the Navy tried to strike even these two, employing the following ruse. The Navy was well aware that the state of New Jersey was very anxious to acquire its namesake battleship as a museum, a move that had widespread public and political support in that state. The Navy offered New Jersey members of Congress the following deal: New Jersey would get its namesake battleship if they persuaded the SASC to strike it and the other ship (USS *Wisconsin*) on the NVR from the NVR. It then turned out that, in violation of the law, the Navy had neglected to place *New Jersey* on the NVR. The Navy quickly corrected this "oversight." Some of us battleship supporters then suggested to the SASC that *New Jersey* be donated to its namesake state and that USS *Iowa* be substituted for it on the NVR. This worked, and the Navy was foiled in its clumsy attempt to finally get rid of all battleships. This bought a seven-year respite for the two battleships on the NVR. However, Congress was still to play unhelpful games with the two battleships.

Led by Sen. Barbara Boxer (D-CA), the "California delegation" sought to move *Iowa* to San Francisco for purely civilian use, which would have been illegal. In a Fiscal Year 1999 Defense bill there was nonbinding "sense of Congress" language calling for *Iowa* to be "homeported" in San Francisco. (Never mind that only active ships can be homeported.) Then as the Fiscal Year 2000 Defense Appropriation Act was being wrapped up, someone from the California crowd slipped in $3 million for moving *Iowa* to the West Coast. This move was made just before midnight when no one was paying attention. Citing these two congressional actions, neither of which was legal, the Navy opted to move *Iowa* from Middleton, Rhode Island, to the Department of Transportation's Maritime Administration (MARAD) facility at Suisan Bay, in northern California. The move of the *Iowa* "had no military utility," said the CNO. It was not only a waste of taxpayers' money, but also potentially was harmful to the ship. Nevertheless, the move, initiated during the Clinton administration, was begun under the new Bush administration, on March 8, 2001. Chair of the House Armed Services Committee (HASC) Bob Stump (R-AZ) tried to persuade Secretary of Defense Donald Rumsfeld to cancel this needless and potentially harmful transfer. Stump, one of the most conscientious, knowledgeable, and decent members on the Hill, was rudely brushed off by Rumsfeld, who said the Navy claimed it was too late to stop the transfer, which was patent nonsense. From this time on, I had little regard for Rumsfeld and often wondered why it took Bush so long to get rid of him. At the time, I felt that any secretary of defense who didn't know any better than to so fob off the HASC chair, actually a friend and ally of the new Bush administration, was going to be bad news.

At the suggestion in 1999 of one of our fellow battleship promoters, Lt. Col. Greg Pickell, USA, I formed the United States Naval Fire Support Association (USNFSA), a public-interest (nonlobbying) entity incorporated in Maryland to give some standing to our loose coterie of battleship advocates and to raise some money through tax-deductible donations. None of us stood to benefit monetarily in any way from USNFSA activities on the Hill or elsewhere. Its salient purpose was to try to ensure that Marines and Army soldiers had adequate NSFS support in future littoral conflicts. I made myself the association's executive director. (We're still in business.) The Navy kept coming up with and then discarding NSFS solutions: the Arsenal Ship, the DD-21 destroyer, and finally the DD(X) (later DDG-1000) destroyer. The Navy also had long been involved in developing an ERGM (extended range guided munitions) round to increase the range of the Navy's 5-inch guns, the only guns left in the fleet. Normal 5-inch range is about fifteen miles, but Navy doctrine mandates that its vulnerable ships remain at least twenty-nine miles (twenty-five nautical miles) from any hostile or potentially hostile shore. In March 2000 a senior Marine Corps general testified on the Hill that 5-inch guns, including ERGM, "lacked lethality" needed to meet Marine Corps' NSFS requirements. (What is more important in a weapon than its *lethality*?) Nevertheless, the Navy persisted in pursuing the constantly troubled ERGM project, which it finally had to abandon in 2008 after having squandered $600 million on it.

In an interview in the June 2000 issue of the *Armed Forces Journal International*, Marine Corps commandant Gen. James L. Jones stated, "As for their warfighting capability, I regret we took them [battleships] out of service before we had actually fixed the naval surface fire support problem." Prior to that, he testified before the SASC on March 1, 2000, "We Marines have been at considerable risk . . . [since the last battleships were retired]." (In SASC hearings, April 12, 2003, then–Commandant Gen. Michael W. Hagee testified that the absence of NSFS placed Marines "at considerable risk.") Just prior to his becoming commandant, then–Lt. Gen. James Jones wrote me (in a mailed letter) that *battleships provide one solution to the NSFS gap.* The Marines had long hesitated to incur the ire of the Navy, on which they depend, by openly advocating battleship reactivation. This changed in the November 19, 2004, Government Accountability Office (GAO) Report on NSFS, in which the Marines finally had the temerity to support the reactivation of two battleships. I can only imagine the thumping Commandant General Hagee must have gotten from the Navy for this courageous Marine Corps statement.

The Navy undoubtedly (and correctly) saw battleship reactivation as a major challenge to its expensive, questionable, futuristic DD(X) (later DDG-1000) destroyer touted to solve the Marines' NSFS problem. It is therefore significant, but not surprising, that the officer mainly responsible for this program, Rear Adm. Charles Hamilton, would launch a full court press, and ultimately successful, anti-battleship campaign on the Hill to take the two reserve battleships off the board permanently—saying, in essence, "the hell with the Marines." He opened his campaign with a March 15, 2005, briefing in the office of Roscoe Bartlett (R-MD), Chair of the House Projection Forces Subcommittee (of the HASC). After a not terribly well-organized pro-battleship presentation on my part (I was actually not very well at the time), Hamilton, a likeable, personable, and articulate briefer presented his staff-prepared professional PowerPoint briefing. It was clearly David versus Goliath, with David lacking an adequate sling. Hamilton's briefing was replete with misinformation about battleships and about the Navy's NSFS programs.

A fundamental flaw was his insistence that the DD(X) (later DDG-1000) and ERM (in other words, ERGM) programs, both far in the future at best, could meet Marines' NSFS requirements. (In the end, Hamilton's much-vaunted DDG-1000 program was reduced from thirty-two ships to three, and those may well be dropped since each will cost from $3.5 billion to $6 billion [as estimated in

2010]. As noted above, the ERM [ERGM] program was cancelled in 2008, leaving the Marines with no NSFS at all.) A real howler came with Hamilton's attempt to ascribe vulnerability to the world's least-vulnerable ships. To make his point, Hamilton alleged that the Japanese super-battleship *Yamato*, which he insisted had armor plate equal to that of the *Iowa*-class battleships, was sunk (in April 1945) by "an American aircraft." In reality it took 386 U.S. aircraft hours to sink this ship, which had armor plate, as well as design and damage control features, that were far inferior to that of our battleships.

Ultimately, alas, Admiral Hamilton's misinformation campaign succeeded, and Congress agreed to strike *Iowa* and *Wisconsin* to be donated to California and Virginia, respectively, to be museums—completely ignoring the language of Public Law 104–106, which sought to keep the two battleships on the NVR until the Navy certifies it has in the fleet an NSFS capability equaling or exceeding that provided by the battleships. The Navy was, and still is, nowhere near meeting that criterion. We studied the battleship language in the Fiscal Year 2006 National Defense Authorization Act (NDAA) and discovered that it stipulated, in probably standard language, that, when the president declares a national emergency, these ships could be returned to the Navy, obviously for active service. We concluded that this made them "mobilization assets" that must be preserved for possible reactivation. We pointed this out to the HASC, which drafted a report, House Report 109–452, with detailed instructions to the Navy to preserve the two battleships intact and to preserve their infrastructure. It also requires the Navy to prepare plans for a possible rapid reactivation. The report's instructions are referred to in the Fiscal Year 2007 NDAA. We had hoped that this would provide increased protection for the two ships, despite their losing the protection afforded by being on the NVR; however, in 2010, the Navy totally disregarded these congressional instructions on preserving battleship infrastructure and ordered the destruction of all battleship spare parts, essentially rendering it impractical to reactivate these ships. The Navy had, for all intents and purposes, finally succeeded in sinking the battleships for good.

Since things continued to look unpromising for battleship reactivation, this effort received a very substantial boost from a long-overdue and unprecedentedly exhaustive, well-documented, and extensive NSFS study that emerged from the Pentagon's Joint Advanced War Fighting School (JAWS) at the Joint Forces Staff College. That study received an award for excellence from the National Defense University Foundation. Basically prepared by Army colonel Shawn A. Welch, aided by much expert advice and information, the study focused on the advantage of major caliber guns (12 inch and above) in providing fire support for our troops in littoral conflicts. The study posited the future construction of four essentially modern battleships called capital surface warships (CSW) with 16-inch guns firing advanced projectiles that had already proven feasible; with brilliant [advanced guiding systems] weapons and long-range ones, for example, 16-inch scramjet projectiles that would go 460 miles in nine minutes, a performance declared "feasible" by Pratt & Whitney experts. In addition to these guns, there were 5-inch guns firing extended range rounds.

The feasibility of major-caliber guns, specifically on CSWs, was put to a rigorous test in a simulation scenario involving a hypothetical conflict in Korea. This scenario was developed by the Marine Corps Combat Development Command and was approved by the Defense Department's Joint Staff J-8 (Force Structure Resources and Assessment). It also was recommended by the Army's Training and Doctrine Command's Capabilities Integration, which had participated in several Navy analyses. The research and evaluation analytical tool used was the well-tested and proven FireSim XXI designed and built by the U.S. [Army] Field Artillery School and Center at Ft. Sill, Oklahoma. The Army's Aberdeen, Maryland, Proving Ground experts provided 16-inch lethality data. All told that was clearly a serious test designed by highly capable experts. It is not surprising that the two CSWs involved clearly outperformed the smaller DDG-51 and DDG-1000 destroyers. Most significant was that they clearly outperformed a carrier's (CVN) forty F/A 18 E/F aircraft plus one B-52 heavy bomber. For example, against armored vehicles they were 79 percent effective whereas air strikes were 36 percent effective against the same target. In any twenty-four-hour period, one CSW (or *Iowa*-class battleship) could lay down a weight of ordnance exceeding that delivered from a carrier that costs far more to build, has several times the maintenance and operations costs, and requires several times more personnel. The study estimated that it would cost approximately $1 billion to reactivate, completely modernize (including installing in each 96 VLS missile cells), and support each of the two *Iowa*-class battleships, each one of which could provide many times the firepower of one $6 billion DDG-1000 in addition to many other advantages especially survivability and show-of-force capability.

The significance of this is that the Navy has long insisted that it could effectively provide fire support for our troops with air assets alone. In littoral conflicts, 16-inch gun platforms have a clear advantage over aircraft in being far more responsive, in being unaffected by weather that can impede and even ground aircraft, and in being invulnerable to enemy SAMs. Moreover, these ships are far less costly to purchase, crew, and operate than are carriers. An intrinsic element of the CSW program is the reactivation and modernization of the battleships *Iowa* and *Wisconsin*. The study effectively demolishes in considerable detail the Navy's case against battleship reactivation, which for the most part is based on a tissue of misinformation. The main Navy argument against battleships has long been that they are too costly to operate and are too personnel intensive. This was cogently and effectively countered by Bob Stump (R-AZ), the chair of the HASC, who quite accurately stated, "*Measured against their capabilities they* [battleships] *are the most cost effective and least manpower intensive ships we have*" (Congressional Record H3394, May 18, 2000; emphasis added).

The 2007 JAWS study subsequently had a significant impact on the Marine Corps as evidenced in a March 18, 2009, report entitled "Amphibious Operations in the 21st Century" and signed by Lt. Gen. G. J. Flynn, Commanding General of the key Marine Corps Combat Development Command, one of the most influential generals in the Marine Corps. This contained a very substantial boost for battleship reactivation. General Flynn noted that the Navy's current short-range guns cause "an over-reliance on more expensive—and weather dependent—carriers and aircraft." He then drew attention to the 2007 JAWS study: "A 2007 study concluded that re-commissioning battleships with improved gun munitions and missile systems the desired blend of [fire support] capabilities could be achieved in a cost effective way because the need to fill the Navy's current shortfall in aircraft carriers and aircraft would be eliminated. The recently initiated 'Joint Expeditionary Fires Analysis of Alternatives' should give due consideration to such ideas in quest for a comprehensive solution."

In the JAWS study, Adm. Harry Train, former NATO Supreme Allied Commander, Atlantic, was quoted as saying, "They [battleships] would be greatly underutilized if restricted to [the] NSFS mission set." In fact, reactivated battleships would be most useful as diplomatic or political *visible* show of forces instruments. For example, there is reason to be concerned about the security of the Persian Gulf, especially after the January 6, 2008, confrontation at Hormuz, which rightly should have led to a thorough evaluation by the Navy of its position in the Gulf. As now constituted, our 5th Fleet is ill-equipped to maintain dominance in the Gulf. Al Qaeda's near-sinking of the USS *Cole* in 2000 dramatized the vulnerability of our warships. This led, on June 22, 2001, to a rapid 5th Fleet withdrawal to sea in the face of just an al Qaeda threat. In fact, one off-target al Qaeda rocket chased two U.S. warships from Aqaba in August 2005. As noted above, Navy doctrine requires that our vulnerable ships must remain at least twenty-five nautical miles (twenty-nine miles) from a hostile or potentially hostile shore. (Our ships' 5-inch guns, however, have a range of fifteen miles.) Also our harmless-appearing ships, with only one small gun showing, look more like merchant ships than warships. When NSFS was needed in southern Iraq littorals early in the Iraq war, only the 4.5-inch guns on British and Australian destroyers could provide it. It was fairly effective against personnel, but would have been marginal in dealing with well-fortified enemy troops.

While carrier task forces can provide a formidable presence in the Gulf, in the face of any potential threat, they would quickly withdraw to far out in the Arabian Sea. (In any case, the relatively shallow Gulf is ill suited to carrier operations.) It is well known that the Iranians possess a very large arsenal of deadly antiship missiles The Navy's claim that they could be neutralized by airstrikes presupposes they can be found, a flimsy assumption at best. In an August 2002 Joint Forces war game, Millennium Challenge 2002, the Red Team (Iran), led by ace war-gamer Lt. Gen. Paul Van Riper, USMC (Ret.), sank sixteen U.S. ships, including a carrier. This score was disallowed, and the game results still remain close-hold. Iranian weaponry is now substantially more formidable than it was then.

U.S. dominance in the Gulf can only be ensured by deploying the reactivated and modernized battleships *Iowa* and *Wisconsin*. They are the least vulnerable and most powerful ships in the world, and the Iranians know it. These massively protected ships are the only ones we have capable of risking a *visible* show of force in high-threat situations. Calling far-distant carriers a show of force is oxymoronic. To those targeted they become simply abstractions when far over the horizon. As 38th Commandant and "father" of CENTCOM Gen. P. X. Kelley put it, "There is no weapon system in the world that comes even close to the visible symbol of enormous power represented by the battleship." In the turmoil of the 1980s "tanker war," when *Iowa* entered the Persian Gulf, "Everything would go quiet," as its skipper related.

This was the view of the late Hume Horan, once State's leading Arabist and a former ambassador in Riyadh, who told me that "nothing impresses the Arabs more than a battleship which would be a major political asset in the region." The Sultan of Oman told P. X. Kelley that a battleship (not a carrier) in Muscat Harbor would ensure the security of Oman. As noted above, he later offered to finance operating and maintaining two battleships as long as one spent at least nine months a year in the Gulf. His offer was ignored. Simply our announced intention to reactivate battleships would have a significant impact in Iran. Warren Zimmermann, our last ambassador to a united Yugoslavia, once told me that if we had had a battleship off Dubrovnik in October 1991 ready to open fire on the attacking Serbs, the whole tragic conflagration, which racked the entire region for years, might well have been headed off. In March 1996, when China was lobbing missiles into international sea-lanes in the Taiwan Strait, U.S. carriers remained hundreds of miles away. A battleship, however, could have risked steaming in those sea-lanes with great effect. A battleship off Kuwait City in July 1990 would most probably have discouraged the Iraqi attack on Kuwait that launched the Gulf War. Timely shows of force actually headed off Iraqi attacks on Kuwait in 1961 and 1973.

The Soviets, and now the Russians, have made their ships look warlike for political or psychological effect. For example, the *Peter the Great* battle cruiser, begun under the Soviets and later commissioned in the Russian Navy, bristles with visible ordnance of the kind we hide in our harmless-looking ships. It looks warlike. The Russians and the Soviets before them have had a fine appreciation of the political or diplomatic gains from timely naval shows of force. The classic successful naval show of force was the deployment of the *Missouri* in 1946 to Istanbul in the face of Soviet threats to Turkey. It had the desired deterrent effect on Moscow.

An important political/diplomatic instrument is the ability to effect forced entry from the sea at times and places of our choosing, which is especially useful in dealing with countries like Iran. Without the naval surface fire support that only battleships can provide, any amphibious forced entry capability we might have lacks credibility. Then, too, there is the oft-repeated Pentagon mantra, "We will never again do another Normandy landing." (That is, amphibious warfare is finished.) This overlooks the simple fact that most of the world's population lives in littoral areas.

The JAWS study cited above included an Australian Navy criticism of the U.S. Navy's inability to provide NSFS for littoral operations in southern Iraq in 2003, leaving this task entirely to ships of the British Royal Navy and the Royal Australian Navy. This raises the hotly debated question of whether we should have gone into Iraq in the first place. I am no doubt in the minority in believing that this operation, though clearly initially bungled, was necessary. President Bush has been repeatedly excoriated for believing that Iraqi leader Saddam Hussein had weapons of mass destruction (WMD) that justified removing him from power. Prior to our attack on Iraq in March 2003, however, there were convincing reasons to believe that these WMD did indeed exist. It is highly significant that Hussein's own generals believed he had WMD right up to the eve of the invasion of Iraq and were nonplussed to discover he had none.

In point of fact, Hussein, for political or diplomatic reasons, wanted everybody to believe he had WMD, and for that reason he blocked external efforts to find these WDM. Indeed, shortly before he was executed, Hussein told interrogators that he wanted Iran to believe he had WMD, and intended to reconstitute his nuclear program to be able to compete with Iran and Israel in nuclear weapons. It is noteworthy that Swedish Ambassador Rolf Ekeus, who played a major role in ascertaining Iraq's compliance with the UN edicts on WDM, believed that if Hussein didn't have nuclear WDM he would certainly strive to get some. (See below.) In point of fact, we were not certain that these WMD did not exist until we had had months to finally actually explore on the ground every possible hiding site in Iraq. It was small wonder that our intelligence on this was so unclear. I wouldn't be too hasty in calling this "an intelligence failure" because I believe we did the best we could in this regard. That intelligence analysts differed on this did not surprise me. Moreover, we had known that Hussein had used chemical WMD against both Iraqi Shiites and Kurds and against Iranians in the 1981–88 war with Iran. This, coupled with the fact that Hussein was a Hitler-type monster who persecuted his people and who had executed hundreds of thousands of innocent Iraqis and had attacked two of his neighbors—Kuwait in 1990 and Iran in 1981—certainly seemed to justify attacking Iraq with its impressive oil reserves and its key geographic position in the Middle East. The most one could argue is that we did the right thing for the wrong reasons and initially in the wrong way.

In any case, early on there was strong congressional and public opinion backing for our going into Iraq. In 2003 a strong case for military intervention in Iraq was made by former executive chair of the United Nations Special Commission (UNSCOM) on Iraq ambassador Rolf Ekeus of Sweden (chair from 1991 to 1997) who wrote in the *Washington Post*, "To accept the alternative [to military intervention in Iraq]—letting Hussein remain in power with his chemical and biological weapons capability—would have been to tolerate a continuing destabilizing arms race in the Gulf, including future nuclearization of the region, threats to the world's energy supplies, leakage of WMD technology and expertise to terrorist networks, systematic sabotage of efforts to create and sustain a process of peace between the Israelis and the Palestinians and the continued terrorizing of the Iraqi people." (When he wrote this, Ambassador Ekeus was chair of the Stockholm International Peace Research Institute.)

Although I am still head the U.S. Naval Fire Support Association, I now largely leave it to my able deputy Ted Yadlowsky to take our battleship case to the Hill. I mostly advise from the side and write on the subject. (For example, I had a battleship-related article in the December 2008 *Marine Corps Gazette*.) I am blessed or perhaps cursed with having a broad, if sometimes shallow, spectrum of interests and fancy myself a would-be polymath of sorts. So I have long allowed myself to pursue a variety of interests apart from battleship reactivation. These subjects will be addressed on my Web site, www.williamlstearman67.com.

Index

Trusty, Virtle Ethyl. *See* Stearman, Virtle
Ethyl Trusty (mother)
Tuskegee Institute, 4
Twain, Mark, 3

U-2 spy plane, 22, 135, 136
UAVs (unmanned aerial vehicles), 40
Udet, Ernst, 26
Ukraine, 205
United States: America First campaign, 28,
53; Communism and McCarthyism
in, 112–14; differences between
Americans and Europeans, 160–64;
Germany, war against, 52; Great
Britain, support for during World
War II, 53; lifestyle and mentality of
Americans, vii, viii, 160–62; political
maturity of, 163; religious beliefs in,
164; return to after living in Europe,
vii, 147–48, 161; return to after
Vietnam, 180–81; Spanish language
and illegal immigration problem,
163–64
United States Information Agency (USIA),
115, 181
United States Information Service (USIS),
115, 180
University of California at Berkeley, viii,
55–56
University of California at Los Angeles
(UCLA), 54–55
university-level teaching in Saigon, 179–80
Up From History (Norrell), 4
Up From Slavery (Washington), 4

Valkyrie operation, 130
Varney, Walter T., 21
Venendahl, "Curley," 25
Vienna: blockade of, concern about, 102;
celebrities, encounters with in, 110–11;
courtship of Eva in, 104–6; homesick-
ness for, 117; Hungarian Revolution
and return to, 122–27; Hungarian
smuggling operations in, 104; important role of, 117; life in, vii, ix; living
arrangements in, 103–4; move to, 101,
102; as music capital, 42, 118; post-war

conditions in, 102–3; Soviet Embassy,
reception at, 109–10; summit in, ix,
139–40, 150; travel to while in graduate school, 95; war destruction in, 95;
zone divisions in, 101, 141
Vietnam (French Indochina): battleship operations off coast of,
239–41; China's assistance to North
Vietnamese, 166, 190; coup in and
destabilization of, 157; expertise
and intelligence on, 165–67, 169–71,
186–87, 189; fact-finding trip to,
186–88; Japanese invasion of, 51–52;
Kennedy's policy toward, 156–57;
Land to the Tiller program, 175;
North Vietnamese, negotiations
with, 108; North Vietnamese Affairs
Division position, 165–80; NSC staff
director position on, x; Saigon, landing
in, 165; Saigon, life in, 172–73, 175,
178–80; Soviet assistance to North
Vietnamese, 190; Soviet involvement
in, 157; terrorist activities in, 172–73;
troops sent to as advisers, 156–57;
university-level teaching in, 179–80;
World War II entrance because of,
52, 193
Vietnam Memorial Wall, 197
Vietnam War: allies in, betrayal of, x;
battleship fire support during, x, 196;
Cam Ranh Bay, 73–74; casualties of,
77, 191, 193–94, 197; chopper trip to
landing zone, 171–72; cost of to South
Vietnam, 193–94; defeat of enemy
during, ix; defecting enemy troops,
uses of, 171, 195; Easter Offensive,
185–86, 216; funding for and assistance for South Vietnam, 190–91;
Hue massacre, 174; leaflet operations,
167–69; media coverage of, 173–78;
mistakes made during, 194–97; My
Lai massacre, 174; negotiations to end,
188–90, 196–97; opinion about, 158;
psychological war operations during,
ix, 158; Saigon, evacuations from, 191;
service during, viii; Swift boat operations, 172; tactical defeat but strategic

About the Author

WILLIAM LLOYD STEARMAN grew up in aviation as the son of an aviation pioneer. He saw considerable combat in World War II after which he attended graduate school in Europe. He then became a diplomat stationed in Austria, Germany, and Vietnam. He taught at Georgetown University and spent seventeen years in the White House on the NSC staff.